OPTIMIZING SPECIAL EDUCATION

How Parents Can Make a Difference

OPTIMIZING SPECIAL EDUCATION

How Parents Can Make a Difference

Nancy O. Wilson

INSIGHT BOOKS

Plenum Press • New York and London

Library of Congress Cataloging-in-Publication Data

Wilson, Nancy O.
    Optimizing special education : how parents can make a difference /
Nancy O. Wilson.
        p.   cm.
    Includes bibliographical references and index.
    ISBN 0-306-44323-6
    1. Special education--United States. 2. Educational law and
legislation--United States. 3. Educational equalization--United
States.   I. Title.
LC3981.W58   1992
371.9'0973--dc20   92-17239
                                                           CIP

This book is a guide to help parents find special services for children with disabilities. For legal advice, parents should consult attorneys who specialize in special education law or civil rights.

ISBN 0-306-44323-6

© 1992 Nancy O. Wilson
Insight Books is a division of Plenum Publishing Corporation
233 Spring Street, New York, N.Y. 10013

An Insight Book

Printed in the United States of America

With deep gratitude to my husband and sons for their
support when I was writing this book

ACKNOWLEDGMENTS

The author gratefully acknowledges permission to reprint excerpts from:

"The Neurological Impress Method of Reading" by R. G. Heckelman, Ph.D., pages 113 to 118 in *How to Write an I.E.P.* by John Arena, copyright (©) 1989. Reprinted by permission from Academic Therapy Publications, Novato, California.

The Misunderstood Child: A Guide for Parents of Learning Disabled Children by Larry B. Silver, M.D., copyright (©) 1984 by Larry B. Silver. Pages 104 and 127 used by permission from McGraw-Hill, Inc., New York, New York.

When All You've Ever Wanted Isn't Enough by Rabbi Harold Kushner, pages 186 to 189, copyright (©) 1986 by Kushner Enterprises, Inc. Reprinted by permission of Summit Books, a division of Simon & Schuster, Inc., New York, New York.

Educational Handicap, Public Policy, and Social History by Seymour B. Sarason and John Doris, page 46, copyright (©) 1979 by The Free Press, a Division of Macmillan, Inc., New York, New York.

Images of the Disabled, Disabling Images, edited by Alan Gartner and

The author wishes to thank individuals who took time to discuss Public Law 94-142 and education for children and youth with disabilities:

Frank E. New, Catherine Bregar, and Ellen Frasca at the Division of Special Education, Ohio Department of Education in Worthington
Cindy Gilligan in Ashland, Ohio
Gretchen Beattie in Hudson, Ohio
Darlene Cunningham at the Rehabilitation Services Commission in Columbus, Ohio
Nancy Archey for help in writing an IEP
Marge Goldberg at the PACER Center, Inc., in Minneapolis
National Information Center for Children and Youth with Disabilities in Washington, D.C. (NICHCY)
National Committee for Citizens in Education in Washington, D.C. (NCCE)
Sandra Berger at the ERIC Clearinghouse on Handicapped and Gifted Children in Reston, Virginia
HEATH Resource Center in Washington, D.C.
Coordinating Council for Handicapped Children in Chicago

This book would not have been possible without the editorial expertise and guidance of Norma Fox, Executive Editor and Frank K. Darmstadt, Assistant Editor at Insight Books, and Judith A. DeCamp, Senior Production Editor at Plenum Publishing. I am deeply grateful to my husband and sons for their support in writing this book.

INTRODUCTION

Is your daughter in special education? Do you want to increase or change her services? Does your son flounder in regular classes but tests reveal his learning problems are not severe enough for special education? Would you like your child with a handicapping condition to participate in more regular school environments or regular classes? This book will show you how to get *more* or *less* education or *change* education to suit your child's needs.

My son, Todd, has learning disabilities, including dyslexia. In the early years, when Todd was seeing therapists and tutors, I leafed through advice books. I thought the authors had enormous energy to put so much knowledge into practice while rearing a handicapped child of their own. (They also had cooks and gardeners.)

Although parents today have access to a wide range of resources, they cannot examine every educational theory. Many of the ideas presented here are after the fact: after rearing my child and after talking with other parents. It is my goal in *Optimizing Special Education: How Parents Can Make a Difference* to explain how laws work to educate disabled children, and to offer you, the parents and guardians, tools to help schools utilize the best resources while your child is in school.

There are more than forty million people with disabilities in this country, and many are children whose learning problems, such as attention deficit disorder (ADD), go unnoticed or are not severe enough for special education. Other children have disabilities that require special services from birth. Yet many parents are unaware of all the help available through Public Law 94-142, the *Education for All Handicapped Children Act of 1975*, and most of it is free.

SPECIAL EDUCATION LAWS CREATED CHANGE

Public Law (PL) 94-142 was passed shortly after Todd entered public school. The changes were dramatic. No longer were Todd and his classmates separated from other kids during lunch and on the playground. Kids in special classes were now included in school assemblies, health programs, and field trips. The idea of equal education had begun.

How did Public Law 94-142, an important, even controversial, law come into being? In September of the bicentennial year, 1976, I sat with parents and teachers in an auditorium listening to a superintendent of schools explain a new law for educating handicapped children. The superintendent said the passage of the law meant every child with disabilities would receive an education equal to that offered to nonhandicapped children. The law required school districts' accountability, that is, they had to keep track of how dollars were earmarked for special children. The law said schools would seek out young unidentified children in the community who were disabled or suspected of needing help. The children would be tested and an education plan written for each, no matter how severe or unusual his or her disabilities. The parents of a handicapped child would be included in creating the plan.

Further back in the auditorium sat a small group of parents. These were parents of handicapped children whose problems varied widely. Some were mildly impaired, such as a learning disabled boy with a few classroom problems. Others were severely disabled: children with multiple physical and mental impairments. Some of the children were in regular classrooms. Others had never seen the inside of a school building but were in hospitals and institutions.

We owe a lot to these parents who laid the groundwork for special education today. They were around during the early years when state laws varied widely in educating handicapped people. The parents joined teachers and administrators in demanding special services through local and county school districts. They traveled to state capitals and to Washington, D.C. They campaigned for new laws and helped write them. Eventually, as local and state laws led to federal support, they succeeded in providing for their children.

LAWS WORK FOR PARENTS AND KIDS

The following information is for parents discovering special education laws and for parents of special-needs children in public and private schools. It will explain what you can expect from:

- Public Law 94-142, the *Education for All Handicapped Children Act of 1975*
- *Education of the Handicapped Act Amendments of 1986* for preschoolers with disabilities
- *Handicapped Children's Protection Act of 1986*
- *Education of the Handicapped Act Amendments of 1990* (title changed to *Individuals with Disabilities Education Act—* IDEA)
- *Section 504 of the Rehabilitation Act of 1973*
- *Family Educational Rights and Privacy Act of 1974* (Buckley amendment)
- *Americans with Disabilities Act of 1990* (ADA)

This book talks about related services and mainstreaming, how laws protect you (due process) and how to find an attorney, and how to use an IEP (individualized education plan) to design your child's vocational future. It discusses homework strategies, working with teachers, and the use of family communications to strengthen a child's social skills for a mainstreamed society. It explores the need for satisfactory parent–professional partnerships from early intervention to vocational training. This book concludes with a selection of helpful books and periodicals, a "dependable dozen" list of agencies and support groups, and a glossary of commonly used special education terms.

FAMILY FEELINGS AND EXCEPTIONALITY

We also talk about our feelings in rearing a child with special needs. Until recently it was believed that parents eventually got over or accepted their child's disability. Recent studies show that disappointment is a natural component of parenting a disabled child. Feelings of fear, disbelief, self-pity, and mourning are normal. Acceptance may be too strong a word, in fact. Affirmation is difficult—that indelible moment of knowing. Parents do not accept, but they eventually adjust to their child's losses as certain events reawaken the pain of learning about the handicap.

Grief can be refreshed by normal evaluations. A special education supervisor used to ask, "What can Todd do? What are his skills?" I would think about the words and phrases used to describe his impairments and answer, "None. He has no skills that I can see." Todd *was* making progress, but the seriousness of his problems made it difficult to notice his abilities.

Not long after Todd's diagnosis, I began watching *Kung Fu* reruns with my after-dinner coffee. I rarely missed an episode. Perhaps the *Kung Fu* philosophy helped, but it was more likely the kicking.

As a parent of a child with disabilities, I understand your anger and grief, your questions and doubts about parenting a special-needs child. I continue to have doubts. As Caine, the Shaolin priest, says, "I don't have all the answers. I'm still trying to understand the questions."

It is normal to feel emotional about rearing a child with

disabilities. You may be tired from looking for specific services or from *choosing* services. An increase in government help means you have more to take advantage of, including fitting services into family life.

In 1984, Canadian parents Terry and Tannis Jarvis said in their booklet, *You Are Not Alone*, that we need to look out after our emotions because the anxieties that result from having a child with a handicap can play tricks on us. When we have been hurt we tend to crawl into ourselves, strike out in anger, or react in any number of contradictory ways. When we feel confused and help-less, the ways we react to our situation can either compound our problems or lead to the discovery of solutions. How we see ourselves in relation to our child, our spouse, and everyone else can influence our well being.

The Jarvises ask, "Are you feeling guilty because your child may be disturbing to others? [I would add that parents of impul-sive learning disabled and retarded children justifiably fear what their children are going to do or say next.] Are you feeling nervous, angry, defensive, aggressive or apologetic because you are parents of a handicapped child? Do you feel hurt because strangers on the street are giving you and your child a nervous or pitying sidelong glance? If you can answer 'yes' to these ques-tions, you are part of a large group of 'typical' parents who are reacting in a perfectly 'normal' way. You may not be reacting the way you 'should,' you are simply reacting the way you 'do.' It's nothing to be ashamed of."[1]

It is important to remember you are the same parent you were before your child was born with a disability or became disabled later. You have the same value in your parenting style and efforts. In other words, never doubt your ability as a parent.

PARENTS SHARE IN EDUCATIONAL DECISIONS

For more than fifteen years I have been talking with parents through a referral line in northeast Ohio and at local parent meetings. I believe parents know about PL 94-142 but are unsure of their role in special education. Parents still ask, "What is an IEP meeting and how often is it held?" (IEP is an individualized education program for each child with a disability, and the meeting is annual unless parents or the school request another meeting.)

Children attend school about twelve or thirteen years. My purpose is not to list a number of exhausting procedures for busy parents. Rather, I want you to use this book one day—one step at a time—to enhance your child's education.

A 1988 Robert Wood Johnson Foundation study of five metropolitan school systems revealed that less than half of the parents attended the IEP meeting. I think that this segment, parents who participate, improve services for their children. In a 1987 talk to Ohio parents and professionals, Margaret Burley, director of the Ohio Coalition for the Education of Handicapped Children, said parents' best tools are persistence and knowing the laws.[2]

You don't need an education background or law degree to get the best from special education, but you can apply what you learn. Getting the best for your child is known as advocacy. Advocacy, a synonym for support, is not the same as militancy or "Put up your dukes." Advocacy means using your knowledge to improve your child's education experience and to take advantage of his or her educational years.

A HISTORICAL PERSPECTIVE

Thirty years ago many disabled children did not go to school. Schools told parents that teaching handicapped children would harm normal students. In 1980, Albert Shanker, president of the American Federation of Teachers, wrote that early admission to special education depended on geography, wealth, or luck. Severely handicapped students were placed in public institutions for largely custodial care. Children with wealthy parents and those supported by charitable organizations attended private schools.

The rest were excluded from public and private schools.[3] Today, specialists who study children's learning patterns know that every child, no matter how severe his or her problems, can benefit from education.

Beginning in 1965 more than a dozen bills were passed to educate special children. In 1971 a parent victory was won by the Pennsylvania Association for Retarded Children. The association filed a court suit on behalf of thirteen retarded children, arguing they should receive an education of equal value to that of normal children.

One brief paragraph, written in 1973, guarantees each handicapped child his or her civil right to an education. This paragraph is Section 504 of the Vocational Rehabilitation Act. It says a handicapped child cannot be discriminated against by any education program or school receiving federal funds.

The result of these efforts for handicapped children was PL 94-142, the *Education for All Handicapped Children Act of 1975.* "PL" means it was the 142nd public law passed by the 94th Congress. PL 94-142 is stronger than previous laws. First, it is permanent. Second, it spells out what states and school districts must do to carry out education for special children. Finally, and most important, it includes parents in making decisions.

British Prime Minister Winston Churchill once said about democracy, "It is the worst form of government except all those other forms that have been tried from time to time."

The same thought applies to PL 94-142. It is flawed but at least is better than what we had before. The purpose of PL 94-142 is to make good education available to all handicapped children instead of a few and to meet the unique needs of each. The far-reaching purpose of PL 94-142 is management of special education from the top down: federal government, state levels, and local school districts. In addition to this, the federal government provides assistance (funds) to states and school districts to help their programs for the handicapped. States must comply with and may go beyond federal laws and regulations.

PEOPLE-FIRST LANGUAGE

In September 1990, the reauthorization of the EHA, or Education of the Handicapped Act (PL 91-230, 1970), changed the name to IDEA, or Individuals with Disabilities Education Act (PL 101-476). The Act says from now on schools, agencies, and other service providers will more appropriately replace the word "handicapped" with "children with disabilities."

In recent years attempts have been made to soften the word "handicapped." People with disabilities are referred to as "special," "exceptional," and "special-needs individuals," to name a few. We use these terms interchangeably, but most of the time we refer to children or adults with disabilities. At the same time, we remember that no person should be identified solely for his or her disability. He/she is a human being who happens to have a significant impairment, one that makes a difference in his/her abilities.

SPECIAL EDUCATION AND HUMAN RIGHTS

Since laws to educate disabled children culminated in the *Education for All Handicapped Children Act of 1975* and the recent amendments, questions have arisen about the amount of money needed to educate handicapped people. Do disabled children receive more expensive services than nondisabled children? Should they? Do nonhandicapped or "typical" children suffer as a result of state and local funding for children with disabilities?

There is little doubt that the numbers of children receiving special education services have increased. The 1990 twelfth annual report to Congress on the implementation of the *Education of the Handicapped Act* reported that the number of children identified as learning disabled has risen 152 percent. Of all students classified as handicapped, 95 percent are learning disabled, speech/language impaired, mentally handicapped, or emotionally disturbed.

It is true that special education costs more than regular education. The Robert Wood Johnson report says the practice of taking children out of regular classes for additional instruction in a special class raises costs. Special classes with or without some regular class instruction are even more expensive.

The federal government has not significantly supported states and local school districts financially. Nationwide, states pay about 54 percent of the average per-pupil cost of special education, and local schools pay about 35 percent. Although the federal government originally promised to states funding of 40 percent of the average per pupil expenditure, it presently contributes less than 8.5 percent nationally.

Knowing what we do about the difficulties in providing effective classroom interventions, not to mention the cost, is it worth our while as a country to educate disabled people, particularly those with severe impairments?

A decade ago educators anticipated a backlash from parents of nonhandicapped children in regard to funding special education. They wondered if parents of nonhandicapped children would ask for IEPs. When will parents of slow learners insist on remedial reading and math classes? What about programs for gifted children? Are citizens of this country willing to support quality educational programs for *all* children?

The answer is at the heart of human rights practices we have strived to achieve since we formed a government under the premise that all persons are created equal, and their destiny not measured by birth, gender, color, or class.

In his 1986 book about the laws and disabled children, *Free Appropriate Public Education*, attorney and special education professor H. Rutherford Turnbull III answers some of the questions concerning education for disabled individuals. In a reply to the statement that government is doing too much, that handicapped children should be placed in institutions or in special schools with their own kind, Professor Turnbull says, "Besides the fact that the states have a legal obligation to educate handicapped children and have violated the state and federal constitutional rights of those children, it is definitely in the public interest to educate them outside institutions whenever possible. Only with education can the handicapped contribute to society rather than be dependent on it. All the evidence shows that they can learn if appropriately trained, and appropriate training usually occurs outside of institutions."[4]

But what about expensive services for children and youth with disabilities? Professor Turnbull says monies spent on the more costly job of maintaining handicapped persons in institutions during the school-age years and beyond can be reduced and diverted to their education. What's more, the long-term cost of maintaining handicapped people at public expense is far greater than the short-term cost of educating them as children.[5]

Frank E. New, director of the Division of Special Education in the Ohio Department of Education, says special education can pay for itself: "When a child for whom we provide an appropriate education gets a job, that child becomes a taxpayer. Even disabled students in work–study programs begin to pay taxes equal to what we spend on their education."[6]

Director New believes any backlash or objection to funding for special education services is an outgrowth of states' serious budget deficits and a search for ways to reduce spending. He adds, "More of an issue is the concept of inclusion where parents of more severely impaired children want to place their children in regular classes versus pull-out programs and special classes. Over the last couple of years, there has been a push toward collaborative teaching models with regular education and special education working with groups of children who are disabled and non-disabled. There is also a strong move by parents of children with attention deficit disorders to include them as a population under the Education of the Handicapped Act."

Is the investment worth the return in educating children with disabilities? "Special education has been the major vehicle in integrating people with disabilities," says Mr. New. "We are witnessing tremendous shifts in society's perception of how much disabled people can do, what and where they can learn. In a short time we have progressed from the concept of putting them away with people like themselves, to today where we think the best situation is a normal environment for everyone."[7] Director New says a great change is occurring in the public belief that people with disabilities can function more effectively in society.

The taxes we allocate for special education and related services for disabled children *today* and *in the future* will eventually reduce the tax burdens of entirely supporting disabled adults. In other words, the federal, state, and local funds we use for special education and vocational training translate into more jobs and independence for disabled individuals and fewer future dollars for SSI (Supplemental Security Income) and additional supports.

The idea behind *Optimizing Special Education: How Parents Can Make a Difference* is to help you obtain the most effective services directed to your child's eventual independence.

The *Code of Federal Regulations*, Title 34, Parts 300 to 399 is the primary reference used for amendments to the Education of the Handicapped Act (EHA) in this book. Readers can obtain a copy of the regulations for $14.00 from the Superintendent of Documents, U.S. Government Printing Office, Washington, D.C. 20402, or at one of the twenty-four branch-bookstores located in major cities. Ask for the Federal Regulations for "Education," July 1, 1990, Title 34, Parts 300 to 399. Libraries carry copies of Federal Regulations.

CONTENTS

Contents

OPTIMIZING SPECIAL EDUCATION

How Parents Can Make a Difference

Chapter 1

WHO BENEFITS FROM SPECIAL EDUCATION?

Are you puzzled by special education terminology: IEP (individualized education program), auditory learning, etiology, and other terms? You wonder, "What's in this for my child? Will the school provide extras? I know about *my* child's problems, but what other disabilities are included in the law? Does my child need a label or category to get special services?" Perhaps you wonder about special education for a child who is not fluent in English.

Public Law (PL) 94-142 addresses these questions. Every disabled child is to receive an education. Public schools are to educate children who are mentally retarded, hard of hearing, deaf, speech impaired, visually handicapped, seriously emotionally disturbed, orthopedically impaired, or health impaired in other ways. Included in special education are children with LD (learning disabilities) or SLD (specific learning disabilities). The Education of the Handicapped Amendments of 1990 expanded services more fully to include children with autism and traumatic brain injury.

TERMINOLOGY IS NOT FOREVER

One of the most explored topics in our parent group has been terminology. How do these terms affect children? Must kids be labeled in order to receive services?

When early-identified infants and preschoolers begin school, their parents have had more time to assimilate the idea of a disability. In cases of learning disabilities or mild mental retardation, it's hard to accept "specialness" when one's child looks about the same today as on the previous Friday. Only a diagnosis has changed. One mother said that, at first, parents can't absorb the purpose of long-term remediation because the idea is overwhelming. Remediation is nearly always a new world for parents.

Some parents worry that a special education label will limit what teachers think their child can achieve. Will early interventions become a part of their child's life-style? Will a diagnosis of mental retardation, hearing impairment, or orthopedic handicap categorize their child forever?

Special education is not a brand. Many children receive partial services or need services only for two or three years. Whether children have mild impairments or require special services throughout school, they are more like other children than not like them. They will grow up to be much more than a category that needs to be provided with special help. A law was written to specify children who are eligible for special services. Children who are evaluated as having a disability receive special education under PL 94-142. They cannot receive special services unless they are evaluated and receive an individual plan, the IEP.[1]

WHO QUALIFIES FOR SPECIAL SERVICES?

The following students qualify for special education:

Children with *mental retardation* are those from birth to age eighteen who develop at a below-average rate and experience difficulties in learning and social adjustment. Mental retardation is measured with intelligence tests and adaptive behavior tests. Adaptive behavior is how a person adapts to normal levels of independence and social responsibility of other persons about the same age. A child with mental retardation is one with a low level of intellectual ability. Social-emotional development is slow. A retarded child learns at a slower rate than other children. Retardation hinders learning by the same general methods, without adaptations, as those other children use to learn in regular classes.

In the language of education, *mildly retarded* children are quite similar to their peers—their differences become more visible as they grow older. (Their IQs fall within the range 52–68 by Stanford-Binet tests; see Chapter 6 about IQ and testing.) Children who are *moderately retarded* (IQ 36–51) are more obviously handicapped, and their retardation is usually apparent before school age. *Severely retarded* (IQ 20–35) or *profoundly retarded* (IQ below 20) children have severe intellectual impairments and, frequently, other disabilities, such as cerebral palsy, blindness, or deafness.

Depending on the severity of their condition, children with retardation can still learn self-help, social, academic, and work skills. Mental retardation is not the same as mental illness. It is not a disease, and in most cases the reason is unknown. About 3 percent of the population is mentally retarded.

In public schools, moderately retarded students are referred to as TMR (trainable mentally retarded), and mildly retarded students are referred to as EMR (educable mentally retarded). In 1982 the rules for special education changed the name of educable mentally retarded programs to *developmentally handicapped* or DH programs. DH programs include children with moderate or severe retardation.

A *hard of hearing* child may not be totally deaf, but hearing loss affects learning efficiency. The hearing loss can be permanent or can vary. A *deaf* child's hearing problem is so severe that voices and sounds cannot be understood with or without a hearing aid. Special education for a deaf child includes sign language and other communication skills.

A child who is *speech impaired* cannot make himself or herself understood or communicate well. The child may stutter or mispronounce words. Perhaps this lack of language or a voice handicap interferes with daily needs, including education.

A child who is *visually handicapped* has no sight or can see little, even with glasses.

Orthopedic refers to physical disabilities. An *orthopedically impaired* child is physically disabled enough to have adjustment problems in regular settings. Physical problems may result from the absence of an arm or leg or stem from cerebral palsy. Perhaps special needs were brought about by polio, spina bifida, tuberculosis of the bone, or physical injuries.

Also included in special education are children both deaf and blind. These children do not qualify for sight impaired or hearing impaired classes but receive special education fitted to their disabilities.

Multihandicapped is the term used for a child with combined disabilities, such as being mentally retarded/blind or mentally retarded/orthopedically impaired, to such a severe degree that an individualized special program is required. The term does not include deaf/blind children.

Children with *serious emotional disturbance* exhibit their problems over a long period of time. Their problems are basically emotional and not due to retardation or other health disabilities. Because these children show unusual behavior, sometimes including physical symptoms, they are not able to learn at normal levels, get along with other people, and adjust to ordinary school routines. Their emotions may relate to extreme fears, anger, or unhappiness. Some disturbed children show symptoms of schizophrenia.

Children with social maladjustments are not included in the category of emotional disturbance. Social problems of young children can be temporary. A child might be troubled or depressed because the family is moving or parents are divorcing. Family members may be saddened by the death of a grandparent or, more upsetting, a parent. Perhaps there is illness in the family or another situation causing social problems that are temporary or long lasting. A family may be stressed if parents are out of work or homeless, a common occurrence these days. But these problems, however troubling for the child, are usually not considered serious emotional disturbances.

Children need special education services if they are *other health impaired*. They may be afflicted with such conditions as rheumatic fever, asthma, hemophilia, or leukemia. Other health-related problems are sickle-cell anemia, uncontrolled epilepsy, lead poisoning, insulin-dependent diabetes, AIDS (acquired immune deficiency syndrome), and ARC (AIDS related complex). A child may be unable to attend school regularly because of infectious hepatitis or cystic fibrosis requiring therapy.

Childhood autism is not an emotional illness or schizophrenia but a serious disturbance of behavior, usually beginning in infancy. These infants or young children have problems communicating. They seem insensitive to activities and people around them. They may become unmanageable. More importantly, they cannot relate normally to the world outside themselves. Because of these differences, children with autisticlike characteristics need special education. They are sometimes included in classes for children with behavior disturbances.

LEARNING DISORDERS: A NEW CONCEPT IN EDUCATION

Children with SLD, or *specific learning disabilities*, are new to laws for special children. These are youngsters whose school and social problems are attributable to disorders in thinking. In school situations they cannot listen attentively, reason very well, talk, read, write, spell, or work math problems in traditional classes. Government regulations say these disorders "include . . . perceptual handicaps, brain injury, minimal brain dysfunction, dyslexia, and developmental aphasia."[2]

Learning disabilities vary widely, depending on the person. Serious learning disabilities reveal themselves early if toddlers are slow developing. Less serious learning disabilities become obvious as children move through school. All learning problems affect children profoundly, however.

Learning disabilities, known as "invisible or hidden handicaps," are not the same as learning problems caused by vision or hearing disorders, motor handicaps (muscle or body activity), mental retardation, emotional disturbance, or home environment. The Learning Disabilities Association (LDA), the national organization for learning disabled people, tells us that children with these disorders have trouble understanding. Their frustrations arise from incorrect mental processing of what they see and hear. Some have memory deficits: They can read but cannot remember what they read or recall instructions or class routines. They have trouble sequencing, that is, remembering the order of letters and numbers. Others have a poor sense of direction, that is, telling left from right, and learning how to get to a new place. (In the spring of 1989, the name of ACLD [An Association for Children and Adults with Learning Disabilities] was changed to LDA.)

ADD, or attention deficit disorder, is a recent term used to describe children who are unable to pay attention or function well in normal classes. ADD can appear with hyperactivity, depression, or other emotional difficulties. Students with ADD are usually restless, easily distracted, and consequently frustrated. They cannot pay attention or follow instructions. They seem to have few or none of the organizational skills required for getting along in class or doing homework. ADD is not included as a category in the recent reauthorized version of the Education for All Handicapped Children Act.

The boundaries remain fuzzy between LD, SLD, and ADD, although learning disordered children are usually behind socially as well as academically. Recent reports say between 10 percent and

20 percent of LD children are ADD; between 50 percent and 90 percent of ADD students are also learning disabled.[3]

Other terms for learning disabilities include educational handicap (EH), perceptual impairments, hyperactivity, hyperkinetic disorder, language disability, specific learning disabilities, organicity, word blindness, and the recent specific developmental disorder (SDD). Learning disabled children receive special education based on the discrepancy, usually two or three years, between their intelligence and achievement tests. States differ in discrepancy formulas for deciding which children qualify for services. (See the Glossary—*Standard deviation*.)

Under the Education of the Handicapped Amendments of 1990, new discretionary (meaning optional or voluntary) programs were created. These included special programs on transition (education to advance the passage of special students from school to independence), a new program to improve services for children and young people with serious emotional disturbances, and a research-information program about attention deficit disorders.

Not every disabled child needs special classes. There are children with cerebral palsy who can handle regular academic work. Other youngsters with moderate physical problems can successfully work in regular classes. Mildly affected LD children working with enlightened teachers can excel in regular classrooms. These teachers understand learning disorders and modify academic activities for an LD child's needs.

Special education is not just for children with mental retardation or physical disabilities but also for every child whose condition interferes with learning. This includes children who speak a language other than English who also happen to be disabled. The federal regulations say that all communication with a child in special education (including testing) is carried out in a language normally used by the child and not that of his parents, if there is a difference between the two. Also, if a child is deaf or blind or has no written language, communication is carried out in whatever mode he normally uses, such as sign language, braille, or oral communication.

SPECIAL EDUCATION AND CULTURAL DIFFERENCES

Recent questions have arisen about students from different cultural backgrounds. Are they more likely to receive special education or at least be subject to more tests? How are students' placements in special education affected by the use of black vernacular English (BVE) or limited English proficiency (LEP)? How will children of immigrant populations be affected by special education services?

In passing the 1990 legislation, Individuals with Disabilities Education Act (IDEA), Congress provided new information about the high dropout rate among minority students. Although minority children are frequently overly included in special education programs, few minorities are enrolled in teacher training programs for special education.

Schools also need to focus on improving relationships with minority parents. A 1987 report from NICHCY (National Information Center for Children and Youth with Disabilities) says insensitivity to the cultural differences of minority parents has created barriers to parent participation in the schools. Parents are often reluctant to interact with school personnel, who may not understand them, their values, or their life-styles. For example, minority parents and extended families do not always react the same way majority parents do to having a disabled child. Professional relationships with minority families can therefore differ from those with majority families.[4]

Historically, studies have shown that among all disabled children, minorities are the group represented about as much as the child population as a whole. Nevertheless, children of social, cultural, and language minorities continue to be overly represented in special education. Because of this trend, the Office of Special Education Programs began a three-year study in 1990 to examine problems in delivering services to students with disabilities who are from nonstandard English, limited English proficiency, and/or minority groups. The purpose of these studies is to help both mainstream and regular classroom teachers strengthen and improve the use of classroom or standard English by nonstandard-English-speaking children.

SPECIAL ED AND ALPHABET SOUP

Laws are almost always interpreted with acronyms, otherwise known as alphabet soup. PL 94-142 is no exception. The law says a child with disabilities should receive a free appropriate education. FAPE means free appropriate public education in an LRE, or least restrictive environment. LRE means every handicapped child should be educated with nonhandicapped children to the greatest extent appropriate, unless it is clear that a special class or other special accommodations are better.

FAPE is important for parents. It means they do not pay extra for special education evaluations and services other than normal taxes. If a school cannot educate a child close to home, there is no cost to parents, and parents do not pay for transportation. If the child is educated in a private school, there is still no extra cost for parents.

When the law mentions parents, it can also mean guardians or other persons acting as parents, the persons legally responsible for a disabled child. A grandparent, stepparent, or foster parent is included in the definition of parent.

The idea of being appropriate includes timing. Special education was to be available to every disabled child of age three to twenty-one by September 1, 1980 (unless individual state law did not provide for children ages three to five or eighteen to twenty-one).

Teachers are appropriately trained in special education methods. They have the required university degree, and the school provides additional programs to help them. Materials and equipment should be up-to-date. No child who qualifies for special education waits for a special program: Waiting lists for special classes are not allowed. A comment in the federal regulations says there can be no undue delay in providing special education and related services to a child who qualifies for special education.[5]

INTERVENTION FOR PRESCHOOLERS

An important event took place in October 1986, when President Reagan signed into law the EHA (Education of the Handicapped Act) amendments of 1986. This new legislation, Public Law 99-457, encourages states to establish preschool programs for all handicapped children ages three to five. This program is Part H of the Education of the Handicapped Act and includes grants to encourage states to serve handicapped children from birth to age two. These services can take place in a child's home, a clinic, neighborhood center, or the local health department. Services can range from prescribing glasses for a two-year-old to physical therapy for an infant with cerebral palsy.

By the school year 1992, all states applying for preschool money under Public Law 94-142 must provide an education for all handicapped children ages three to five or risk losing federal funds. States receiving funds under Part H of this law must serve children through age two.

Under the new regulations, parents of very young children have the same rights as parents of older children. If your infant or preschooler has a handicapping condition, Part H wants your involvement in services provided by professionals using the IFSP, or Individualized Family Service Plan. Infants and preschoolers are eligible for help if they have delays in cognition (understanding and perception), physical skills, language and speech, psychological-social skills, and/or self-help skills. They are eligible if they have a physical or mental condition that can lead to slow development. The purpose of PL 99-457 is to strengthen future learning and social skills of disabled infants and toddlers. Early intervention is a term used to help very young children.

The infant-toddler program established by PL 99-457 gave the states five years of federal planning money to set up state methods to help infants and toddlers and their families. The fifth year was completed in 1991.

In a 1987 talk to the ARC, or National Association for Retarded Citizens, Assistant Education Secretary Madeleine Will said two challenges face the new childhood programs. One is a shortage of personnel qualified to provide these services to infants and preschoolers with handicaps. The other is the degree to which agencies can help the very young without isolating them from regular kids. Mainstreaming young children with special needs is not required, but it is an important issue in local communities.[6]

Parents in the military can find out about programs and services for military families through: Specialized Training of Military Parents (STOMP), 12208 Pacific Highway SW, Tacoma, WA 98499; telephone number (206) 588-1741. (Military parents can call this number collect.)

PARENTS AND LEGAL FEES

Until recently, parents who took legal steps with school districts were financially on their own. Another law, the *Handicapped Children's Protection Act of 1986* (PL 99-372), was also signed by President Reagan. This law allows courts to awarded reasonable attorneys' fees to parents or guardians of a disabled child or youth "who is the prevailing part," meaning winning the litigation. This act applies to cases initiated after July 3, 1984.

If your state receives money for programs for the handicapped under EHA-B, all school districts should provide special education to handicapped students. EHA-B means Part B of the Education of the Handicapped Act. In fact, Part B *is* Public Law 94-142. In their 1979 book, *Educational Handicap, Public Policy and Social History*, Seymour B. Sarason and John Doris say even if there

is no special class in a child's school district to fit his needs, the
school must find special education for him if his state receives
EHA-B money for such programs.[7]

Other expressions in special education include *public agency*,
which means any state agency or local school district providing
special services to disabled children. SEA is the state education
agency. LEA is the local school or local education agency.

FAMILIES NEED CLEAR EXPLANATIONS

The special terms that identify children can help parents too.
When your child has been recently evaluated, it is difficult to
explain his or her problems over and over. When you are getting
used to the idea of having a disabled child, this process refreshes
your grief. It is not unusual for parents to explain a disorder and
then hear, "I don't understand. What's the matter with her?"

The mother of a son with multiple disabilities says people
who love your child will be shocked by the diagnosis, but they are
genuinely interested. You can avoid painful repetition by writing a
couple of paragraphs in layman's terms describing your child's
problems. Maybe your doctor or parent support group can help
you. Make copies for relatives and friends. You can tell them this
up-to-date material explains these problems more fully and accurately.

A child once told Todd that he was going to become a drug
addict because he was in a special class. As they grow older,
children who are verbal need the ability to explain their disabilities. Todd has been comfortable with the word "dyslexia" to
explain his difficulties with reading and writing.

Kids with special problems need help to understand the
difference between a disability and a disease. We are moving away
from the misconception that mental disability is synonymous with
mental illness. Talking with your children dispels myths and
rumors. A sibling may hear from someone outside the family to

"be glad you're not handicapped." The child is glad and probably feels guilty about it.

When you take your daughter to a tutor, does her brother go along? Do you feel somewhat anxious before doctors' appointments or school conferences for your special-needs child? Does it show? Siblings need compassionate talk about the physical or mental disability, the special class, and the therapy. They need to know "where we are going today."

A sibling can feel different conflicts over family identification with "specialness." Feelings can be shaped by the type and severity of the disability. How much has the special child been able to compensate for his problems, for instance? Is the disabled child an infant newly diagnosed with Down syndrome, a younger child with physical disabilities, an older brother or sister with behavioral problems, or an older child with troubles at school?

The range of emotions siblings feel in a single day confuse them. At the breakfast table they talk with their disabled sister, and they laugh at a TV cartoon. Later at the supermarket, they are embarrassed by their sister's behavior. They feel uncomfortable if their sister's disability is visible. They are frightened by the intensity of their feelings about a disabled sibling's acting out in public. Other times they are troubled by confusing emotions toward families without such unusual problems. They watch neighbors prepare for a picnic and wish their family could be like that too.

An older nondisabled sibling begins to notice societal reactions to the disability. Sarah, age eleven, is more perceptive about her brother's multiple disabilities. She asked her mother, "Why do people look at Bobby, or they look away like they don't want to see us?" Sarah overhears her parents worry about the time required for Bobby's therapy. At the shopping mall another child asked Sarah, "Is that your brother? What's the matter with him? Why can't he walk?"

You don't need prepared speeches, but you can answer questions as they arise. As our two sons grew older, we tried to tailor discussions to their maturity. Sometimes we were successful in explaining learning differences and dyslexia. Other times we were not, especially when family members were feeling emotional about a specific incident. I believe we gained from trying, however. As parents we can't expect to succeed in every effort to impart sensitive information to our children.

Do not be put off by your typical child's concerns, his sometimes blunt observations. Siblings cope better with straightforward but simplified explanations about family resources—meaning time, money, and energy. When your children talk with you and explain how they feel, they learn that their reactions are normal.

CHILDREN AND FEELINGS

All children, including siblings of disabled children, need permission to be sad, angry, or confused. Frances Dwyer McCaffrey and Thomas Fish, authors of *Profiles of the Other Child: A Sibling Guide for Parents*, say there are two issues: one, you need to recognize your own feelings and say how you feel; two, you need to find ways to let your children talk about their feelings whenever they're ready.[8]

Not all children (and siblings) want to talk about their feelings, but they do need to know that it's okay to get mad "when people ask them dumb questions," or that "It's not always fun to take John to the playground, is it?" But you don't want to put the sibling on the spot by saying, "So, how do you really feel about your brother/sister?"

It is also helpful to let the sibling know that there is no right or wrong way to feel. Feelings aren't bad, but they are individual. It's what we do or don't do about our feelings that makes a difference. How you, as a parent, express and cope with your feelings will have a significant impact on the other child's ability to cope.

Sometimes parents inadvertently expect different things of their typical (nondisabled) children than they might otherwise if there wasn't a disability in the family. This isn't uncommon or unnatural. But it can be very difficult for the "normal" child if displaced expectations interfere with his or her individual needs and emerging personality. Unfortunately, isolation is a common phenomenon in families with disabled children. This, in turn, can be exaggerated by a tendency to compare one's own family with other families and see only the difficult differences.

Like individual children, families are unique. Try not to compare your family with anyone else's or to live your life according to someone else's idea of what it should be like. Your family is probably succeeding and excelling in ways not apparent to other people.

Communication with your children can clear the air. It can stop misinformation about disabilities and hidden insecurities about being disabled or being the sibling of a disabled person. Kids with learning problems, in particular, are often relieved to learn that their inability to perform in school is not caused by illness or "weakness" or lack of effort.

When children with disabilities know the truth they are not so vulnerable. They are more open to learning when they are not consumed by the questions, "Why am I in a special class? Why do I need help with my speech? What is the matter with me that I can't learn like the others?"

A good place for brothers and sisters to air their feelings and read about other siblings is the *Sibling Information Network Newsletter*. You can also order the booklet *Profiles of the Other Child* from the Nisonger Center in Columbus, Ohio. See Resources, p. 253.

Chapter 2

A PERSONAL PROGRAM

We need to get away from the idea that special education is peopled by designer suits. Special education is administered by people who usually have families and problems like yours; too much month at the end of the money and wondering what to do about the guinea pig Martha brought home over Christmas vacation.

Special education, including early services, requires a plan. An IEP or individualized education plan (also known as an individualized education program) is the guide to your child's schoolwork for the year and is the most vital part of PL 94-142. It is like a prescription telling what the school is doing for your child.

NEED HELP? DO THIS FIRST

First, if you suspect your child needs special help and you want him or her tested, *write* your principal or director of special education. The school must reply in writing to your request within thirty days.[1]

The school will then evaluate your child. If tests reveal he or she needs special education, help must begin immediately. A short delay is allowed over summer vacation or to make transportation arrangements.

If the school refuses to test your child, it is saying he or she does not qualify for special education under the requirements mentioned in the previous chapter, such as being visually impaired, speech impaired, other health impaired, learning disabled, and so on. Therefore, the school must explain in a written notice why it said no. This written notice should include an explanation of your rights under PL 94-142. It is very important that you keep this letter.

INDEPENDENT EVALUATIONS

Next, if your child has received assessments and school tests reveal his or her problems are not severe enough for special services (but you still think he or she needs them), you can locate independent tests through a private psychologist or clinic, child guidance agency, your local Special Education Regional Resource Center (SERRC), Special Education Training and Resource Center (SETRC), or parent resource center. Call your state department of education, community hotline, or appropriate parent support group for telephone numbers.

You can pay for independent evaluations yourself, or you can request in writing that the school pay. Federal regulations say, "A parent has the right to an independent educational evaluation at public (meaning school district) expense if the parent disagrees with the evaluation obtained by the (school) public agency."[2] Contact the supervisor of special education (or a comparable official) of your school district. Your letter should state that you are requesting an outside assessment at public or school expense. Some insurance plans pay for evaluations. Check with your insurance agent or employer. In some cases, coverage of expenses is retroactive. You can get the tests and then ask to be reimbursed. (Make copies of all letters *you* send.)

The school district can respond in one of two ways. It can agree to pay and help you arrange outside evaluations, or it can say no and move to a hearing in order to prove its assessments were correct. If you request information about independent evaluations, it is to tell you where such evaluations can be found.

If a hearing determines the school evaluations were correct, you still have the right to an independent evaluation, but not at school expense. After your child is tested again, the results of school and independent evaluations must be included in determining the appropriate type of education.

Sometimes school and outside tests show the same thing, that a child's problems are not severe enough for special education. If this is the outcome, you and the school can combine strategies to address these problems. More about this in Chapter 9. Remember, you cannot realistically challenge what the school says about your child unless you get more tests.

If tests reveal your child needs special education, he or she receives an IEP, and special services begin as soon as possible after the IEP is written.

THE IEP AND PARENTS' RIGHTS

School personnel have additional obligations to you. They must make every effort to invite you to IEP meetings. The invitation should be in a language you understand. If your language is Spanish, the invitation should be in Spanish. If you are hearing impaired, the invitation should be delivered by sign language, TDD (telecommunications devices for the deaf), or any other language you can read. The place and time for the meeting must be convenient for you, and you must be notified well ahead of time to attend.

The IEP invitation should say who will attend the meeting aside from parents. School personnel include the child's teacher, of course, and anyone who recently tested your child and who understands test results, such as the school psychologist or a special education supervisor. Parents may invite others to an IEP meeting if they wish. Would your child's doctor be willing to attend if his or her knowledge would contribute? (The new family practice MDs are particularly interested in early childhood education.) Do you know a teacher, friend, or relative who could help?

If possible, both parents should make an effort to attend the meeting. If neither of you can attend, the school will try to arrange an individual telephone meeting or a conference call.

If you are single, by all means, take a friend or relative to the meeting. Two interested parties are better able to share a child's educational, social, and emotional needs with the IEP team.

IEP meetings can be stressful. If you're worried you'll forget something, bring a tape recorder with you. You can tape the meeting if you want. If the recording is maintained by the agency (school), it is considered part of your child's educational record. Courtesy, however, indicates you tell the school beforehand that you plan to record. Some parents take notes and jot down key phrases during the conference. When they get home, or even while still driving back, they fill in the details.

EVALUATING THE WHOLE CHILD

Before the initial IEP meeting, a child receives tests on different fields, given by different specialists, who pool their findings. Educators refer to tests as "instruments." Evaluating a child with more than one test is called multifactored evaluation. This means several tests explain how well your child is learning. The law says no child's IEP should be written on the weight of one test.

The situation differs somewhat for a child who has only a speech impairment. Federal regulations say, "Children who have speech impairments as their primary handicaps may not need a complete battery of assessments (e.g., psychological, physical, or adaptive behavior). However, a qualified speech-language pathologist would evaluate each speech impaired child using procedures . . . appropriate for the diagnosis and appraisal of speech and language disorders and . . . make referrals for additional assessments needed to make an appropriate placement decision."[3]

For children with physical problems, medical information is added. Other information is added by psychologists and education specialists. This information collection is called an inter-disciplinary or multidisciplinary assessment. Specialists from several disciplines do the evaluation.

If your child's tests reveal his or her disabilities and he or she is not receiving special education, an IEP meeting must be held within thirty days.

PREPARING FOR MEETINGS

IEP meetings become easier as you become more experienced, but how do you prepare for the first one? List services you think your child needs. If you are unsure of terminology, write down skills you want to improve. You need not sound like a textbook. Goals are improvements or changes in a child's performance or behavior. The idea behind the IEP is to help you and the school see your child as a whole person. Do you want teachers to work on one aspect of behavior if your child is emotionally immature? Do you want speech therapy or physical therapy? Todd needed help to cope, in and out of class. His goals, which changed through the years, combined academics with organizational skills, social maturity, and later vocational training.

Margaret Burley says parents should take their own sets of goals into each conference. She says, "Writing down more objectives than you think you'll get gives you something to negotiate."[4]

In Melissa's case, for example, another idea would be to make an outline of what you think her IEP should contain based on her personal evaluations and her parents' contacts with other professionals. What do teachers and the school psychologist say about Melissa's behavior in various classrooms? At what times is she learning (or not learning)? Which school environments make her comfortable or uncomfortable? Her parents take the outline to the meeting. They discuss their concerns early in the meeting instead of waiting until the meeting is almost over.

PARENTS' IDEAS COUNT!

Before you see the IEP for the first time, you should have participated in planning the listed goals. Perhaps you had talked on the phone with teachers, the special education supervisor, and school psychologists, or you had previously met with them at the school.

Sometimes school staff are unaware that they cannot prewrite an IEP or ask you to sign a blank one. A discussion of the IEP in the federal regulations says the agency (school) should not present a completed IEP to parents for their approval before there has been a full discussion with parents about their child's need for special education and related services and what kinds of services the school will provide. It is appropriate for school staff to bring to the meeting evaluation findings (results from testing), statements of present levels of your child's educational performance (how well he or she is doing academically), plus recommendations for annual goals, short-term goals, and the kinds of special education and related services to be provided. At the same time, the staff should make it clear to parents that these are only recommendations for review and discussion.[5]

The IEP meeting is for listening and planning, for explaining what is going to be written on the IEP. You and the IEP team are getting together to discuss your child, not a group of children. The meeting should not include other families.

How long should an IEP meeting last? There is no required length—perhaps thirty minutes to an hour—but it should be long enough to cover the topics that will affect your child in the coming year. Meetings may be longer for a child just beginning special services or for one with more complex needs. IEP meetings are shorter for an annual review or when a child needs fewer services.

The IEP meeting is an opportunity for you to establish your child's native language. With recent immigrations, this problem has intensified. Is your child bilingual? In which language does he learn best? Until your child is comfortable with English, neither programs nor evaluations should be carried out in this language.

An IEP should explain your child's working levels. What are his academic levels in math and reading? How is he doing with spelling? Children with learning problems rarely stay at one level in all areas of development. The IEP should name which tests were given to establish these academic levels.

The IEP should say how your child gets along with children and teachers, his personal-social evaluation. The IEP should mention any health problems (food allergies, for instance) that interfere with learning. Can your child keep track of school belongings? Button his coat? Take himself to the bathroom? The IEP should explain self-help skills.

Let's assume the IEP meeting has begun. Everyone is relaxed (more or less). The speech therapist is talking, but soon you are lost in his comments on encoding. What are phonemes?

Ask about points you don't understand. Teachers and others who see your child on a daily basis want you to know what is going on. It's okay to say, "I don't understand," or "I want to think about that a moment." How many parents new to special services know off hand what a WISC-R is? (See Chapter 6 about testing.)

WHAT ARE GOALS AND OBJECTIVES?

The IEP includes two kinds of goals. The long-term or annual goals tell what your child should accomplish in a year. The short-term goals (also called "short-term instructional objectives") are smaller steps taken on the way to annual goals. The IEP goals and objectives should focus on offsetting or reducing problems resulting from a child's handicap that interfere with learning and educational performance in school.

Goals should be measurable. A child, within his or her *abilities*, should reach most of the annual goals. If he or she easily reaches all goals, the IEP asks too little. If he or she cannot reach any goals, they are beyond the child. An IEP should encourage your child to stretch.

In a report, the PACER Center, a parent advocacy coalition in Minneapolis, gave examples of general and specific IEP objectives (goals). "Susie will be able to give and follow instructions" is too general. The PACER Center says, "This objective does not explain what kinds of instruction the child is to give and follow: Simple, short, spoken instructions or longer, more complex written ones?" A more precise objective is, "Given a simple, two-step verbal instruction, Susie will be able to follow instructions 80 percent of the time."[6]

SPECIAL SERVICES AND MODIFICATIONS ARE WRITTEN ON THE IEP

The school is not responsible for a child reaching all goals written on the IEP, but it is responsible for providing all services written on the IEP. An IEP can consist of two or three pages or run as long as six pages or more, depending on how much information is needed.

This seems like a lot of information for one or two sheets of paper. Is every moment of your child's school day written into the IEP, you wonder. Not necessarily. Your child's total education is not written on the IEP unless a profound or severe disability exists that requires total special education. For a child receiving therapy for a mild speech impairment, the IEP would pertain only to speech therapy services. Only special education and related services are written on an IEP, plus the extent to which your child can take part in regular education.

How much time during the day can your daughter spend in regular education, and what subjects or activities are suitable to her needs? The IEP explains this. Can she take physical education, consumer education, music, or art? Can she go to regular lunch, playground activities, and regular assemblies? How about field trips?

Modifications to accommodate your child in regular education should be written on the IEP. Does the classroom need to be rearranged, a door widened, or a ramp built to accommodate a wheelchair? Does your child need an aide in the classroom? Does your child with hearing or vision impairments need a desk closer to the teacher?

Does your child need related services: speech, physical, and occupational therapy? (Related services are examined in Chapter 3.) The IEP should explain what the therapy includes and why. It should spell out a time sequence for extra help. For instance, speech services will be given two half hours a week, to begin in September and end in May. All related services needed should be mentioned. A school is under no obligation to carry out services not written on the IEP.

If Jennifer goes out of class for a special service, what will she miss? She should not receive auditory training in place of social studies or be taken out of math for speech therapy, for instance. She should have access to academic subjects, plus her related services, even if a longer day is needed.

What other means can you use to ask for services? If you want to add a goal or related services to an IEP, a parent coalition, the Coordinating Council for Handicapped Children in Chicago, says you can prepare a written statement of what you want, make enough copies to hand out to all attendees at the meeting, and read the statement out loud. "This will ensure that all your concerns will be heard."[7] The council says it isn't the parents' job to write an IEP or stipulate what kinds of materials should be used. Your main objective is to present views of your child.

WHY AND WHEN TO SIGN AN IEP

The IEP meeting has ended, and the IEP team asks for your signature. Why and when do your sign? Parents' or guardians' signatures are required at only two instances: (1) before your child is evaluated to determine the need for special education, and (2) upon the first placement of your child in a program providing special education and related services. Once your child is placed, any changes in your child's special program require only that you are notified.

In the spring of 1990, the OSEP (U.S. Department of Education's Office of Special Education Programs) ruled that parents can seek a change in their child's special education program at any time. Before such a change occurs, however, your child's IEP must be modified. If you request a change at a time other than the annual IEP meeting, the OSEP suggests it would be appropriate to ask your school district to schedule another meeting. Your school district is not required to grant your request or even comply within a specific time, but the OSEP advises school officials to grant "reasonable" requests for a meeting. Although parents must be involved in IEP meetings and decisions, there is no "explicit" rule under PL 94-142 that says parents must be part of the group that makes placement decisions. On the other hand, parents must be notified of their right to a due process hearing if they object to a change in placement.[8]

If your signature is required only twice, why should you show up at all? Because your input means so much. A speech therapist told me that caring, concerned parents always make an impact on a child's school years. Your regular appearance at IEP conferences, your obvious interest, and your signature (on IEPs that meet your approval) carry more import than if you appear occasionally.

What about Jennifer? Does she notice your efforts to meet with teachers and involve yourselves with the IEP? I think so. Even kids with serious problems recognize parental interest. You can include your child in conferences. Even if you choose not to, your child benefits from learning how you and his or her teachers are trying to make school a more satisfying place.

A PRIVATE OR PAROCHIAL PLACEMENT, WHO PAYS?

Some school districts cannot provide, within their resources, the right services for everyone. In rural or sparsely populated areas, a disabled child's problems can be too complex for the school. If so, the IEP team may recommend a private school. If the school agrees to place your child in a private school, a residential school, or one outside his district, your district must assume the cost. It must pay the entire cost (not just the tuition), including transportation. But if the parents select a private school for their child *against* the wishes of the school district, then those parents must bear the cost.

If you choose to place your child in a private or parochial school, the public school is not required to pay for his or her education, but your state is still required to make special education and related services available. A public school must provide special education and related services to private school disabled children who live within the jurisdiction of the public school.

A special education student in a private/parochial school is also educated with an IEP. A representative from the private school should be present at the IEP meeting, but if he cannot attend, he should participate through an individual or conference call.

PARENTS CAN USE THE IEP

Parent participation can be added to an IEP. If you, the teachers, and/or related service providers are interested in combining school and home strategies to help your child with social skills training, for instance, the plan can state how you will go about it. In other cases, parents and teachers may want to write on an IEP the program they are using to teach self-feeding skills to a severely disabled child.

It isn't necessary to immediately sign an IEP. You can study the paper at home. Special education teachers I talked with believe it is a good idea to take the IEP home for an overnight study. Perhaps a concerned relative or friend could read it. You should return it the next day or so. Although federal law does not *require* your signature, most schools request parents to sign, to indicate they agree with the IEP services. After you sign an IEP, one copy is yours.

After all this attention the IEP gets, it is still a working tool, not holy writ or carved in stone. An IEP can be redirected and rewritten. In 1982, I used the IEP and my knowledge of Section 504 of the Rehabilitation Act of 1973 to redirect Todd's vocational training. I asked that the IEP be rewritten to focus more on work skills than the academic skills we had written in the past. Before I signed the IEP, I requested another meeting with vocational teachers as well as special education teachers and the special education supervisor. The meeting took place in August, before the fall semester.

You can use Section 504 to safeguard your child's right to an education in the least restrictive environment. For example, Ray, a child with spina bifida, lives two blocks from his elementary school. For the first few years Ray was bused to special classes for students with orthopedic handicaps—classes located on the other side of the city.

Ray's parents believed that Ray's physical strength had improved, and since he could use crutches, in addition to a wheelchair, he would be happier and more productive in his neighborhood school. School administrators hesitated, however, reasoning that the school had no ramps, and Ray would need an aide to get to his fourth grade class on the second floor.

At a meeting with the elementary school principal, the director of pupil personnel, and a special education supervisor, Ray's parents pointed out that Ray could not be prohibited from his regular school because he could not walk as other children or because the school did not have a ramp. School officials agreed, and the fourth grade class was moved to the first floor. A ramp was added later. The situation ended satisfactorily because parents and school officials resolved the problem and because the parents understood their rights.

IS THE IEP WORKING?

How do you find out if an IEP is working? When you meet with teachers and visit the classroom, ask yourself if the classroom instruction is utilizing special services mentioned on the IEP. Is your child receiving special services and related services? Is he receiving them as often as stated on the IEP? Although most school districts want to carry out an IEP that you and the IEP team have developed, various problems can arise. For instance, no therapist may be available, a teacher may fall ill and substitute teachers may be needed, or there could be an unexpected change in enrollment or changes in the school building itself. If you are not following your child's program, you may not realize the IEP is not in effect. Don't be a pest, but if you notice discrepancies, ask for a meeting to review services.

Another means of requesting a service is to write it on the IEP. I gained this valuable information from a university professor of special education. After learning this, I wrote a request for extra-curricular activities on Todd's junior high IEP. In the fall Todd received a school work program and extra participation in sports.

IEP meetings take place at least once a year. If your child already receives special education, the IEP meeting probably takes place in the spring, to prepare for the following year.

SCHEDULING IEP MEETINGS

A difficult situation in educating special children has come about through changes in society. Many parents do not participate in IEP meetings because they cannot take time off from work. The same employer who would allow a mother to take her sick child to the pediatrician may not let her attend an IEP meeting. To this person, it is just another school conference; he or she does not understand its importance.

The ability of parents to take off from work to attend IEP meetings depends on a number of factors, including the type of job they have and access to transportation. Teachers I talked with say they have held IEP conferences as early as 7:00 a.m. and as late as 5:00 p.m. in order to accommodate parents' schedules.

In some cases, parents have been successful in explaining to employers that the IEP is like an educational prescription, and the school wants them to participate. If informed that the IEP conference is held annually, an employer might also allow a parent to attend.

Occasions may arise when your advocacy has little to do with an IEP. When Marilyn and the IEP team decided her learning disabled son was ready for integration into ninth grade classes, she made appointments with regular teachers and guidance counselors. She told them David was primarily an auditory learner, that he could rarely follow written directions and could follow only one or two spoken ones. She explained the methods junior high teachers used to help him compensate for this problem. She said David had trouble taking notes from the blackboard, and she told them what alternatives had helped. She explained to guidance counselors that large classrooms distracted her son, and noisy assemblies made him crazy. She added that these characteristics (listed on an information sheet about learning disorders) were not his alone but common to children and adults with learning disabilities and attention deficit disorders.

The intervention paid off, and David began high school with small classes.

TRANSITION SERVICES AND THE IEP

In 1990, the Education of the Handicapped Act Amendments added services to promote independence, also called *transition* and *assistive technology* services, as new definitions of special education services to be included in IEPs. Assistive technology can mean anything from computer-adapted devices for students with vision impairments to reading aids for students with learning disorders. Transition services are "a coordinated set of activities for a student . . . (that) promotes movement from school to post-school activities, including post-secondary education, vocational training, integrated employment (including supported employment), continuing and adult education, adult services, independent living, or community participation."[9]

In *One Miracle at a Time,* Irving R. Dickman and Dr. Sol Gordon comment on the importance of IEPs for vocational and college education: "The IEP is also the right place to make sure that the student is provided with whatever special aids or equipment are required. For students with certain types of disabilities, the advent and widespread use of the computer and word processor are a special boon, alone or in combination: for blind students, for example, they may easily be hooked up to inexpensive 'talking machines' that give the results vocally."[10] Dickman mentions other helps, such as special typewriters for students with cerebral palsy or cassette recorders for students who cannot take notes, all of which can be written in an IEP.

It is important for parents, and sometimes students themselves, to request special equipment for vocational education, if needed. Ask to include it on the IEP, or write it yourself. Students with disabilities who begin their work experience in high school gain a valuable skill—how to adapt to work. Surveys show that disabled people who have a marketable skill have greater success finding work.

AN EARLY PLAN (IFSP) FOR INFANTS AND TODDLERS

Early special services also begin with a plan: Infants and toddlers and their families receive an IFSP, or individualized family service plan. Early intervention services include speech-language therapy, occupational and physical therapy, psychological and health services, case management, and home visits. The IFSP is similar to an IEP except that it includes families more fully—with provisions for parent training and counseling and medical diagnoses. An IFSP should contain the child's level of development, strengths and needs, services required, major goals and outcomes expected, date of the next evaluation, and the starting date of the present IFSP. Parents do not pay for this early help, except where federal or state laws provide a system of sliding-scale fees. The IFSP is evaluated yearly and reviewed every six months or more.

From now on, parents of special-needs children are going to be more involved in preschool programs. Dr. Oliver Hurley, chairman of the Department of Special Education at Georgia State University, says this means teachers and home visitors need to be sensitive to the dynamics of being a parent of a child with handicaps. They need skills to help parents manage behavior and routines; they have to know how to refer the parent to another professional. Personnel also need to learn how to respect the dreams, goals, love, guilt, intelligence, and humanity of these parents.[11]

An IFSP should be a sensitive tool to help parents of developmentally at-risk babies. In *Early Intervention*, the quarterly newsletter of the Illinois Early Childhood Intervention Clearinghouse, Sue Walter writes of her vision for her daughter, Jennifer, who is developmentally delayed. She says, "In the beginning I naively assumed that everyone—doctors, therapists, educators, etc.—knew each other, and would naturally share in our family's vision for Jennifer. The path we have traveled instead has been bumpy and sometimes seemingly impassable. Even though my vision for Jennifer seems fairly common in the world of the family, the extent of her disability makes that vision seem unique, if not unattainable, in the world of service delivery."[12] Sue Walter says it took tremendous effort and perseverance to navigate "the system" while at the same time preserving faith in her daughter's abilities. She offers these suggestions for successful coordination of early services for children with disabilities:

> *Services must be family-focused for maximum effectiveness.* Professionals at all levels must believe that families—whatever their makeup—are the constants in a young child's life and best create the atmosphere in which a young child can thrive. Family needs should be met in such a way that family competence is increased and the focus is on enablement and empowerment. Parents should be considered equal team members with the ability to participate at a level they desire and feel comfortable with.

Programs and services must be community based. Young children and their families should be able to receive services in the most natural environment possible, which means being included where their normal peers would be. A service delivery system . . . should look at existing day-care programs and other types of community-based programs, in addition to home-based programs to meet the needs of this population.

Services should be geographically and culturally accessible. One of the most common problems challenging families is the fact that what they need always seems to be somewhere else. This means packing up and going to the source of help—across one or more counties or perhaps to the other side of a major city—provided you have a means of transportation. . . . We also need to allow for diversity, and respect not only a family's value system but their primary cultural values as well.

Services should be comprehensive and coordinated. An early intervention system should include an array of services for the child and family. Health and social services in addition to education should be combined to benefit the total child and family. We must strive for high-quality services from all professional fields. Families should also be assured that they will receive services as frequently as their situation necessitates. We must avoid creating a "watered down" service system where children receive a little of what they need, but not enough to make a real difference.[13]

PRESCHOOLERS AND THE PRIMARY CARE PHYSICIAN

Children with disabling conditions see doctors often—specialists who deal with the disability, plus their pediatricians, if only for colds and earaches. You want to give extra thought to how you choose a pediatrician for your disabled infant or preschooler. A professional relationship with a child whose needs are unusual can be difficult. Yet your child needs to be able to communicate with the doctor or, if too young to do so, develop a sense of trust with her or him. Older children and teenagers with disabilities need input into their medical decisions and concerns, and they need to be comfortable talking with a physician who understands them. Therefore, you need to find a doctor who can look past impairments and treat your child as a whole person, as she or he would any other child.

A primary care physician is the doctor who coordinates your child's health care needs. This doctor is concerned about your child's whole health and development, including school adjustment. He or she should know what area services are available and be able to refer you to other specialists and clinics as you need them. Physicians can't always answer all your questions, but they should be able to say, "I don't know, but I can help you find out," and/or recommend specialists who they think would be comfortable with your child.

How do you find a suitable primary care physician? A 1990 NICHCY (National Information Center for Children and Youth with Disabilities) paper, *A Parent's Guide: Doctors, Disabilities, and the Family*, says the first step is to identify your needs. Do you need several doctors and therefore need each to be open to discussions with the others? Do you need a doctor more frequently than other families and therefore want someone close to home? Do you need a wheelchair-accessible office? Circumstances surrounding your young child's disability are easier to manage when you find a suitable physician who provides continuity and is willing to work with the IFSP team members and later, the school.

The NICHCY guide to doctors says if your young child's needs are very unusual or extreme, your regular pediatrician may not be suitable. You may need a specialist. You can look in the phone book under "developmental pediatricians," or you can phone the department of pediatrics at the closest hospital. You can call a children's hospital and ask for names of developmental pediatricians. The NICHCY paper adds:

> When asking for a referral to a local pediatrician, there are several important steps. Be sure to request a referral rather than ask for a recommendation; it is difficult if not impossible for someone on the phone to recommend a doctor to someone he/she has never met. You can say, "I have a child (age) who does not seem to be developing like other children his/her age. Do you see such children in your practice?

Is this an area of interest for you? If not, can you refer me to a pediatrician whose special interest is children with possible developmental difficulties?" Be specific about your child's needs; if this is a child whose behavior is very difficult, be honest about this. After all, you are looking for a doctor who is accepting and comfortable with such conditions.[14]

The booklet discusses the use of public health clinics and of Indian Health Services (including who is eligible to use Indian Health Services). For a thorough analysis and guide to choosing your child's doctors, write NICHCY, P.O. Box 1492, Washington, D.C. 20013. Ask for the free booklet, *A Parent's Guide: Doctors, Disabilities, and the Family.* (In 1991, the NICHCY name changed to National Information Center for Children and Youth with Disabilities.)

HELPING PARENTS—A NEW APPROACH

Another thought about helping parents of children with disabilities. During the early years parents normally see many professionals, from diagnosticians to education specialists, such as physical therapists, speech therapists, and tutors. Parents nearly always want to share their joys and challenges with someone else—other parents and understanding professionals.

By the same token, professionals who work with parents of developmentally disabled children are interested in the circumstances that cause parents to either interact enthusiastically with agencies and specialists, attend appointments indifferently, or not show up at all.

When our children are young and/or recently diagnosed, almost none of us knows how to get from point A to point B. Parent education includes learning how to manage our child's disability and behavior and how to take advantage of school and community services. One idea is to make parent education flexible and informal. When Todd was young, there were issues and problems I wanted and *needed* to share, such as conveying the characteristics of his disability to friends and relatives and managing his impulsiveness and hyperactivity. I tended to forget about meetings where groups of parents sat in rows on straight-backed chairs, facing a lecturer. But I nearly always attended sessions when someone said, "Let's get together for coffee and talk about our kids."

Several years ago at a summer camp for children with learning disorders, our local chapter of the Learning Disabilities Association offered the children a special session, "Social Skills and Hygiene." (Did any kid ever like the word "hygiene"?) The problem was no one showed up. After changing the name of the session to "How to Get a Date," everyone piled in, including the eight-year-olds.

A similar concept easy to change is the idea and perhaps the name, "parent training" attached to what would be beneficial programs if parents took advantage of them. A forty-year-old mother of four (one has mental retardation), who already knows quite a bit about mothering, may feel cynical about "training" but receptive to "family education." Families are more receptive to parent-education techniques that do not demean self-esteem.

One sunny morning, Todd and I headed downtown on the Route 8 expressway. I realized with a shock that I had no idea where we were going. It took me five full minutes to remember we had an appointment with an ophthalmologist.

After acknowledging my son's learning problems, my feelings about his disabilities were similar to those of other young parents. Because I had recently discovered the word *remediation*, we had more appointments than time to keep them. Sometimes my frustrations were totally unrelated to anything going on in school. Before one IEP conference, Todd gave us a sleepless night. He broke a good plate while eating breakfast. When the school bus arrived, he was nowhere to be found. I arrived at the conference in a frantic, disheveled state while everyone else there was poised and collected, including Todd's father.

We know that special kids usually need more energy, money, and patience. They need more of the little things—more special equipment, glasses, or doctors' prescriptions. Parents become frustrated when professional appointments or advice add stress to family life. The physical therapist recommends an evening exercise. Teachers may ask parents to help their child carry out school-related tasks. A quandary arises with conflicting opinions or overlapping responsibilities. Parents are particularly frustrated by duplicate testing, a situation remedied when professionals from all disciplines communicate on behalf of a child.

"In every handicap specialty it is essential that parent and professional actively work together on the child's behalf," wrote John Gliedman and William Roth in *The Unexpected Minority: Handicapped Children in America.* "Cooperation may be essential for medical reasons; medication not given the child by the parent is medication that may as well not be prescribed. Cooperation is necessary for the child's sake because neither parent nor professional has a monopoly on the truth."[15]

PARENT CARE IS CHILD CARE

You also need to take care of yourself practically as well as emotionally. If your child is undergoing a combination of therapies which are stressful to family life, you need to make changes. You may want to stop for a while to reassess your child's most important needs, your need to be a family. If you are confronting this situation, communicate with professionals. Explain the problem with current intervention routines. Ask for help to reschedule programs. Sue Walter says accessibility and transportation are major barriers to services for families that must and can be removed. Even when a parent (usually the mother) has a car and can get to a program, she usually pays for parking. Add the stress of taking an infant or preschooler along to intervention appointments. The hurdles can be monumental if she takes public transportation. Early interventions are necessary, but not at the expense of family cohesiveness. Easy access to services is the tool to help families using an IFSP.

Never feel you lack expertise to participate in IEP meetings. Most parents, regardless of education, have trouble understanding the nuances of special education, until they experience it for a while. Every question is a good question when it concerns your child's personal programs. You can be flexible and negotiate, but you need to hang on to the essentials.

An IEP contains five basic items:

- statement of your child's present educational performance, i.e., how he or she is doing academically
- statement of his or her annual or short-term goals
- statement of special education and related services your child will receive and the extent of his or her regular education
- projected dates of annual services and how they are carried out
- which evaluations are used to determine your child's progress

At the end of the book we include a sample individualized education program. The short-term objectives, though, are incomplete, that is, insufficient to achieve mastery of the annual goals. This plan is meant to show you the appearance of an IEP.

Chapter 3

WHEN YOUR CHILD NEEDS EXTRA HELP

When our children were young, we had few words to explain learning disabilities. Parents today have access to abundant medical and psychological information that they can convey to people who see their child on a regular basis.

A child's survival can depend on talk. In his book about learning disabilities, *The Misunderstood Child*, Dr. Larry B. Silver says parents need to explain their child to adults who operate preschools, day-care centers, summer camps, and Sunday schools. He says you may have to explain the whole thing, that your child is not bad or lazy. The disability is simply invisible.[1]

EXPLAINING YOUR CHILD TO OTHERS

In explaining your child's special problems, you can encourage activities promoting success. Does Timmy swim better than he ties knots at day camp? Try to find a group activity that strengthens Susan's social skills. One skill, no matter how small, leads to new skills, particularly if a child has low self-esteem. Look for flexible programs and directors willing to adjust activities to children's varied learning styles. To help matters, carry a short description of your child's learning patterns and skills. Ask teacher(s) and persons who tested your child to help you write a couple of paragraphs.

How much do we tell and how much do we leave out when we explain our child to virtual strangers? When I explained Todd's learning disabilities to a summer camp director, the director said Todd should instead attend a camp for children with disabilities. Later, my reluctance to explain Todd's perception problems to a driving instructor resulted in emotional trauma for Todd. The instructor told Todd he would never learn to drive because he had a "thick skull."

What we tell depends on who needs to know and for what reason. Do we explain our child's disabilities to excuse his or her acting out or to find ways to help the child control unusual behavior? Ellen described to our parent group how her hyperactive son frequently walked home from school, roof to tree to roof, his feet never touching the ground. Once Todd and another boy climbed the fence above a busy freeway to look for returnable pop cans. They slipped around the steep, grassy slope, oblivious to the danger.

Although Todd was young when we learned about his problems, I still suffered from his behavior. I took family comments personally. I wish someone had told me this about parenting a disabled child: Your child is not to blame for his problems, and neither are you. Nevertheless, it is painful to be the mother or father of a child who rarely succeeds in the classroom and who operates on the periphery of school and neighborhood life. What's more, you know other parents in the neighborhood know about your child.

We explain our children when it is necessary to help them compensate, to manage a social or learning situation, and to help others comprehend the reasons behind their behavior. Although it is one of life's toughest jobs to speak up for these children with so many problems, our support makes a big difference.

YOUR CHILD AND EXPLANATIONS

Todd has occasionally been asked to talk to parent groups about his life and education. He declines because the idea of public speaking makes him anxious. He adds, "I have dyslexia, but I am not handicapped."

How soon and how much should your child discuss his disabilities with other people? In her book, *Parenting Plus*, which is about children with special health needs, Dr. Peggy Finston says parents need to use discretion in letting a child decide when he or she wants to talk about his or her differences. A child can learn to discuss the handicapping condition, but the outcome depends on the type of impairment, the child's age and maturity, and, of course, the circumstances. Dr. Finston says another issue is when the child should say it and how much control we exert over this process. "Parents can go too far in their efforts to have their children be unapologetic about their condition and accepted for who they are. . . . Sometimes a child wants to talk about his difference, but it has to be on his terms and in his time." She says when it is a question of a health risk (such as epilepsy), your peace of mind is important. "Don't withhold information from others that you believe *might* endanger your child's health. His anger at your disclosure will be much easier to live with than your guilt over some unfortunate event that you could have prevented."[2]

RELATED SERVICES ENHANCE SPECIAL SERVICES

The people who wrote PL 94-142 knew that children need developmental, corrective, and support services, that is, *related services*, to get the most from special education. You can share your child's personality with school personnel who provide these services. You don't need to use the language of diagnosticians, but you can explain when your child seems to be learning, which activities he or she prefers or dislikes, and how he or she relates to other children.

Related services are social work, audiology, early identification of handicapping conditions, diagnostic medical services, child and/or parent counseling, transportation, speech therapy, occupational and physical therapy, psychological services, recreation, school health services, and supports such as interpreters for the hearing impaired.

Ideally, a *social worker* follows your child's history. This person is familiar with community resources and offers parents current information on such areas as financial help. As a child grows older, the social worker recommends job opportunities and training. Social workers connected with schools are to provide a social or developmental history on a handicapped child and group and individual counseling to a child and his or her family. They are to help families work with home and neighborhood problems that could affect their children's school adjustment and utilize school-community resources to help the children benefit from education.

In reality, few school social workers provide all these services, and many families rarely know of other social workers unless they use state or community service agencies for disabled children. Parents who want a social worker's help can schedule an appointment with a community clinic. Social workers are usually employed by hospitals, special schools, and clinics, in addition to local schools and state agencies. Families receiving help from PL 99-457, the Education of the Handicapped Act Amendments of 1986, are more likely to use the services of social workers through an IFSP.

Another related service is *early identification*, including physicians' examinations. Your child may receive a medical evaluation from your family doctor or pediatrician—or may be evaluated though in-hospital tests administered over two to three days. Hospital examinations include blood tests, urinalysis, EEG (electroencephalogram, a test to measure brain function), EKG (electrocardiogram, a test to measure heart function), tests for glandular disturbances, plus vision and hearing tests.

Medical examinations are only one part of an early identification. Your child may be given a psychological exam by a certified school psychologist. This assessment covers your child's intellectual, social, adaptive, and emotional development. A school social worker may look at family, school, and community factors contributing to school problems. A speech pathologist or therapist may assess your child's language skills.

An *audiological* assessment refers to hearing tests. An audiologist is not a physician but a hearing specialist who determines how well a child hears. This specialist can examine a child to see if the child reacts to sounds within certain ranges. (He or she can determine if a child's hearing is essentially normal but there may be gaps that cause some words to sound unclear.) After testing, the audiologist may recommend treatment, such as the use of a hearing aid or speech therapy.

Early identification of your child's special needs is carried out by a team that includes clinicians, parents, teachers, representatives of the school district, and the child (if appropriate) in order to produce an IEP.

Occupational and physical therapy can overlap. Both provide activities to help your child cope and learn, including communication. An occupational therapist teaches a child to change clothes, use the toilet, take a bath, eat with utensils, and play with toys. The physical therapist teaches your child exercises and the use of muscles to improve balance and coordination.

Other related services not mentioned here can be added if they help your child benefit from special education. Parents who want related services should know these services cannot be offered to a child *not* in special education. The purpose of special education via an IEP is to focus on reducing problems resulting from a child's disability that interfere with learning and school performance. If your child's need for a related service is mentioned in the IEP, then the school must provide it. If services are unavailable from your local school district, they must be procured from another school district or agency.

In some cases a school system may ask the family to use their private insurance to pay for services such as physical therapy. "Parents do not have to do this," says the Ohio Coalition for the Education of Handicapped Children. "Consider the long-term effects, such as lifetime limits on coverage, before agreeing to use the family's insurance."[3] Related services are included in a free appropriate public education.

Psychological services are tests to gather information about a child's learning and behavior. Some of these tests measure educational achievements. How well does the child read, for instance? Is he or she learning math concepts? School psychologists and education specialists administer these tests, including your child's intelligence test. The number given for your child's intelligence quotient, or IQ, is not the final word on this subject. One intelligence test does not cement a child's abilities for the rest of his life. An IQ test roughly indicates a child's intellectual functioning at a given time.

TRANSPORTATION IS A RELATED SERVICE

Do you wonder why *transportation* is considered a related service, especially if your child rides the same school bus as other neighborhood children?

Tom is a child with mild cerebral palsy. His education is managed by an IEP, but he is able to keep up with classmates in a regular schoolroom. He continues to need physical therapy for coordination. PL 94-142 says if Tom needs therapy to help him benefit from education, the school must include transportation to and from related services. Sometimes parents drive the child to school or to related services, and the school provides a gasoline allowance.

Your child should not be subject to a shortened school day or an unusually long one because of transportation needs. Philip R. Jones says in *A Practical Guide to Federal Special Education Law*, "Creative planning and scheduling is vital to make certain the education of handicapped students is not slighted by a shorter school day where transportation equipment is utilized first for nonhandicapped children."[4]

If your child receives special education in a parochial or private school, in another district or county, or in a residential school, he or she must still be able to avail of transportation services.

WHEN IS COUNSELING A RELATED SERVICE?

Counseling is a related service. The concept behind parent counseling in PL 94-142 is to help parents understand their child's needs and provide them with information about child development. Counseling by a school psychologist, social worker, or guidance counselor is no indication a family cannot handle their problems. One purpose of counseling is to help a family through a particularly rough time or to help a family member with a troublesome problem. The 1990 reauthorization amendments (PL 101-476) added *rehabilitation counseling* to related services.

Some leeway is allowed schools in providing professional services. Counseling services can be provided by social workers, psychologists, or guidance counselors. Psychological testing can be carried out by qualified psychological examiners, psychometrists, or psychologists, depending on individual state standards.

Robert, a ten-year-old with mild retardation, is learning steadily but is behind other children academically and socially. Other children tease him because he is clumsy. Robert comes home in an angry mood. He slams the door and kicks the cat. His family "catches" what he suppresses on the playground.

Some days we understand our child. Other days we wonder where our child leaves off and the disability begins. Sometimes reading books and listening to speakers are not enough.

If daily life with your child overwhelms you, you need to locate help from a school or community counselor who understands children's disabilities. An effective counselor, trained to understand the whole family, can give you tips on managing typical problems.

Counseling can help you explore relationships with grandparents, relatives, or neighbors, if you feel the disability is causing divisions. You may need help in finding financial assistance for your child's prosthesis (leg brace or other body support). You may need help with physical therapy or advice on talking with your children. These days counseling means getting help when it is needed—for a variety of reasons. If money is a factor, look for a clinic with sliding-scale fees. If a counselor is ineffective, or you feel he doesn't understand families of special-needs children, look for another.

DIAGNOSES AND PARENT COUNSELING

Rarely do parents receive counseling in the form of emotional support on hearing that their child is going to be disabled. It is true that parents of special-needs children experience grief the same way as other families faced with significant loss. A child's diagnosis can create subtle changes in parents. They're confused and wonder how they can help.

Some parents find themselves having to educate grandparents while trying to control an uncontrollable child. Parents may be subject to family criticism before the problem is eventually discovered. They too would like their child to learn and behave if they only knew exactly what to do to be of help.

Our efforts to cope with our feelings may be reflected in our interaction with teachers and related services providers. We can feel defensive, angry at times, and frustrated that not more is being done.

Some parents carry their burdens to the teacher. While a teacher is confused by parents' complaints about their child, he or she may be unaware that complaining about one's child can be a cry for help. A mother who criticizes her child may echo family members. She details her child's foibles to stay on the good side of her husband and grandparents. To take the child's side is to risk alienating her only support system.

Because Todd was educated in a special unit for learning disabled children, we felt separated from normal school activities by the intensity of his education and by our feelings about his developmental delay—a type of isolation commonly experienced by parents of handicapped children.

It took a long time for my husband and me to come to terms with parenting a special-needs child. Although we spent considerable time discussing Todd's development, we avoided mentioning his specialness. Not wanting to upset each other, we skittered around the real issues. After reading about special parenting and talking with other parents, I eventually concluded that my sense of loss was normal. Our acceptance began the day we decided our child was no less cherished because he is disabled.

In his book about loss, *Your Particular Grief*, Wayne E. Oates says many parents react differently to the same pain. One parent realizes the impact of special parenting sooner or feels angrier or more frustrated than the other. "Marital distancing" is a hazard related to the stress of living with a handicapped child. Oates asks parents if they haven't the right to experience some feelings individually.[5] It is normal to feel your own feelings in all respects concerning the disability.

Additional related services are *school health* and *recreation*. Health programs include school-offered dental checkups or access to a qualified school nurse during school hours. Sex education films and speakers, including AIDS education, should be offered to children with disabilities as well as to other students.

RECREATION CONTRIBUTES TO GROWTH

Recreation is an important but often overlooked related service. The law says recreation includes assessing and providing leisure and extracurricular activities, therapeutic recreation services, and recreation programs in schools and community agencies.

While growing up, your child needs guidance in using leisure time, in finding activities that are fun and contribute to growth. Recreation can be a dilemma if some kinds of recreation are closed to students with specific disabilities. Although a physical disability has traditionally been viewed to limit access to sports, that concept is changing to include activities for disabled kids such as horseback riding, gymnastics, camping, swimming, and in some cases, skiing.

Competitive sports are generally unsatisfactory for children with disabilities. Unless special accommodations are made to integrate a disabled child into a program, conventional sports leagues, such as soccer, football, or baseball (especially Little League) can challenge a child with delayed development in areas where he is most vulnerable: gross motor control, instant decision-making, and speed.

Todd was frustrated by neighborhood ball games, complex board games, and coordination games such as Ping Pong. But he and his younger brother enjoyed family outings—miniature golf, camping, eating out, bowling, and taking day trips to museums and local historic sites.

Recreation depends on what enhances children's skills and what they truly enjoy. You can check out programs at the YMCA and YWCA, Indian Guides, Boy Scouts, and Girl Scouts. Special Olympics is a recreation.

So how *do* we entertain children with delayed development or more complex disabilities? The public television shows *Sesame Street* and *Mr. Roger's Neighborhood* continue to provide entertainment as well as valuable learning for children with special problems.

As children grow older, recreational opportunities can pop up from unexpected places. Before Todd could drive solo at age twenty-one, he learned to ride the metro bus around the city. It was his idea. It is normal (but nothing to be ashamed of) that parents tend to shortchange children's abilities. I feared crime and drugs. I feared Todd's determination to learn bus routes. I feared he would get lost. After much teeth grinding Todd finally learned to carry enough change and to change bus lines in order to get to his favorite mall where the video games were better.

One afternoon Todd was riding a city bus when a gang fight broke out between rival high schools.

"What did you do?" I asked, preparing a speech to ban bus rides.

"I sat in a corner and tried to be invisible," he answered.

Todd drives now, but he takes the bus when his car breaks down or he fears snowy streets. The bus gave him freedom during his teen years, and he learned to take care of himself.

You can be realistic about related services. The mother of a child with serious retardation wanted to write on an IEP that her daughter, who was receiving speech therapy, would be talking in sentences by March. Related services are not miracles on the road to normalcy but strategies to help your child gain the most from his/her education.

A positive relationship between parents and related service providers is vital to special education. Most school districts operate on good-faith principles. They continue to search for creative ways to reach children with and without special needs. These districts want to involve parents as much as possible. If you are fortunate enough to live in such a district, you must take advantage of efforts to include you. When a teacher or related service provider asks about your child, try to reply honestly. If your child demonstrates unhappiness or troubling behavior, don't picture the child as someone he or she is not. It is unnecessary to reveal your private life to these professionals, but you owe them the courtesy of a genuine appraisal.

PARENTS HELPING PARENTS

When Todd was young and acting out, or his activity level increased, I usually believed it was something I did or did not do to manage him. Should I be firmer about his impulsiveness? Why couldn't he get to sleep at night? What did I do to cause this? My mind churned with questions.

Nearly always, Todd's behavior changed, whether because he caught a cold, or because of some outside pressure I knew nothing about. When his speech came slowly and not too clearly, I had to decipher these problems myself. As he grew older, he could tell me about incidents on the school bus or playground. Even now I can tell when a social or work situation is causing him stress.

Special parenting *is* labor intensive. We see no immediate solutions to large problems. We are troubled by the future. Friends and family may be unable to help because they are too close to our situation.

Parent groups are exceptional in supporting parents through disheartening scenarios. Where else can you ask other parents what they are doing about their child's inability to play with neighborhood kids? Where else can you ask how to explain attention deficit disorders or learning disabilities or the need for special education to extended family?

Among worthwhile developments for families of disabled children over the past twenty years are parent-to-parent support programs. These programs are found in every state and are sponsored by chapters of the Association for Retarded Citizens (The ARC), children's hospitals, school districts, and health departments. One program, "Parents Educating Parents" (1985), focuses on education, especially parent-teacher relationships. Hospital-based programs tend to focus on parents whose disabled children are identified at birth. Parent-to-parent programs offer help with transportation, financial advice, sharing special equipment, and child care. The groups operate with a sense of mission and a vision that certain universal experiences are shared by parents of disabled children. These parents offer an understanding that comes only from those who have been there.

RESPITE = PARENT REST

Another thought about recreation includes parents getting away from their children. You, of all parents, need respite. You need to interrupt child care, even for twenty-four hours. Respite should be directed to you either as a couple or single parents.

Parents with preschoolers, one of whom is delayed and/or physically disabled, often lead volatile lives filled with child care, work, and household responsibilities. Although more than 60 percent of American moms work outside the home, the care of preschoolers is usually left to them. Mothers who do not work outside the home can be equally stressed from lack of relief.

If continued proximity to small children is causing you stress (I have rarely met a mother of a special-needs child who didn't need some relief), you need to build your own support system—to get away from your children several hours a week. Use the time for yourself to browse through stores, watch a movie, sit in the library, or exercise—whatever stabilizes and contributes to emotional strength. Be honest with family and relatives about your need to refresh. At a local parent support group a young mother said that her twenty-four-hour involvement with two overactive, impulsive children made her fear she would strike out and hurt them. Don't let your stress get this far. Do something now.

How can you tell if you or your family could benefit from respite care? Do these questions apply to you?

- Is finding temporary care for your child a problem?
- Does caring for your child sometimes interfere with scheduling appointments for yourself or your family, or with completing personal projects?
- Is it important that you and your spouse enjoy an evening alone together, or with friends, without the children?
- If you had appropriate care for your child with special needs, would you use the time for a special activity with your other children?
- Are you concerned that in the event of a family emergency there is no one with whom you could feel secure about leaving your child?
- Do you avoid going out because you feel you are imposing on the family members and friends who care for your child?

If you can answer "yes" to any of these questions, you and your family could benefit from respite services.

How do you find respite? Can you arrange to swap child-care hours with other mothers in the neighborhood, with relatives, or with some members of a support group or of your church? Call your YMCA or YWCA and ask about summer getaway camps for moms. Contact your pastor or a human service group, such as the United Way, the Community Chest, the Red Cross, the Easter Seal Society, the United Cerebral Palsy Agency, or the Association for Retarded Citizens. Call your city or county health department and social services department. As your child grows older, he or she will benefit and you will find relief through sheltered workshops and summer camps.

You may need respite for reasons other than recreation. Families use respite for emergencies such as a death in the family, for taking care of family business, or for pursuing an education. Several types of programs provide relief. The Kalamazoo, Michigan Parent Respite Care Co-op is a *parent cooperative*. In this case, a small group of parents obtained funding for a respite program from the State Department of Mental Health, in cooperation with the Kalamazoo Association for Retarded Citizens and the Family and Children's Services of the Kalamazoo Area.

In Toronto, Canada, a parent group obtained government funding to recruit host families to provide *community home care*, through a program called Extend-a-Family.

Respite foster care is provided by the State Office of Mental Retardation in Hartford, Connecticut and by the Kansas Children's Service League in Kansas. In Utah, the Early Childhood Research Program and Utah State University provide a family home respite day-care program.

Group Respite Care Residences are programs in which the child or adult with disabilities stays in a group residence designed for respite care. This type of program is used in Philadelphia and in St. Louis, the latter sponsored by the St. Louis (Missouri) Association for Retarded Citizens. Children and adults with disabilities stay for a few hours or longer. They receive individual, personal care from nurses and trained child-care aides who work on shifts. Parents pay on a sliding scale.

Other community arrangements include *teaching homes*, where children with severe and profound handicaps are taught basic living skills. *Group homes* for adults with disabilities are becoming more accepted. The group home concept provides a more normal residential environment than the institutions of the past.

For a comprehensive report, write NICHCY, P.O. Box 1492, Washington, D.C. 20013. Ask for *News Digest*, April 1986, about alternatives for community living, family support services, respite care, and related topics.

PARENT ENCOURAGEMENT LEADS TO HOPE

In earlier books about rearing kids with disabilities, parents were often commended for their detachment. Now we know parents can expect to feel varied emotions in rearing disabled kids. You need to be kind to yourself in regard to your parenting skills. Although you are doing the best you can, there is no rule that parents of special-needs, difficult children have to be better parents.

Of course you worry. You are deeply concerned about social and academic lags. Your children suffer too. They are desperate for you to understand what they are going through. They need to know you are willing to listen to them, even when their observations are unrealistic and immature.

Although our children need extra help to benefit from special education, individuals outside the handicap experience often wonder why parents do not embrace every innovative school of thought or remediation. As parents we *are* open to new thought, but we are stopped by constraints of money and time. How do we feel when a well-meaning relative or a casual acquaintance tells us about a new teaching technique, a special school, an electronic device, or even a diet, each guaranteed to: (1) nearly cure our children's impairments, or (2) remediate them to near normalcy?

Angry? Frightened that so much time has passed without our trying these strategies? Parents are sometimes led to believe that children can be helped by one program, one medication or treatment, or perhaps a single, charismatic therapist. Naturally we want to learn all we can about our child's impairments in order to understand them, but we have learned through experience that there is no magic. We parents have a tendency to stick with a course of action showing positive results. Our child's combination of remediations may be slow, but it's helping. Besides, changing horses in midstream is perilous and takes more energy than we can muster. What if we try another program and find it ineffective? What if the program shows promise, but the teacher is opposed to it and our child hates it? What if the drive to this new specialist takes another chunk out of our money and time? And certainly not the least consideration, what will be the effect of this new effort on family life, on siblings?

The most valuable services are directed to your child in specific situations at home and at school. A child with disabilities thrives on family acceptance and a resourceful exchange between parents and professionals.

You need to avoid situations that drain you of hope, however. One of the greatest favors you can do for yourself and your family is to focus on professionals, other parents, and family and friends who understand what *you* are going through.

Fortunately, I have met only one professional who continually intoned, "Todd is a seriously delayed little boy." Even parents new to disability understand the gravity of delayed development. The years following a diagnosis are rough. Parents are constantly exposed to intervention terms: delayed development, working-far-behind-other-kids-in-this-class, low verbal skills, and the frightening "at risk."

In other words, good news is rare. Parents who fail to appear for another educational test, who cannot seem to follow through on a continuum of psychological assessments pointing to mental retardation or acute learning disorders, may not be denying a disability but taking a break from another round of emotional distress.

It is difficult when one hears repeatedly from informed specialists how much one's child differs from other kids. Parents who act unaccepting or oblivious may be gathering strength. We see what we can see. Then we wait and see more. "He will never go to college. . . . She will not climb mountains" are among the most devastating opinions parents can hear—and most *are* educated opinions based on a variety of assessments.

Our powers and prayers need a foundation. How can parents work to improve their child's meager skills if they believe there is no hope? How can we add a dimension of hope to evaluations, to annual meetings with teachers and other specialists?

Parents, particularly mothers, need to hear their children are making a little progress. They need to hear *they* can make a difference. They do not need conditions ("Yes, your daughter is doing okay, but she can do better if you change the therapy or increase her vocabulary words"). Jan Mariska says in *Acceptance Is Only the First Battle*, "We do not need false hope, but we do need hope—and the fields of medicine and early intervention are ever-changing, sometimes from year to year. Few of us have any expectation that our children may someday be 'perfect,' but we *work* to help them become less imperfect."[6]

Parent and author Betty Lou Kratoville says in light of the total experience, counselors might admire the remarkable re-silience that keeps parents going and looking for answers. "A counselor truly interested in establishing a relationship of integrity might be moved to say with absolute honesty, 'You know, *you* are the best thing your child has going for him. You are the only person who sees him as he truly is. Teachers and doctors and people like myself see him only in certain circumstances, under controlled conditions, in fragments, while you see him at his best and at his worst. You are the continuity of his life, and how marvelous that he has you.' "[7]

Encouragement leads to hope and to improving our parenting skills. When we suffered over Todd's continuum of diagnoses, a close relative strengthened us by saying, "Look how well he's doing now—all because of *you*."

Through the years we've made critical decisions. Because the idea of learning disabilities was new, we were unsure of our judgment. Eventually we learned that growth is frustrated by constantly retracing one's steps. "We should have. . . . If we had only. . . . Why didn't we?" are futile questions. Trust in your love for your child and your wisdom as a parent. You aren't responsible for all the bad things that happen or for the good things either. Learn what you can, but evaluate what you learn.

Chapter 4

MAINSTREAMING
A Regular Life

Most adults with disabilities want to belong, without fanfare, to a regular society. They want to shop, eat out now and then, rent a video, work, and complain about the cost of gasoline, like everyone else.

Disabled children are no different. Todd's declaration, "I am not handicapped," is not a bias. Todd understands he has learning disabilities, but he wishes to be part of community life.

Parents of both disabled and nondisabled children are concerned about educational mainstreaming. Parents whose children are not disabled wonder about the cost and quality of mainstreamed or integrated programs. In many situations, opposition to mainstreaming has come from parents of disabled children, who are satisfied with their children's special classes but wonder if schools are ready to integrate special-needs children.

These fears are justified. In 1985, Stanley J. M. Vitello and Ronald Soskin, authors of *Mental Retardation: Its Social and Legal Context*, said the limited number of trained teachers, the lack of related services, and a lack of acceptance of disabled children all justify parent concerns.[1]

In education circles no recent phrase has caused as much unrest as mainstreaming. Which disabled children can be taught in regular classes? What extra help do they need? Will regular teachers be burdened, and what kinds of support do they need? What about teachers who do not feel comfortable with disabled students? Can severely disabled students be integrated?

In special education language the term "least restrictive environment" means each handicapped child should be taught with nonhandicapped children as much as possible—unless it is clear the child would benefit more from a special class. Handicapped children should also be educated in the same school they would attend if they were not handicapped, unless their IEP targets a better location.

But least restrictive environment (LRE) or least restrictive alternative (LRA) is not the same as mainstreaming. The word "mainstreaming" is, in fact, never mentioned in the law. Mainstreaming does not mean closing special classes in order to return handicapped children to regular ones.

Not long ago, a child with disabilities was routinely separated from his neighborhood school. The idea of an appropriate education means educators are trying to get away from separating children with disabilities from integrated and/or regular programs. The framers of the law said that LRE means some children can be intelligently returned to normal classes while considering the needs of teachers and other students.

Mainstreaming is gradually blending special children into society as well as into public schools. This is what the law says about integrating handicapped children:

> . . . to the maximum extent appropriate, handicapped children, including children in public or private institutions or other care facilities, are educated with children who are not handicapped, and special classes, separate schooling, or other removal of handicapped children from the regular educational environment occurs only when the nature or severity of the handicap is such that education in regular classes with the use of supplementary aids and services cannot be achieved satisfactorily.[2]

The requirements of a least restrictive education also apply to preschool children who are diagnosed as having a disability. If a school district does not provide preschool programs, some alternative methods for meeting the LRE requirements include placing children in programs, such as Head Start, by placing disabled children in private school programs for nonhandicapped preschool children or in private schools that integrate handicapped and nonhandicapped children, or by locating classes for handicapped preschoolers in regular elementary schools.

If special-needs children are moved into regular classrooms, why is everyone so jittery? Because of a misleading idea that mainstreaming simply involves moving disabled children from special into regular classes. And because quite a number of disabled students have already been educated without special classes. The more serious questions are, in fact, not addressed to self-contained classrooms for children with profound disabilities but to students with milder but no less troubling problems. For instance, how much special education is needed for students with learning disabilities or mild to moderate mental retardation?

First, decisions about integrating children into regular classes must be based on each child's needs at the time. We cannot assume *all* children with mental retardation or learning disabilities can be placed in regular classes two hours a day. Nor should all blind children be placed in a state residential school for the blind. Before the idea of least restrictive environment, the trend was to fit handicapped children into existing programs. Under the new LRE concept, if no appropriate program exists, a new or modified program should be developed.

MAINSTREAMING REQUIRES PLANNING

The following elements make up a least restrictive environment:

- Children with disabilities are taught in the same school they would attend if they were not disabled.
- The placement decision is made after drawing up an IEP.

- Whenever possible, children with disabilities are taught in regular classes with their nondisabled peers.
- Special services are provided at regular schools. Lack of these services cannot be used to deny placement in integrated settings.
- Children who cannot be fully integrated into regular classes are integrated to the greatest extent possible. Separate classes are located near regular ones, not in a separate part of the school, and are not given special labels. For instance, "Room 103" is better than the "MR class."
- Positive attitudes and social integration are actively encouraged.
- Junior high students are provided career planning and counseling services and prevocational skills training.
- Secondary students are provided opportunities to learn practical vocational and community living skills at normal community training sites.

Mainstreaming or integrating children with disabilities requires planning. All school staff, parents, the disabled child, and regular classroom children involved should be fully aware of the reasons for a mainstreaming placement. In addition to this, we tell disabled children the reasons behind their placement in a more mainstreamed class. Information for the mainstreamed children depends on their age, maturity, and type of disability. School personnel are also informed. Appropriate in-service education for school staff should take place before a mainstreaming placement.

The main concern of regular teachers is what to do when a special child is assigned to their classes. Before disabled children enter regular classrooms, the regular teachers should have access to their IEPs. Do the teachers understand the characteristics of mild or moderate mental retardation or cerebral palsy? Are they aware of the characteristics of learning disabilities? What do they know about society's pressures on disabled people? How do they feel about handicaps in general? Do they know about convulsive disorders, for instance, or sensorimotor defects? Has the school district made an effort to modify the structures of buildings to accommodate wheelchairs?

In addition to being part of the IEP team, the regular teachers should receive a printed statement as to what the disabled children can do by themselves. This is especially important if they are physically disabled, blind, or hearing impaired. The teacher should have access to a schedule of related services and should know if a particular child will be accompanied by an aide.

Before the teachers are ready they need materials and help to adapt their classrooms to these special children *and* regular students. They need to know *how* to do it. For this reason, the school provides support or assigns education specialists to smooth the integration of disabled students into regular placements. These specialists are known as *resource teachers* or *learning disability specialists*, and *special education supervisors* or *coordinators*. Support staff should check on the children's progress in their regular classes to determine if or when they need more services or a change in services.

A problem arises, however, from the area these support people are required to cover. Special education supervisors are often spread so thinly through a district, that they have little time to spend with one teacher. Regardless of this practice of overextending resource persons, a regular teacher still needs vital information before mainstreaming occurs.

Teachers who integrate disabled students should receive information on the following topics:

- How to write an IEP
- How different disabilities affect children's behavior and how they learn
- Strategies and ideas for classroom use
- Related services the child is using
- Where needed related services can be found, if not in the school district
- How other parents in the school feel about mainstreaming

- Basic knowledge of PL 94-142, plus related laws such as Section 504 and the Buckley amendment (Chapters 6 and 7).
- Classroom help for children with speech and language problems
- Counseling special children
- Teacher-parent rapport
- Preparing nonhandicapped children for a special child in the classroom

One concept of mainstreaming is changing a child's "placement" or moving the child from one educational area to another to enhance LRE and to improve his or her education.

MAINSTREAMING STUDENTS WITH MILD OR SEVERE DISABILITIES

Bill, a student with learning disabilities, is introduced to regular social studies and history. Bill already goes to regular music, art, physical education, recess, lunch, and other "soft" subjects. Mainstreaming for Lisa, a child with emotional disturbance, means temporary placement in a regular art class for part of the day. Lisa spends the rest of her day in a special class.

Circumstances vary. Mainstreaming a severely disabled boy could mean his transfer from an institutional setting to a public school special education unit. Mainstreaming a mildly impaired girl could involve moving her from special classes to a regular class with tutoring, or to a resource room.

An issue of NICHCY *News Digest* further explains integration or teaching students with learning disabilities in regular classrooms:

> Depending on the severity of the disability, the student may be placed in a self-contained special class or may remain in a special class with supportive services. The student who is placed in a self-contained special education class receives intensive specialized help. The class size is smaller than that of the regular class, and the teacher

has been trained to work with handicapped students. Many students in self-contained special classes attend some regular classes, either in academic areas in which they perform particularly well or in nonacademic areas such as music, art, or physical education. In this way, they spend at least part of the school day with their nonhandicapped peers.

Students who remain in the regular class may attend a resource room on a regularly scheduled basis. The amount of time spent depends upon the child's individual needs, but usually consists of at least twenty minutes a day, three days a week. In the resource room, the student receives individual or small-group instruction from a teacher trained to work with handicapped students. In addition to directly instructing the student, the resource room teacher should coordinate with the regular class teacher, sharing information and providing assistance in selecting the best methods and materials to use with the student.

Some students may not need to spend any time outside of the regular classroom. With the help of a consulting teacher, who is a specialist in learning disabilities, the regular class teacher may be able to provide the additional help the student needs.[3]

Parents normally wonder about the long-term value in integrating children with mild or moderate mental retardation. Will their children learn more or less in regular classes? Do their social skills remain the same, or do they copy the behavior of typical kids?

An argument for integration says retarded children model their behavior after normal children in integrated schools. Dr. Daryl Paul Evans says in *The Lives of Mentally Retarded People*, "Although it is difficult to ascertain whether modeling nonhandicapped behaviors is the cause or not, it has been demonstrated . . . that integrated mildly retarded pupils showed more socially appropriate behaviors in school than a matched group of segregated students."[4]

Is integration easier or harder on kids with retardation? Studies based on reports by students who are mildly retarded say they had better attitudes about school than students in special schools. It seems that mildly retarded students in regular classes were better off academically for two reasons. One, special classes may not demand as much from students compared to retarded children in regular classes. Two, regular classes involve more academic work.

A valid argument against mainstreaming retarded students is that some retarded children feel inadequate and frustrated in mainstreaming situations, either because they see normal youngsters as intellectually superior, or because other children are cruel. Critics of mainstreaming say that even if students are integrated and show more socially appropriate behavior or perform better academically, the personal costs are high because integrated retarded students are significantly more anxious over social and academic pressures. Dr. Evans says, "The issue boils down to this: a youngster who has relied on the predictability of a special-school environment can be shocked and bewildered in an integrated setting, and in some cases it is difficult to predict whether a student will adapt or crumble."[5]

MAINSTREAMING STUDENTS FOR A GENERAL ED WORLD

Before PL 94-142 became law, we parents were told that our handicapped children were more comfortable, safer, and better educated in special classes. After the law passed, parents heard the phrase that special ed kids were going to have to function in a general ed world. As our children grew older, we realized the latter is true, that integration is truly all-encompassing. Charles R. Callanan says in his book about his disabled son, *Since Owen*, that after the passage of PL 94-142, many schools grouped similar special students into classrooms away from the mainstream but still with access to exterior doors and bathrooms. Callanan says, "Imaginative administrators, on the other hand, moved the special students out of the shadows and into central locations . . . " where they had access to cafeterias, student lounges, and auditoriums. "[Students] shared such common facilities as lockers, snack bar, library, and school store, offering a realistic but sheltered laboratory for handicapped children to learn such life skills as making change, choosing from the cafeteria menu, using appropriate table manners, being on time for class, using coin-operated vending machines, and operating locks under realistic, integrated conditions."[6]

Perhaps this is what Woody Allen meant when he said that 80 percent of life is just showing up. When disabled children carry out socially accepted tasks in regular environments, they are preparing for a general ed world.

Integrated disabled students continue to receive a free appropriate public education, which means that parents are notified before the children are tested, or their educational setting is changed. Your consent is not required for any program change after your child's first placement, but you always have the right to ask for another IEP meeting and review. In-room changes in teacher planning, lesson plans, and activities do not require parents' approval.

Special students in regular settings continue to receive the related services and support they need to function, such as tutoring, typewriters, tape recorders, large-print texts, or a sign language interpreter. They receive physical and occupational therapy, speech, training in sign language or braille. If only a few students in the school need such services, the school can share these special personnel with one or two other schools or hire consultants to train and work with regular teachers. It isn't your job to scout around adjacent school districts for such related services or support. However, you should take some initiative to see to it that your child is not shut out of a particular subject or an integrated class, or integrated without the needed support, because these forms of support are not forthcoming. Ask your IEP team where accommodations can be found to more fully integrate your child. Ask what you can do to help.

If your child is educated in regular classes, the IEP is reviewed annually or more often, if necessary.

MAINSTREAMING IS ALSO SOCIAL

Integration is social in that children with disabilities adapt to nondisabled behavior. Todd matured appreciably during the months he spent with the high school track team. He took part in masculine repartee. He controlled the acting out behavior he had used in early special settings because he realized the consequences. C. Beth Schaffner and Barbara E. Buswell, codirectors of PEAK Parent Center in Colorado Springs, say that integrating children with special needs contributes to positive relationships with other kids, enhances students' self-esteem, and increases their motivation to learn. They add, "The importance of relationships goes beyond the basic needs all children have for the give and take, the support, and the sense of belonging that comes from having friends."[7]

Can children with severe handicaps be comfortably integrated in regular settings and where is the line between severe and mild disabilities? Emily, a special education teacher of students with autism, believes a least restrictive environment begins socially, even for students with severe disabilities. Emily takes her students into lunchrooms and hallways so they can copy regular behavior.

If teachers are not comfortable with disabled children, how do we integrate disabled kids with accepting teachers? A teacher who feels uncomfortable about bringing a disabled student into the classroom is no less adequate than other teachers but may have less experience with children's differences. Another teacher may feel more accepting of a child with a physical disability than one with retardation or learning disabilities. Philip R. Jones says, "While we would like to believe that all teachers are accepting and understanding, this is probably not the case." Jones says teachers with disabled children in their classrooms should not be overloaded just because they are cooperative or have attended workshops or have taken additional course work.

What do we take into consideration in mainstreaming severely impaired children? Jones says two basic questions must be asked in considering an appropriate program for a handicapped child: One, is the program in the least restrictive environment possible, and two, is the program in the most productive environment possible. He adds that in the final decision, it seems the answer to the second question should receive more attention than the first.[8]

HOW FAMILIES CAN HELP

Children without disabilities usually pick up cultural expressions that help them fit in, first with peers, later with adults. It is not so easy for LD-ADD children or those with mild retardation. Children with learning problems tend to miss out on social give and take, unless they are motivated or someone teaches them. Even children with delayed development and impaired speech can learn to respond with "Thank you" and "Please" instead of "Yup."

One way to prepare for integration is role-playing. We called it rehearsing. We couldn't rehearse everything, but we prepared for wedding receptions and introductions. Todd once escorted me to a retirement reception. We practiced shaking hands. We practiced using table manners. We rehearsed as many stock lines as we could think of. "How do you do? Good to see you. Isn't the weather nice? Dad wanted to be here, but he has the flu. What are your retirement plans?"

Todd has trouble remembering names (as many people do). "How nice to see you again," covers a lot of territory. No one expects you to create an Emily Post, but every positively reinforced social skill is another step toward integration.

As disabled children grow older, social competence includes learning what to tell and what not to tell. Todd eventually became less impulsive, but he continued to share family business and our personal observations with anyone. Consequently, we avoided discussing in his presence how much the car cost or our opinion of cousin Suzy's husband.

As a young adult, Todd has finally decided how much to reveal or conceal. When a policeman asks if Todd knows he is missing a taillight, he replies, "Is that right, Officer? I had no idea."

Social mainstreaming includes disciplining a child with disabilities. We don't like to think about it. Shoppers at the supermarket we go to are horrified by parents swatting a disabled child on the behind because he ran off once too often.

The purpose of compassionate discipline is imparting correct behavior. A tantrum in public is still a tantrum, no matter who is doing it. In *We Have Been There*, Lyn Isbell wrote about disciplining her son, Walter, who has Down syndrome.

> It's easy to say that you'll treat a retarded child just like you treat a non-retarded child. It's great in theory, [but] the way things work out, it's going to be uphill all the way. . . . The message is that it is critical to discipline your retarded child. A retarded brat is a brat. And brats do not go through life winning friends and influencing people. And you have to decide about it; you and your child have to live with the decision. . . . It HURTS people to see you spanking that poor little handicapped child, and people don't like to be hurt. These same people, however, don't live with the vision of the poor little handicapped child growing into a poor large handicapped adult with no idea in the world why he hasn't got much of a fan club. People who throw tantrums to get their way seldom have an extensive circle of friends.[9]

Suit the punishment to the crime. A swat is not always the answer. A younger Todd had a disconcerting habit of wandering away through crowded shopping centers and stores. Although I explained that he was to keep track of *me*, not the other way around, he was unconcerned.

One day at a shopping mall I let him get lost. I doubled back and followed him for a while. He was plenty worried. It took just one episode to convince him that *really* being lost was most unpleasant.

Another day—another shopping mall—I noticed a young retarded woman indulging in a colossal tantrum in a women's coat department. Long coats, car coats, ski jackets flew everywhere with no one paying much attention, including store clerks and the woman's parents. Clearly, everyone was embarrassed. Perhaps the store clerks only wanted the family to leave. Perhaps the parents knew their daughter would get tired and stop.

Whatever our children's abilities, they nearly all develop a talent for misbehaving in public, plus they discover early just where and when, usually in front of other adults. Does it matter how your disabled or retarded child behaves in public? Why is it easier to ignore acting out? Because changing a disabled person's behavior is more difficult and requires more involved strategies than molding the behavior of a nonhandicapped person. Robert Perske says to look away from disagreeable behavior "may be the most hostile thing a parent can do. How will a child learn if he's never faced with it and helped with it? But we might do just that if his actions were misunderstood. It is much easier to face your child when you understand he is not a monster. He merely has yet to learn better judgment."[10]

Aside from this, what happens when parents are no longer present to control or limit a disabled adult's integration, when the community becomes more accepting of mentally disabled persons? Your child needs to learn appropriate behaviors for integration.

Do not regard your child's aberrant behavior as a parenting fault. Parenting a special-needs person is a new and challenging experience for all of us. Nonetheless, if your child's behavior is getting out of hand and is more than you can change through home strategies, you can look into behavior modification programs through local agencies.

You wonder if discipline (or modification) pays off. It does. In most respects, a message, "You are not in control, so I am helping you control yourself," tells children that because they are loved, they are expected to change their behavior. But more is involved than one child's behavior. Do you discipline using the same methods you use with your other children? What do your children think is fair and not fair?

Consistency is important. Parents need to agree on how and

when to react. You decide if the behavior is a by-product of the disability or if the child is just testing the waters. You talk to your child based on his or her reasoning powers. Why is he or she acting out? Is this a form of rebellion? Is it the result of teasing or another unpleasant experience on the school bus or in the neighborhood?

As Lyn Isbell observed about discipline, talking with retarded or immature, perceptively impaired children with short attention spans is easier in theory. If they are verbal, what do they want to talk about? Probably not much that interests you because they have a different and much younger perspective. As parents we eventually face the painful truth that our disabled children can be trying when they are *not* misbehaving—their observations totally inappropriate to the situation. We talk with them as much as we can, however, and accept that we are under no obligation to respond to every comment and complaint.

Okay, so you talk as a family. You talk at dinner, but your special daughter talks more than anyone else about a rock star or a sitcom or whatever comes to mind. You break in, "Don't forget we have to get our clothes bundles to the church by 7:30." She speaks up heatedly, "Well, it was my turn," or worse, she throws a tantrum. Everyone chimes in, "I was talking too. Nobody ever listens to ME." Chaos ensues. Sound familiar?

Time out. Time to explain again, to reinforce the idea of family members taking turns talking about their day. We set a time limit on topics not of interest to everyone. We certainly don't want to put down a child for his viewpoint, and we are entitled to our opinion as well. But when we allow any child, disabled or not, to verbally tyrannize the family, the child fails to learn some important communication skills.

Eliminate "you-messages" when you talk with your kids. You-messages indicate blame and are expressions of parents who see the child as misbehaving. Even when the child is acting out, responses such as "You drive me nuts," "You better listen . . ." and "You eat like a pig," are degrading and make children defensive. You-messages damage esteem and provide children with strike-back messages of their own: "You drive me nuts too and you eat like a cow," thus escalating a discussion into a verbal battle.

Better to talk with "I-messages." I-messages communicate how you respond to your child's misbehavior. I-messages allow you to assume the role of guiding your child on an equal level, which means you respect his or her dignity. Children may get angry because they are not getting what they want, but I-messages do not damage the parent-child relationship.

Start with something the child did right. Being specific with praise is better than generalizing. "I like the way you used nice table manners when Grandma was here." "I like the way you are combing your hair." "Thank you for clearing the table. You did a nice job." "I am proud of how you got yourself ready for the school bus this morning." Rather than "You are a good girl," say, "You were nice to that little girl in the park. I liked the way you helped her on the swing set."

I think it's okay to tell kids they are good people, because they hear so much about the bad ones. This is different from saying, "You are a good boy," which is a vague assessment of behavior. You can explain to your child that he or she understood a situation or another person because he or she is sensitive and is "a good person."

WHEN YOUR CHILD NEEDS YOU—PART ONE

On Monday did your son come home from school in a fury? Did he stand before you so angry, he couldn't speak for screaming? Now is the time he needs you most, when his combination of disabilities is causing him to suffer at school or in the neighborhood. More than likely, even with interventions, school is a difficult place. He needs you to help him calm himself, to express his frustrations.

Discipline is not the same as refusing to hear children vent. School can be rough, both academically and socially, for children with learning problems, even with the best interventions. One of the major stresses on children with hidden handicaps is that LD and ADD characteristics are misinterpreted, and behavior *is* a symptom. Adolescents, in particular, can be intolerant of those who do not fit the mold. Children need their parents to listen to stories about their day without getting excited or criticizing their self-described behavior. Let them get it out of their system verbally rather than physically. Help them find a way to work it off by exercising, running, or taking a fast walk, if that's what they need. Disabled children and their siblings should be allowed to speak their minds, to tell you their viewpoints, even when you disagree. When you cut them off from expressing themselves, they may eventually draw away, feeling you cannot respect or tolerate their opinions.

How *do* parents respond to bad language, writhing on the floor, or jumping up and down and screaming at the community ice cream social? Let's not close our eyes to the truth that foul language, even from the mouth of a disabled child, is socially damaging. Assuming your disabled son never hears a swear word in *your* kitchen, he's eventually going to pick it up from television or his peers. You can tell him which words are unacceptable. Allow him to "try them out" in the privacy of his room.

When your son acts out, try to focus on the act you dislike, rather than say he is stupid or disappointing. Tell him in private. Don't humiliate him in front of relatives, other children, or anyone else.

Remove him and do not give him what he wants. Tell him later, "Your behavior at Aunt Emily's house was unacceptable. You need to talk to me instead of acting like you did. Next time something is bothering you, come and tell me about it." Then make yourself available for the talk.

One way to avoid tantrums is to explain new situations ahead of time. Explain the whole thing: "We are going downtown to a business office. First we will park in a big parking lot. We may have to wait in the office awhile, so we are taking a book and a toy." If your child has memory problems, explain again and again.

Rehearse what is going to happen, and how everyone is going to act at Aunt Emily's house. Keep in mind that some adults cannot tolerate impulsive, overactive children, even when parents are working to change their behavior. If your son is simply too rambunctious to take to Aunt Emily's, arrange to meet her in the park for a picnic.

When is praising children nonproductive? If they are not feeling good about themselves, they are not inclined to believe any word of praise that increases their anxiety. We all say to our kids from time to time, "Just do the best you can." But "Do your best" can backfire if our children are already trying hard. When parents say, "You can do better," they imply that their children are not doing well enough, which *they* interpret as not being good or competent enough.

We should encourage our children to think about how other people feel in various situations, even those they only hear about in the neighborhood or at school. Educators Richard Elardo and Judith Freund wrote in a *Perceptions* newsletter about the effects of parental behavior on children's social development. "When you correct your child for misbehavior, explain to him how the misbehavior affects the feelings and behavior of others. An example of this would be to say, 'I can't let you play your harmonica in the living room right now because my friend and I are trying to talk and your playing makes it hard to hear each other; this upsets us, but you can play it in the bedroom or outside."[11]

Discuss with your child alternate ways of dealing with interpersonal conflicts. If he or she has a problem with a teacher or a friend, help think of different ways to handle the problem. Then discuss various consequences of these solutions. Let your child know you really care how he or she gets along with other people.

Relax. Outside of consistent abuse such as ridicule, sarcasm, or put-downs, what we tell our kids once or several times is not going to permanently damage their esteem. A rule of thumb is to talk to our children as kindly as we talk to our friends.

MAINSTREAMING IS LETTING GO

We parents fear change. Even when a situation is nearly intolerable, it's hard to make changes because of the insecurity involved, because of our inability to know What's Out There. This is why you may hear some comment during your child's growing up years that you are overprotective. It's a normal reaction to involving oneself with a child's development.

Michael T. Yura and Lawrence Zuckerman say in *Raising the Exceptional Child* that the realization that perfect parenting is impossible sometimes comes as a shock to parents. "One of the pitfalls parents are faced with is their feeling of having to deal with every misbehavior successfully. . . . The misbehaviors of children present a difficult challenge to today's child-rearing skills. Parents of exceptional children need to realize that it is impossible always to know the best course of action, the best solution to a behavior. One of the reasons it is impossible is because many of the situations are so complex and may be virtually impossible to correct."[12] The authors say the first step to becoming truly good parents is to realize that parents cannot do everything, cannot solve every problem presented.

The hardest lesson I've learned as a parent, however, is to let Todd either correct or live with his own mistakes. Early on I guided him away from mistake-making opportunities. I didn't want him to fail more than he was failing already. I guarded against hurt.

Parents tend to think of their children as more helpless than they really are. You can keep your child out of danger, but you can't manage his life forever or avoid errors. Even educators who love special kids have a tendency to think people with disabilities have to succeed, that they can't have opportunities to fail. When children are disabled, we tend to think they should do things a certain way instead of jumping into new territory. Todd's autonomy increased when *I* learned to let go. Even now I will myself not to inspect his refrigerator. He isn't going to starve.

Paul, a young man with spina bifida, is educationally and socially integrated. Paul's school is accessible by wheelchairs and has made other classroom adjustments. In summer and good weather, Paul's friends push his wheelchair across the park to fast-food restaurants and in and out of neighborhood kitchens.

Early observers of educational mainstreaming wondered if normal children would be injured by integrating handicapped students. I think the opposite is true. Typical children accustomed to sitting in classrooms and moving through halls with disabled children will be more comfortable with disabled adults in the workplace. There is solid evidence that the earlier mainstreaming occurs, the faster it is for children with disabilities to adapt to regular environments and for nondisabled children to become comfortable with their disabled peers.

Frank E. New, director of the Division of Special Education in the Ohio Department of Education, believes more children with disabilities are going to be educated in regular classes. "With new technology we are going to overcome problems that create handicapping conditions, particularly for individuals with physical disabilities. Opportunities for these people will expand greatly." Mr. New says community housing patterns are also changing from a concept of group homes for disabled people to residential homes and shared apartments.

BEHAVIOR A COMPONENT IN LRE

Of all the factors involved in mainstreaming, a child's behavior is particularly noted. If special children are so disruptive that other students' learning is diminished, then their needs cannot be met in a regular class. If the school insists your daughter disrupts regular classes, you must see for yourself. Observe her classroom and playground behavior on several occasions. You should be able to affirm or reject the school's viewpoint. If she prevents classmates from learning, then it is only fair to move her to a more restrictive environment. But if you feel your child can benefit more from a regular placement than a restricted environment, you should meet with school personnel to resolve the situation. Your daughter and her teacher may need additional support to integrate her into the classroom.

Parents of older children appreciate the benefits of mainstreaming. Blending children into normal worlds is called "normalization," or exposing children to community life and the community to them. Integration is a realistic goal for children who can be placed in normal settings, and outside of severely impaired individuals, *most* qualify. In 1975, *Closer Look* wrote:

> When we talk of the "supports" that have to be provided to the handicapped child in the mainstream, our starting point *has* to be our genuine conviction that there really is no special status we assign to one child and deny to another because of IQ or looks or . . . other differences. Acceptance—a conviction that every child is worthy of the best we can give—is the heart of the matter. We have to really mean it when we say that to be different from the "norm" is not just OK—it's what being human is all about. . . .[13]

Chapter 5

HOW LAWS PROTECT YOU

A woman with cerebral palsy wrote in a transition newsletter that she has always depended on the kindness and paternalism of others, but NO MORE, thanks to the ADA.[1] Why do we need the ADA? The *Americans with Disabilities Act of 1990* mandates social and occupational equality. One purpose of this law is to eliminate myths surrounding people with disabilities by strengthening their cultural opportunities.

Before the ADA, Alan Gartner and Tom Joe wrote, in *Images of the Disabled, Disabling Images,* that one of the most serious obstacles to the progress of disabled citizens is the widespread presumption of biological inferiority, the same presumption used to oppress other minorities. "Just as racial or ethnic groups were once considered genetically deficient and women were regarded as weaker than men, the subjugation of people with disabilities often appears to be implicitly justified by individual limitations or inabilities. In a culture that places an extraordinarily high premium on physical agility, strength, and appearance, the subordination of disabled people might even appear to be natural. Moreover, they live in a world that was planned and constructed almost exclusively for the nondisabled."[2]

Gartner and Joe wrote that architecture and environment are products of public policy, and "The deprivations imposed upon disabled citizens by present environmental features might have

77

been prompted either by the political neglect of their interests and needs or by a deep and unrecognized aversion to this segment of society." The authors say, in a culture that usually regards disability as personal misfortune, few are willing to recognize a situation that results in a denial of constitutional guarantees supposedly granted to everyone.

Thanks to the ADA, PL 94-142, Section 504, and other laws granting equal civil rights to disabled citizens, the rights and privileges of living in this country are accessible to your child, and will be accessible to him or her as an adult. What's more, an appreciation of rights guaranteed by laws designed for disabled individuals will help you and professionals educate your child.

THE ROLE OF DUE PROCESS IN SPECIAL EDUCATION

After my child was placed in special education, I heard about *due process*. At parent meetings and LDA state conventions, due process was cussed and discussed, which led me to believe no one quite knew what it was.

Due process (also called due process of law) is the course of proceedings established by the legal system of a nation to protect individual rights and liberties. In our country, due process is guaranteed under the Fifth and Fourteenth Amendments of the U.S. Constitution. Although due process appeals can be used in any educational situation (such as in regard to discipline, grades, etc.) we apply the term to students with disabilities. In special education, due process applies to steps that are followed to assure a free appropriate public education is available to every disabled child. The people who can take these legal steps are parents of disabled children, parents of children who are suspected of having a disability, or a school district.

There are more than one law guaranteeing important legal steps for children, parents, and schools:

- *Public Law 94-142* says parents must receive a written notice a reasonable time before the school intends to change the child's identification, evaluation, or educational placement (meaning class or building), or before a change in providing a FAPE, or free appropriate public education. Parents may begin the hearing process if they have reason to believe the school is refusing a change in identification, evaluation, or classroom.
- *Section 504 of the Rehabilitation Act of 1973* is a civil rights act. Section 504 says no otherwise qualified handicapped individual in the United States shall, by reason of his handicap, be excluded from participation in, be denied the benefits of, or subjected to discrimination under any program or activity receiving federal financial assistance.
- The *Americans with Disabilities Act*, PL 101-336, signed into law on July 26, 1990, prohibits discrimination against people with disabilities—in employment, transportation, public accommodations, activities of state and local governments, and telecommunications relay services.
- The individual laws and standards of each state.
- The policies of each school district.

PL 94-142 says each school district must follow correct steps in educating children who need special services:

1. Your child is identified as a suspected handicapped child and referred for evaluation.
2. Your child is given different kinds of tests from areas of medicine, psychology, and education. He or she is evaluated as a whole person.
3. Before your child is enrolled in any special program, he or she must have an individualized education program.
4. His or her IEP is reviewed annually.

Before PL 94-142, some states put monetary limits on educating disabled students, reasoning that money was in short supply for all students. The Education of the Handicapped Act says limiting funds for special education is unconstitutional. The 12 percent limit (meaning 12 percent of a state's school-age children) is a limitation on funding only and does not relieve schools of the responsibility of serving more than 12 percent. A comment in the federal regulations says the population of children your state may count for allocation purposes may differ from the population of children to whom the state must offer special education services. "For example, while . . . the Act limits the number of children who may be counted for allocation purposes to 12 percent of the general school population aged three through 17 (in States that serve all handicapped children aged three through five) or five through 17 (in States that do not serve all handicapped children aged three through five), a State may find that 14 percent (or some other percentage) of its children are handicapped. In that case, the state must make a free appropriate public education available to all of those handicapped children."[3]

WHO CAN INITIATE A HEARING AND WHY?

Parents who believe the school has not been diligent in following correct procedures may call for an impartial hearing. You may have your own reasons for requesting a hearing, but these are typical:

- You think your child needs special help but is not receiving it in regular classes. You feel the school is underestimating, ignoring, or has not recognized his or her problems.
- A reverse reason is when the school wants to educate a child with special services against the wishes of parents.
- You believe the school district is not providing an appropriate special education based on your child's needs.
- You object to an evaluation or the way it was carried out.
- You asked for but have not received an evaluation.

- You object to major changes in your child's program; your child's speech therapy has been reduced from two half hours to one half-hour a week, for instance.
- You object to ending your child's special education program.
- You object to the school removing your child from his or her special class, or you were not notified in writing of a change in placement.
- You think your child should be educated in a less restrictive environment.
- An IEP is changed against your wishes.
- You believe your child has been suspended or expelled for behavior caused by his or her disability.
- You are not allowed to add the results of private tests to school records.
- You are not allowed to read your child's records.

The school may initiate a due process hearing for the following reasons:

- You ignore or refuse the school's request for an evaluation. (I urge you not to object to a recommendation for an initial evaluation, which can shed light on your child's problems at school. You still have the right to refuse special services or a special class if you feel they are unnecessary.)
- You refuse the special placement offered by the school.
- You keep your child out of school because you have refused the placement.
- You request another evaluation, but the school feels the original evaluation was adequate.

Charlotte Des Jardins, executive director of the Coordinating Council for Handicapped Children in Chicago, says it is easier now for parents to get services, but more questions are directed to appropriateness of services. She says there are many problems with learning disabilities, primarily because there are many forms of learning disabilities—disorders which are often misunderstood.[4]

PROBLEM SOLVING WITHOUT HEARINGS

A hearing is requested when parents and school have held many discussions and cannot agree. Just as we do not kill a fly with a cannon, we do not use a hearing for minor disputes. You should be able to talk with all concerned parties and resolve differences *before* you initiate a hearing. Keep notes on all that has transpired. Talk to the classroom teacher and other school people such as the counselor, nurse, school psychologist, and social worker. Can any of these people help you make changes? Will they back you up? See your family doctor or pediatrician, the audiologist, neurologist, or similar specialist who has seen your child. Will they express their views on tape, which you can then take to the school?

Make an appointment to see the school principal. Approach the problem as a situation in which both of you are seeking a solution.

If the school is unwilling to change its decision, go directly to your district director of special education or director of pupil personnel services. If no such person (title) exists, see your superintendent of schools. The superintendent is responsible for all school programs in the district and must be involved if other officials are unresponsive. When meetings are held, try to involve other people familiar with your child.

If nothing has transpired thus far, take your complaint to your local school board, which may give you insights on appropriate contacts or locate someone to intervene with school officials on your behalf.

Next, contact your state director of special education. He or she should have information you can use.

Locate your allies: members of state and local chapters of parent and advocacy organizations, such as the Learning Disabilities Association, the Association for Retarded Citizens, United Cerebral Palsy, and similar groups.

Call your state protection and advocacy center for information as to what to do next. See Resources, p. 261, for the address of the National Association of Protection and Advocacy Systems.

Finally, if you think your disagreement with the school is not close to resolution, if you believe what your child receives is wrong, inadequate, or even harmful, you should write a letter to your local director of special education (or equivalent official). Do not threaten or state the problem angrily. The purpose is to request a "due process hearing." Send the letter by certified mail. Request a return receipt. This way, you'll know the letter has arrived. Keep a photocopy of this letter and other correspondence, plus notations of *all* pertinent phone calls.

If you are thinking about challenging your child's placement, the Coordinating Council for Handicapped Children in Chicago suggests you visit your child's program or the program the school has offered your child. "Spend a whole day if you can. Take a notebook along and take notes that will help you document why the program is not an appropriate one for your child."[5]

PARENT-GUARDIAN RIGHTS IN HEARINGS

When the school district requests a hearing or receives your request for a hearing, it must inform you of any free or low-cost legal services available in the area. It is important that you contact support people and gather all pertinent materials before you initiate a hearing. When the hearing is granted, an "Impartial Hearing Officer" (IHO) will serve as a party to hear both sides of the argument. This officer cannot be one who works for the school district or any other agency caring for your child. After the hearing, the officer makes a decision within forty-five days.

If the child is a ward of the state, or parents are unavailable for due process, substitute parents must be found.

The law guarantees you certain rights during the hearing itself. It is your right to be accompanied by counsel (an attorney or someone familiar with laws for the handicapped). You and your counsel have the right to request the presence of witnesses and to introduce evidence and examine witnesses. You have a right to receive a written or recorded report of the hearing and to receive a written decision on the outcome. You can take your child to the hearing if you want. A copy of the final decision is mailed to you.

THE LAWYERS' FEES BILL

As mentioned earlier, the 1986 Lawyers' Fees Bill was passed by Congress and signed into law by President Reagan. Officially known as the Handicapped Child's Protection Act of 1986, the law authorizes the payment of attorneys' fees *to parents who win a PL 94-142 court case*. However, parents can recover lawyers' fees and other court costs, whether the case is settled during an administrative due process hearing or through the courts.

Parents who decide to act as their own counsel should take extreme care with information and procedures. School districts are usually represented by knowledgeable firms with expertise in all forms of school law.

If you are unhappy with the hearing results, or your school district is dissatisfied, either of you may then appeal to the state board of education, the state commissioner of education, or an appropriate state officer. This person will then review the findings of the earlier hearing.

If parties still cannot agree, you may take your case to the courts, to the Court of Common Pleas of your county, or to a Federal District Court. Appeals to the courts must be preceded by an Impartial Due Process Hearing and a state level review.

The steps for due process (after communication between parents and school district has failed) are:

DUE PROCESS HEARING, followed by

APPEAL TO THE STATE DEPARTMENT OF EDUCATION, followed by
CIVIL ACTION or APPEAL TO U.S. DISTRICT COURT.

Hearings are usually the end of negotiations or attempts between school district and parents to reconcile differences about a disabled child's educational opportunities. In a discussion of appeals and hearings, special educator–administrator Dr. Leslie Brinegar wrote, in *Human Advocacy and PL 94-142: The Educator's Roles*, "Most potential appeals can be headed off by improving communications between the school and the home, actively working out truly participatory IEP meetings, giving proper attention to the details of parent notices, and establishing meeting times with plenty of time for parents to make arrangements for attending."[6]

Something is lost in conflict. Children who know their parents and teachers are not getting along because of their class placement, homework, or discipline are probably worrying instead of learning. Hearings can be avoided when (1) parents assume that school personnel are working in their child's best interests, (2) school personnel are willing to listen and act on parent concerns, and (3) both parties try to coordinate home and school learning-behavior strategies.

Winston Churchill said, "To jaw-jaw is better than to war-war." Due process appeals take an enormous amount of energy and time. Before any decisions are made about your child's education, he or she will continue in the current classroom situation unless parents and school agree otherwise. Before you begin legal processes, you and your school should meet and talk, and talk some more.

SSI CAN HELP WITH MEDICAL COSTS

Can you use help for your child's medical costs? Until recently, unrealistic rules kept many families from getting Supplemental Security Income (SSI) and Medicaid for their children with disabilities. A 1990 United States Supreme Court decision, *Sullivan v. Zebley*, changed the eligibility requirements for a number of children with autism, spina bifida, AIDS, cystic fibrosis, other chronic illnesses, and birth defects, who were earlier denied benefits through SSI.

A recent publication from the Mental Health Law Project in Washington, D.C. says, as a result of the Zebley decision, some children who were turned down after January 1, 1980 may be entitled to benefits back to the date they first applied.

In a Zebley review, Social Security must apply its new rules to the child's overall condition. If the child's daily functioning now prevents the child from doing things other children the same age can do, the child will be found disabled. Usually, the Social Security Administration will *assume* the child was also disabled when he or she first applied. The family or child will then receive payments back to the date the child first applied for SSI.

If your child qualifies for SSI, your family's annual income can be $20,000 or more and its countable resources can be $5000—higher limits than for an adult with a disability. A child eligible for SSI can receive *up to* $407 monthly—money the family can spend on the child's behalf. The exact amount of SSI depends on your family's income.

How does Social Security determine if your child is disabled? A child is considered disabled if his or her physical or mental impairment is as severe as a condition that would prevent an adult from working, and if the condition is expected to last at least twelve months or to result in the child's death. Social Security considers a child blind if, with corrective glasses, the child's vision is no better than 20/200 or the child's visual field is 20 degrees or less. However, a child whose visual problems are not that serious can still qualify as "disabled" if the problems are severe and long-lasting.

To apply for SSI, visit your nearest Social Security district office or call that office or Social Security at 1-800-234-5772 (1-800-2345-SSA) to make an appointment. The TTY number is 1-800-325-0778. Call again if lines are busy. Social Security usually takes three or four months to decide if a child is eligible, but once SSI payments start, they will go back to the date the application was filed. Social Security will use the date of the initial visit or the phone call as the application date (as long as the application is filed within sixty days of that visit or call). If you think your child qualifies for benefits, it is important to go or call right away.

When you apply at the SSI office, bring your child's Social Security number, a birth certificate (photocopy) or other proof of the child's age, information about family income, such as payroll slips, bank books, insurance policies, and car registration, names and addresses of doctors, hospitals, and clinics that treated your child. Also be ready with names and addresses of teachers and therapists, social workers and other caregivers, and relatives and neighbors who know your child. Bring along copies of your child's recent IEPs.

For more information about the Zebley case, call the Zebley Implementation Project, sponsored by Community Legal Services of Philadelphia: 1-800-523-0000, toll free.

The National Information Center for Children and Youth with Disabilities (NICHCY) will send you a free resource sheet of legal aid, Protection and Advocacy (P&A), and disability and parent organizations in your state. The number to call is 1-800-999-5599.

You can call your local legal aid or legal services office, and/or your state P&A system.

For more information about eligibility, how to apply for SSI, and how Social Security determines financial need, call your local Social Security office. See Resources, p. 257 for information on ordering the booklet, *SSI New Opportunities for Children with Disabilities*.

WHEN YOU NEED AN ATTORNEY (A SIDEBAR)

What can you do if communication with the school district has failed to resolve any differences? You bring in a lawyer as soon as you decide to challenge your child's educational placement or to protect the violation of his or her civil rights. You call a lawyer when it appears that mediation with the school district has failed and/or when you are going to be involved with the courts.

Which lawyer do you call? You need an attorney who specializes in education law, preferably special education and civil rights of persons with disabilities. A general practice attorney might be competent for some things, but he or she might have to research on PL 94-142 and cases pertaining to it.

Call your local bar association. Contact your local law school or the legal department of a local university. Ask them to recommend a law firm with someone who has expertise in education law and civil rights, specifically PL 94-142 and Section 504.

In their book about using legal services, Gregory Smith and Steven Naifeh say, "A recommendation from someone who has the expertise to assess a lawyer's competence is much more valuable than rave reviews of a neighbor or fellow worker. Good sources of *informed* referrals are other lawyers, law school professors, judges and other courtroom professionals ranging from accountants to bankers to physicians, depending on . . . the specialty of the lawyer you're looking for."[7]

Call your local advocacy group, such as the Learning Disabilities Association (LDA) or the Association for Retarded Citizens (ARC). Ask if they know of an attorney whose specialty is children's educational rights.

If you live in a metropolitan area, an advocacy group may recommend two or three firms. A law firm, rather than a single attorney, will have access to firm resources. If the lawyer handling your case becomes ill or cannot continue for some reason, someone else in the firm can take over.

You can look for a lawyer through a local legal aid society. Legal aid societies can help you on a sliding-scale fee basis. You can contact the American Civil Liberties Union, 1432 West 43rd Street, New York, NY 10036, or the Children's Defense Fund, 122 C Street NW, Washington, D.C. 20001. Or call (202) 628-8787.

You can call a legal clinic, but remember that the lawyer's

knowledge of your problem is much more important than general knowledge of law or the organization he or she belongs to. Don't walk your fingers through the yellow pages.

After you narrow down your list to a few attorneys, set up personal interviews. Assemble photocopies of important documents in order to explain your case. Write down pertinent issues you want to discuss. You conduct your interviews in absolute courtesy, but if a potential attorney is put off by questions about his or her expertise in education law, you probably wouldn't want to use him or her.

As potential lawyers these questions:

"Do you handle cases in education law, specifically PL 94-142, Section 504 and related state laws?"

"Have you handled similar cases in the past?"

"Do you have time to take our case?" If a lawyer can't see you within a reasonable length of time (about two weeks), try another lawyer. Beware of a lawyer who is available to see you anytime, or the one so busy he or she can't see you at all, or for weeks or months.

Ask you potential lawyer, "What is your fee arrangement, and how often will you bill me? What total legal fees can we expect?" (An important question! How much can you afford to lose? According to the Handicapped Children's Protection Act of 1986, parents are reimbursed for legal fees, if they win, but not if they lose.) You need to assess the costs in the event you lose your litigation with the school.

"Will you handle this case personally, or will a partner or associate handle it?"

"How should we go about pursuing this case, and what do you want us to do next? What papers should I bring with me?"

Ask you candidates for references. Call and ask the references if they were satisfied with the lawyer's professional conduct, ability, and fees. No lawyer can predict how a case will turn out, of course, but you can ask references about how they felt regarding *their* cases.

The first six criteria for selecting a lawyer are first impression, education (Where did you attend law school?), experience, reputation, competence, and cost.

After you decide on a lawyer, send the others short thank-you notes.

Your new lawyer will know how to prepare for your case. That's why you hired him. Be honest with your lawyer about what has gone on before. Assemble letters, documents, doctors' reports, IEPs, records of phone conversations—anything pertinent. Better to gather too much than to leave out something important. Photocopy everything you hand over to your lawyer, and keep photocopies in a safety-deposit box.

Chapter 6

KEEPING TRACK OF TESTS AND RECORDS

During the years of a child's education and therapy, some problems are solved, and others appear. In time we understand our children as whole persons. Our expectations change as they change and grow. While we acknowledge some achievements are out of the question, we delight at their progress in other areas.

Acknowledging a child's disability is not the same as giving up. It is only by affirming a disability that we reframe our concept of family and free ourselves to enjoy our children's unique compensations. The process can take weeks, months, or years, depending on the individual and his or her family.

During the first few years of special education and services, our child's needs are identified and treated by tests and evaluations. Tests are measurements, not whole pictures. They tell about your son's or daughter's levels of development. Because PL 94-142 calls for a number of developmental assessments considered necessary for improvement, parents may come to believe their child is a product of test results. Sometimes it is hard to separate him or her from all that evaluation.

EVALUATIONS UNLOCK NEEDED SERVICES

Yet tests *are* important. You are intimately aware of how your son talks at home, how he plays with other children, or how he enjoys riding his bicycle. You live with him and compare him to siblings and neighborhood kids. A professional does not have this advantage. He sees your child for a short time. He evaluates your child's strengths and needs.

Children's tests involve three areas. The tester should select the right tests, should know how to give them, and should be able to skillfully interpret them. If a child's impairments are unusual, the right test may not be available. In that case, a combination of tests is given. Tests are given by school psychologists, education specialists, or psychometrists. (A psychometrist is a specialist who gives psychological, individual intelligence, and achievement measurement tests.) People who evaluate children are found in hospitals, schools, private and community clinics, psychologists' offices, and doctors' offices.

A test is as valuable or as meaningless as the conditions surrounding it: a child who is ill or a tester who does not relate to a particular child. But when conditions are good, and your child relates well to the person testing him or her, an accurate picture develops of your child's unique needs. In a 1985 report about psychological testing, the NICHCY *News Digest* says, ". . . the examiner needs . . . to make the child feel comfortable with the testing situation so he or she can concentrate on the task at hand. At the same time, the examiner must use uniform procedures, presenting each item in the same way to each child."[1] Without uniform tests, it is impossible to discover if a child's problems are due to his or her development or to fluctuations in testing.

As we know, no child should be placed in a special program on the basis of one test. The use of several tests to measure development is often called a multiphasic evaluation. The results of these tests tell how well a child communicates and gets along with other people. They describe education levels in reading, math, and spelling. A child should receive psychological tests to target emotional problems. Test results include the child's health status.

Tests should be given by specialists drawn from more than one field. Evaluations should be made by a multidisciplinary team or group of persons, including at least one teacher or other specialist with knowledge of the child's suspected disability. No test or group of tests can provide a complete picture, but samples of behavior through psychological tests allow a psychologist to make generalizations about the child.

Tests evaluate children on the basis of their age, disabilities and abilities, language, and cultural backgrounds. Children must receive tests in their native language or a language with which they are comfortable. If the child is deaf or blind, this is taken into account. If the child cannot talk, other types of communication are used, such as sign language, gestures, or special boards. Tests given these children should be validated; that is, it is determined if the test measures what it is supposed to measure.

Children bring a variety of experiences and background to testing. Some children with poor school experiences become upset with testing conditions. This causes them to perform poorly on tests. Other youngsters with less exposure to tests may not know how to perform. Children from poor or homeless environments may be unable to focus on procedures because of troubling situations beyond the testing experience.

No child should be tested when tired, especially late in the day. Sick children, or those suffering from allergies, should not be tested until they have sufficiently recovered. Test results are useful when your child's performance on the test is typical of his or her behavior.

TESTING AND CULTURAL DIFFERENCES

Many children have home backgrounds quite different from the person giving the test. Educational psychologists often use evaluations that take cultural differences into account. One test, for example, is designed to "compensate for the 'cultural bias' of standard IQ tests through which . . . children are mislabeled," report Julius Segal and Herbert Yahroes in their book, *A Child's Journey.* This test is given to children ages five to eleven and compares the child's test scores to other children with similar cultural backgrounds. The SOMPA, or *System of Multicultural Pluralistic Assessment,* is a test designed to take into account a child's disabilities and sociocultural background and to be non-discriminatory.[2]

Discrepancies can arise from testing a language disabled child with language-based tests. Care should be taken in giving language-based tests to children with symptoms of dyslexia, for instance. Since many tests require language, a poor reader is defeated before he or she begins. Dyslexic children frequently become accustomed to failure and do not care how they do on any written exam, a defeatist attitude common among older dyslexic children. One young man with dyslexia said about school evaluations, "All those little boxes make my eyes swim."

In 1981, educator Dr. A. Lee Parks of the Department of Special Education, University of Idaho, recommended certain tests as effective and nondiscriminatory. The AAMD (American Association on Mental Deficiency) *Adaptive Behavior Scales* and the *Camelot Behavioral Checklist* for mentally retarded people are tests of adaptive behavior. These are tests that measure how children react to life situations, such as self-help skills, social behavior, and independent functioning. They do not rely on labels.

Dr. Parks recommended "criterion referenced" tests. Such tests measure how well a child performs certain tasks, which is preferable to measuring him or her against other children.[3]

The *Normative Adaptive Behavior Checklist* (NABC) is an individual test for persons beginning from birth to the age of twenty-one. It measures self-help skills, home and independent living, social skills, sensory and motor skills, and language and academic skills.

The *Adaptive Behavior Inventory* is an individual test for children ages six through eighteen. It measures self-care and social skills, communication, and academic and occupational areas of persons functioning in daily living situations.

The *Vineland Adaptive Behavior Scale* for infants and children up to age eighteen interviews parents to determine a child's communication, daily living and social skills, and behavior.

WHICH TESTS FOR WHAT?

Tests and evaluations are divided into types. Some are infant development and readiness tests, preschool and school-age development evaluation, comprehension tests, reading tests, math and language tests, intelligence tests, personality tests, achievement tests, and vocational evaluation.

The four types of tests commonly used in assessments of children with handicapping conditions are infant development scales, intelligence tests, special abilities tests, and personality tests.

"Screening" is a word used by educators to mean *find* or *uncover*. A popular method of discovering early learning problems is through screening. Screening tests are given to large numbers of children in order to locate those with developmental delay.

The DDST (*Denver Developmental Screening Test*) has been used in the United States and other countries. This test was developed in 1967 by two Denver researchers, Josiah B. Dodds, Ph.D., and William K. Frankenburg, M.D. The test compares a child's development with a large number of children of the same age. It is divided into four parts: muscle coordination, speech and language, social skills, and emotional health.

The *Slingerland Screening Tests for Identifying Children with Specific Language Disability* are screens for learning disabilities that relate to reading, writing, spelling, speaking, and listening. The tests include visual and auditory memory sequencing and discrimination.

The purpose of the DDST and other screening tests is to locate children who show signs of developmental disorders.

The *Gesell Developmental Schedules* for children through age six focus on motor and language development, self-help skills, perception, and social/behavior skills. The *Bayley Scales of Infant Development* test motor development, language, and perception of infants through age two.

TOBE, or *Test of Basic Experiences*, is a group test designed to assess preschool, kindergarten, and first grade understanding of language, social studies, science, and math.

The October 1985 *News Digest* about testing (see NICHCY in Resources, p. 260 says that an understanding of how standardized tests are scored is necessary to make sense of results. The first score is the raw score. The raw score is usually the number of "correct" answers. The raw score is then changed to a derived score, which shows how the child's raw score compares with raw scores of the norm group. (Norm means typical or standard.) This comparison is provided in several ways: (1) An age or grade equivalent indicates the age or grade level for which a certain score is the standard. For example, a score of 5.3 means that on a particular test the child got the same score as other children in the third month of the fifth grade. (2) A percentile rank indicates what percentage of the norm group was exceeded by the child. For example, a derived score of 35 percent means the child scored better than 35 percent (or 35 out of 100 students) in the norm group. (3) A standard score shows how far below or above the average score of the norm group the child's score is. A standard score provides information about where the child stands in relation to the norm group.[4]

Two commonly used IQ tests are the *Stanford-Binet* and the *Wechsler* tests. For both tests, a score of 90 to 109 is normal or average, meaning that half the people taking the test will score in that range. A lower score is below average and a higher one is above average.

The *Stanford-Binet* can be used with both preschool and school-age children and is usually administered to children between age two and age eight. The *Wechsler* has separate forms for preschool and school-age children. The preschool form is called the *Wechsler Preschool and Primary Scale of Intelligence* (WPPSI), and the school-age form is called the *Wechsler Intelligence Scale for Children—Revised* (WISC-R).

Both disabled and minority children with normal intelligence may receive below normal scores on IQ tests. One reason is that norm groups often consist entirely of white middle-class, non-disabled students. Even when minorities and disabled students are included in the norm group, the children are still primarily compared to nondisabled and nonminority children. Another reason is that many test items require familiarity with middle-class values and experiences. Even items that appear on the surface to be nonbiased are not necessarily without bias. For example, a child who is used to playing with blocks similar to those used in the *Stanford-Binet* block-building task is likely to do better than a child who has never played with blocks. Similarly, a child with normal intelligence who has eye–hand coordination problems will have trouble with the block-building task, but for physical rather than intellectual reasons.

The *Detroit Tests of Learning Aptitude-2* are individual tests for children ages six to eighteen, and measures learning aptitude, ability, innate or acquired capacity, talent, readiness in learning, and intelligence.

The *McCarthy Scales of Children's Abilities* for children aged two and a half to eight and a half is made up of three subtests: verbal, perceptual/performance (nonverbal thinking and problem solving), and quantitative (number knowledge and reasoning). The McCarthy perceptual/performance subtest can be used with preschool children who are bilingual or bicultural, or have specific language or visual problems. This test is preferred to the *Stanford-Binet* if a child within a specific age group is thought to have learning disabilities.

Tests are given to determine children's achievement levels in language, math, reading level and comprehension, spelling, and general knowledge. Certain tests can be used to determine achievement levels. Three of these are the *Peabody Individual Achievement Test* (PIAT), the *Stanford Achievement Test Series*, and the

Wide Range Achievement Test. These tests determine the children's achievement for their age or grade. The *Peabody Individual Achievement Test* measures academic achievement in reading, spelling, math, and general knowledge. The *Wide Range Achievement Test* (WRAT) is a screening test for academic skills in reading, spelling, and math from preschool through college levels.

The *Illinois Test of Psycholinguistic Abilities* is a language test for children ages two to ten years. The ITPA measures children's communication skills and how well they receive information from their environment. The *Peabody Picture Vocabulary Test* (PPVT) tests children two to eighteen years old for verbal intelligence and hearing vocabulary.

Personality tests are used to determine a child's emotional and social development. These tests provide a child with hypothetical situations based on real life. Responses allow the tester to gather information about the child's personality. The *Personality Inventory for Children* is an objective test for younger children. The *Minnesota Multiphasic Personality Inventory* can be used for adolescents and adults.

In picture-story tests, children are asked to tell a story about each picture. In the *Children's Apperception Test*, children interpret animal pictures. In the *Thematic Apperception Test*, older children and adults interpret pictures and respond with stories.

As children grow older, they will receive vocational assessments to determine their skills and interests. The *Singer Vocational Evaluation System* for special-needs individuals from the age of seventeen to the age of thirty focuses on aptitude, interest, and work tolerance. The *Wide Range Interest–Opinion Test* for individuals or groups focuses on vocational interests and attitudes.

TESTING AND TOLL ON FAMILIES

Periodic testing—medical, educational, or psychological—can be draining. You may not sleep well during procedures. Your mind is full of questions. Even when testing personnel understand your concerns, you worry about the outcome. "How serious is my child's learning problem? When will my child learn to read? Do these tests show why my child is having trouble at school?" Most parents in our LD-ADD support group ask sooner or later, "Can these kids really become independent?" (Yes.)

In many families, the father spends time at work and the mother cares for young children, including the one undergoing evaluations. Stress arises if the diagnosis is vague or parents disagree over treatment.

SPECIAL PARENTING IN THE REAL WORLD

Parents themselves say that a factor in accepting the fact of a child's disabilities is the attitude of family and friends. It isn't easy being the parent of a child who may not look like other kids and has limited potential. There is no question that parents suffer, especially when they see other children excelling socially or academically.

A disability can create invisible social barriers with people who feel uncomfortable with differences. Friends may keep quiet, fearing they will do or say the wrong thing. Grandparents and other family members may want to help but feel afraid if an infant or young child is fragile or displays unusual behavior. The mother of a son with severe handicaps says her parents said and did nothing for a long time after the child's problems were diagnosed. She says, "I think they were too stunned to react."

Parental acknowledgment of learning and/or attention disorders is particularly difficult if extended family members are not open to a diagnosis, deny the child's disabilities, or believe the child's school problems are a product of bad parenting skills. Even people you know intimately can be frightened by discovering that a disability is part of the family picture. The mother of a son with autism says, "Friends and relatives tend to stay away, or they ask, 'How are the children?' hoping I won't mention Ray. No one asks about Ray."

What matters most is how *you* feel about attitudes. There are some attitudes you can change with information and talk. Others remain the same. Nevertheless, healing cannot grow out of negativism. When your child is not like other children, you need to focus on people who react positively to you and your family. Of the people who are able to "tune into" your situation, many will be other parents, of course. Many of *our* parents, brothers, and sisters will do anything they can to ease the burden of our current situation. Others are teachers, neighbors, or members of your church. They can be married or single, with children or without. A young single woman we know has always shown an interest in how Todd is doing in school or at work. She genuinely cares.

But is it possible to control our feelings about other people's reaction to our children's disabilities? What about people we see in stores and restaurants, even in church? You'd have to be stuck inside a sensory-deprivation tank not to feel *something* when strangers stare or ask inappropriate questions.

Sometimes strangers are interested in our children for valid reasons. A mother said an older man at the supermarket asked her a number of questions about her special infant car seat. "We stood in the hot sun and talked for almost an hour about his granddaughter who was recently diagnosed with symptoms of cerebral palsy."

If you feel hurt when others stare at your child or act embarrassed, make your feelings temporary. Consider the consequence of smoldering resentment. Your emotional–physical health is more important and bears directly on family health and well-being. If someone, most likely a child, asks you why your son is in a wheelchair or can't talk very well, you answer truthfully and calmly, "My son has Down syndrome (or other accurate diagnostic term)."

Resolve to focus on your child's contributing, loving qualities, on his gradually improving skills (even small ones), and on people who love him. Recognize and deal with unpleasant emotions churning inside your body. Talk them out with an understanding spouse, friend, or relative, or with your pastor.

In a discussion about families of mentally retarded children, Janet Carr wrote that respect for parents has increased over the years. "No longer are [parents] seen as anxious, guilt-ridden, rejecting and over-protective of their children but as resilient people who have real problems . . . and some angry parents may have had something to be angry about."[5] Carr says the present need is to examine more closely what handicapped people and their parents need at different times in their lives.

WHEN YOUR CHILD NEEDS YOU—PART TWO

When we want to enjoy our children, it's normal to be upset with someone who causes daily havoc. Your son wants to please you. You cannot excuse undesirable behavior, yet he can be exasperating. (Why can't he dress himself right? Why is his coat missing? Will he ever remember his lunch money, or phone number, to keep his hands off other kids? The teacher called again. Why didn't he get on the bus like he was supposed to?)

When school is a source of constant conflict for your son, he is sorely confused. He receives so many covert, along with the overt, messages during the day, he wonders if he ever does anything right. (Wish I could open this milk carton. Why am I always late? What's she yelling about now? I hope the teacher doesn't call. Is that Rodney wearing my coat? Think I'll take the long way home.)

When Todd was in fourth grade, his teacher sent home a note, "Todd wants to know why he is in a special class. He is asking questions only you can answer." Todd was asking me too, but I was too busy to answer.

One day when we could avoid the issue no longer, Todd and I went out for a hamburger. On the way, I brought up his disability. I didn't know why he had learning disorders, but I tried to say how much we love him and how important he is to his father and me.

He responded angrily. He sobbed to learn he is indeed handicapped. As I cried with him there at the McDonald's parking lot,

I knew our conversation was one of the most difficult I would ever have.

Something changed that afternoon, though. The air was cleared of secret imaginings. I was amazed at his questions about school and learning and about other people with disabilities. Now we were able to assess the future in the light of his strengths. I could honestly explain why some jobs were not realistic but some he could handle. And we agreed to forget the word "never" because someday he might want to try more difficult tasks.

How do we prepare to explain an impairment to our child? When is he or she mature enough to understand? How do we reveal this kind of information without becoming upset ourselves?

The only right way I know is with honesty, kindness, and effort. The topic need not be belabored. The parent should begin when the child is young but has developed sufficient reasoning ability to understand a simple explanation. Then, later, when the child is a teenager, the questions may be more matter-of-fact than volatile. A parent willing to share a child's sorrows over losses, as well as joys, becomes vulnerable to the child's pain. Therein lies the mystery of a disabled child and his or her family, a bonding often obscure to those outside the handicap experience.

KEEPING TRACK OF RECORDS

Do you remember the evaluations mentioned at your last IEP meeting? Remember the day you discussed your daughter's test results with the school psychologist? Do you know where those facts are stored?

You have important rights related to your child's records. The school that provides your child's educational services must allow you complete access to his or her educational records. The regulations say, "Each participating agency (meaning school) shall permit parents to inspect and review any education records relating to their children which are collected, maintained, or used by the agency. . . . The agency shall comply with a request without unnecessary delay and before any meeting regarding an individualized education program or hearing relating to the identification, evaluation, or placement of the child, and in no case more than 45 days after the request has been made."[6]

What are these records? They are the information gathered about your child throughout his or her school years. This information is stored in a confidential file or cumulative record (or similar term) in your school district. Records can be printed, handwritten, on tape, or on computer disk. Some of these records are:

- test scores
- medical information you released to the school
- copies of all IEPs
- the results of IEP meetings (that is, in what program was your child placed as a result of each meeting?)
- report cards and/or copies of grades
- discipline folders
- personal notes added by teachers, counselors, and other staff members
- any material identifying your child, such as a photo, Social Security number, or student identification number
- results of tests taken outside the school, such as private psychologists' tests

What if you don't want to see all the records, but you want to know what and where they are? At your request, the school must list the records and tell you where they are kept.

If you want to see test results, you have the right to read all or any of them. Records should be explained to you. Test results can be complex. You may not understand everything. Again, ask if you don't understand test results or any other part of the records.

What is the first step in obtaining copies of your child's records? First, write or telephone the business office of your school district. The best approach is a phone call followed by a letter. (Make photocopies of all typed and handwritten letters.) The business office will put you in touch with the person in charge of student records.

When you are contacted, make an appointment to visit the office and obtain copies of the records. In some districts, records are computer-stored. It may take several days to get them. A school can charge you for copies, but no more than the cost of copying and mailing.

Now that you've seen the records, ask if they are complete. "Is there other information about my child stored elsewhere in the district?"

FERPA = PARENTS' RIGHTS TO RECORDS

You also have rights to information about your child because of the Buckley amendment or federal privacy act passed in 1974. This amendment gives you some rights while taking away others.

The Buckley amendment is a short name for the Family Educational Rights and Privacy Act (FERPA). This 1974 law gives parents of students under eighteen years of age, and students over eighteen or attending postsecondary schools, the right to inspect and review all of the student's education records maintained by the school. Any school district receiving federal funds from the Office of Education (OE) must comply with this law.

Under the Buckley amendment there is information you *cannot* see:

- the records of another student
- a teacher or counselor's personal notes made for his or her own use
- records made by school security police *if* this information is stored separately from other school records, and security people do not have access to other school files
- information about school employees, such as their personnel files

A student cannot see his or her psychiatric or treatment records but can ask his or her doctor to look at them. Nor can a student see the financial records of his or her parents or read confidential letters of college recommendation.

Parents worry about the school's ability to destroy important information. The school can destroy records, but once you request to see your child's records, the school may not destroy any of them. The school is under no obligation to make copies (although most schools will make copies for you as a courtesy). The final regulations pertaining to FERPA say that the school should copy the records if failure to do so would effectively prevent the parent or student from exercising the right to inspect and review the records.

You can read the records. The Buckley amendment does not specifically give parents the right to bring someone to inspect records, but it does allow you to authorize others to see them. The school may ask you to sign a statement saying a friend has been given permission to see the records.

Suppose, while reading the records, you discover a couple of surprises. Do you see information you believe wrong or biased toward your child? If you want to remove these records, the first step is simply asking school personnel to do so. FERPA says if parents believe information in school records is inaccurate or misleading or violates the privacy or other rights of their child, they can request the school to amend the information. Ideally, they remove it in your presence. If they agree, that ends it.

If they refuse, they should advise you of your rights to a hearing. If you feel the situation warrants a hearing, write a letter to your principal or appropriate school official. Request a hearing concerning your child's records.

But what if the school agrees to a hearing? This is another part of due process. This hearing is a meeting between you and school officials and is presided over by an impartial hearing officer (IHO). Incidentally, an IHO can be a person or a committee. The hearing allows all parties to present their evidence about the records. Here too, you can bring your attorney or someone familiar with education laws for disabled students. The hearing should be granted within a reasonable length of time.

You have another alternative, should the decision go against you. You may insert a written statement in your child's records, saying you object to leaving in specific information.

The Buckley amendment controls who sees your child's records. In this way it protects each student's privacy. Although no one can see these materials without your written permission, there are exceptions:

- teachers and other school personnel who have a "legitimate educational interest"
- school officials from the district to which your child is being transferred (They may receive the records only after you have read them and had an opportunity to challenge them.)
- a research organization helping the school; all information is confidential, of course
- anyone responsible for student financial aid
- a court order
- an agency of the government, if it is enforcing federal laws
- anyone to whom the school must report information as required by state law
- in an emergency situation, anyone needing information about the health or safety of your child

THINK BEFORE SIGNING

NOTE: It is important to think before you sign. If a school wants your signature releasing records, ask who needs the records, why, and which records. You can refuse permission if you feel releasing the records would damage your child in some way.

You'll want copies of records if you are moving. Because these records are sent to the next school district, you want to know what they're getting. As soon as possible, read through the records. Is there any information you don't want sent ahead to the next school district?

You should know that police, probation officers, and employers cannot see records without your consent. There is a catch! If your state has a statute that went into effect before the Buckley amendment passed (November 19, 1974), which says the school can open files to these individuals, then you cannot object. If you are concerned, check it out with school personnel.

Do not sign a blanket form covering all the years your child is in school. The school should contact you each time it wants to release records to someone. Again, you ask the question "who," "why," and "which." Parents may also ask the school for a list of people requesting information throughout the school year, but this probably won't reflect names of school employees who have seen the records.

As soon as your child graduates or leaves school for other reasons, you should ask for copies of records because: (1) you need to know about information on file before it is destroyed, and (2) you need to keep this information on hand for vocational training, technical school, college entrance, or a job search. Copies of IEPs and results of testing may help you get SSI for your child if you haven't done so already.

After your child has left the school district, the school should tell you when records are no longer needed, and those records may be destroyed. The school will keep only a remainder record of the name, address, phone number, grades, attendance, and grade level completed. It is stated in the federal regulations that "personally identifiable information on a handicapped child may be retained permanently unless the parents request that it be destroyed. Destruction of records is the best protection against improper and unauthorized disclosure. However, the records may be needed for other purposes [such as] social security benefits."[7]

You have a valid complaint if your school releases records without your consent, if they refuse to let you see the records, or they refuse to let you add a correction to the records.

If you feel there has been a breach in the law, write to the following:

Family Policy and Compliance Office
Department of Education
400 Maryland Ave., SW
Washington, D.C. 20202-4605
(202) 732-1807

There is no standard letter of complaint, but you should provide as much detail and evidence as possible to support your allegations. Support material includes copies of letters, memoranda of telephone conversations, pertinent statements from other individuals, and a sufficiently detailed and specific description of events. Your letter should include the following:

- the exact name and address of the school and school district
- the name, title, and telephone number of the chief officer (superintendent, president, chancellor, principal, or other title)
- names of students who are the subject of the complaint
- names and titles of the school officials with whom the complainant has had dealings
- complainant's complete address and daytime telephone number
- all pertinent dates and circumstances surrounding the school's denial or violation of the complainant's rights (If the complaint pertains to your right to inspect and review education records, you should then include the date of the request for access to records. The school has forty-five days to respond to your request.)

If you phone with questions about registering a complaint, have all pertinent information on hand. Say you are calling long distance and need information right away, or you need to know whom to contact.

For more information about tests, write NICHCY, P.O. Box 1492, Washington, D.C. 20013. Ask for the October 1985 *News Digest* about psychological tests for children with disabilities. *Assessment: Special Education Tests: A Handbook for Parents and Professionals* lists tests currently used in special education and helps parents understand their purpose. To obtain a copy, send $4.00 to PACER Center, Inc., 4826 Chicago Avenue South, Minneapolis, MN 55417-1055.

Chapter 7

WORK, HIGHER EDUCATION, AND DISABILITIES

I used to ask teachers and other school people if they could give me a handle on the future. Would Todd graduate from high school? Would he learn to drive, to become independent?

Most answered, "I don't know," or "It's hard to say," reflecting a reluctance to give me false hopes or an uncertainty about his prospects.

Finally I asked a summer camp teacher. What did she think he could do? She said, "Todd will graduate from high school, probably use vocational training, and then work."

Right or wrong, her answer was one I could live with. It gave me hope. Todd has done all that and more.

It is difficult to think of your young and immature child as an employee. Regardless of your child's disabilities, you should start talking early, preferably no later than ninth grade, with the school about further training and education. Keep in mind that the 1990 amendments say IEPs should now include statements of needed transition services (to smooth the passage of students into independence and work) beginning no later than age sixteen and every year thereafter. IEPs should also include transition services when appropriate for students fourteen years of age or younger. By September 1, 1980, states were to provide an appropriate education to all handicapped children from ages three to twenty-one. An exception would be a state that does not authorize funds to educate *non*handicapped children in that age group.

Do you know what kinds of vocational experiences are available for your child? Look into vocational testing and training offered by your district. Your school district should offer job evaluation and training in several areas in order to match your child with a suitable program. If not, it should liaison training programs and transportation with neighboring districts. Does the school maintain contact with local rehabilitation agencies? Do not hesitate to ask school personnel if they periodically study the community labor market. Which local governments, businesses, private industries, hospitals, and restaurants are receptive to hiring young people with disabilities? Ask about adding technical, employment-related devices to the IEP. At IEP meetings, discuss your child's skills in terms of future work.

For more information about using current technology and adding assistive devices to an IEP, write NICHCY, P. O. Box 1492, Washington, D.C. 20013. Request the *News Digest, No. 13, 1989,* which is about assistive technology.

Ask your son now and then what he wants to do, and do not be put off by a reply of "astronaut." Take family tours of local businesses, factories, shopping centers, and grocery stores to see what interests him.

You are not alone in your concern over your daughter's vocational prospects. You are frustrated and frightened with her incomplete academic and social skills. You ask yourself, "How can she get this old and STILL NOT KNOW?" Because she is impaired perceptively if she has learning disorders. A child with physical disabilities may not have had opportunities to gain important work-social skills either.

STEPS TO INDEPENDENCE

First, disabled kids usually need more time to get ready academically, which means they may stay in school until age nineteen or longer. If your children are delayed, will they leave home on schedule? Probably not. Kids sense this too. A young man with learning disabilities said he feared his parents would make him move out at age eighteen. (They didn't.) Learning disabilities are not outgrown anymore than other types of disabilities are outgrown. Children learn strategies to compensate for their disabilities and to strengthen their abilities.

Second, be approachable to your child during adolescence and young adult years when he or she is vulnerable to other influences. Children need to learn about social skills, sex, and drugs from their parents, not other young people whose ideas are not accurate either.

Third, independence begins at home. While disabled children live at home, parents can help them develop a "memory method" of self-management that is easier to live with than constant monitoring (i.e., nagging). Children can be responsible for what is appropriate for their abilities. A boy can post a chalkboard in his room to keep track of appointments, assignments, due dates, meetings, and classes. He can buy a large monthly calendar, the kind with a large square for each day. He can write "to do" or "pay _____ today" in the squares. He can jot down when he needs to clean his room (not a joke), wash his bedding and replace it on his bed, carry out his trash, and get a haircut. He can learn the steps for doing his laundry. He can throw away clutter that contributes to disorganization.

Sometimes during Todd's growing up years, especially adolescence, I felt we were on an emotional roller coaster. We shared exhilarations as well as sorrows. After Todd began cross-country track, he entered a local Octoberfest "Fun Run." The joy on his face the day he walked into the kitchen carrying a large trophy was worth everything we had gone through.

We also suffered through two years of distress when Todd could not find work or vocational training. We discovered that a learning disabled young adult is second to none in taking out his unhappiness on his family. Now he was verbal! We tried to answer his questions. We looked everywhere for help. We gritted our teeth through interviews and training programs that resulted in nothing. (This is why I have five library cards. Libraries have comfortable couches when I had to get OUT, when we needed time away from each other.)

Our experiences were not unique. A 1989 HEATH Resource Center paper says a number of parents and professionals have been phoning HEATH about a group of young adults with learning disabilities and other special needs. Most of these young people had IEPs in high school. Some were mainstreamed and graduated with their peers. Others have dropped out or entered unsuitable training programs. Most have left public schools by age eighteen, although services were available to them until age twenty-one, or later in some states. These young people function far below grade level because they do not have the academic skills necessary to complete a college degree program, even if they are offered tutoring or instructional adaptations.

The HEATH paper says, "Many young people in this group are unable to enter a college, a career school, or a full time job right after high school. They frequently stay at home well into their twenties, trying one short-term job after another. Some spend many lonely hours at home with nothing to do. They are often depressed, and they tend to have no sense of what work might be meaningful for them or even how to search for employment. Too often, families do not know how to help them. A [1986 Louis Harris] poll of persons with disabilities estimates that two-thirds of this population are unemployed."[1]

TRANSITIONAL PROGRAMS *WORK*

If you think your son or daughter will not be able to find work on his or her own, it is never too early, or too late, to investigate federal–state vocational rehabilitation programs in your area. Don't give up. Transition programs are in place for your child. If you are experiencing this difficult situation, or you believe it is over the horizon, contact every agency and resource you hear about. Explain your child's abilities as well as disabilities. Talk about things he or she can do. If people at the agency feel they can't help you, ask if they can refer you to someone else. Sometimes word gets around, or one contact leads to another.

Explain *to your adolescent or young adult* that the program he or she begins may not end up as his or her chosen vocation. Young people sometimes balk if they think they will be bound the rest of their lives to the first job they will take. It is possible to change one's mind. Many people change careers more than once.

What if your child eventually finds work but you consider the conditions unsatisfactory? Unless the work environment is dishonest, potentially dangerous, or environmentally unsafe, almost any employment teaches a few work skills and may lead to another job.

Do you wonder what training and employment options will be open? Will your young person be stuck in menial work or will work use his or her abilities? Many factors in the community affect a disabled young person's ability to find work, including the local economic climate, attitudes toward disabled people, and the number of people looking for work. One key factor in hiring, however, is a marketable skill. When special education students *do* work, other crucial factors seem to be previous part-time or summer work or volunteer work, a high school diploma, and some reading and math skills.

Special education students who are employed have used special education work experience programs that target good employment habits plus communication and job search skills. Their vocational programs focused on realistic employment in the community. Vocational service providers assessed students' interests and strengths, they tried to match student abilities with appropriate programs, and then they decided on accommodations needed for employment.

An important issue in employing people with disabilities is matching abilities with appropriate training programs. In 1985, Dale Brown wrote for the President's Committee on Employment of the Handicapped that learning disabled people should not do tasks in which their disabilities play too large a role because this handicap is not obvious to the casual observer. "For example, people with perceptual motor problems could have difficulty working on a car engine or laying bricks or building bookshelves. People with a tendency to transpose digits due to visual sequencing problems should not be data entry operators where lines of numbers must be accurately copied. Persons with auditory perceptual problems should not work as telephone switchboard operators where they spend their day taking messages. On the other hand, many learning disabled people can do well provided they are working in their area of strength or have received remedial assistance and . . . overcome their disabilities."[2]

Dale Brown says the confusion between learning disabilities and mental retardation can lead to bad matches between people and jobs because many successful retarded people have stronger perceptual motor abilities than most learning disabled people.

Darlene Cunningham, a rehabilitation program specialist at the Rehabilitation Services Commission in Columbus, Ohio, says some Ohio school districts are using transition programs in compliance with the new education amendments. Others are not, which means there is little consistency throughout the state in implementing the amendments. Cunningham says the new amendments indicate a need for training educators because schools are going to be responsible for addressing transition services and involving other agencies. More important, says Cunningham, vocational training should focus on what is available in the labor market. "Many times we make plans for our children and adults with disabilities. They complete a training program, but the chosen area is not marketable. Students need career planning and exposure to community jobs. The outcome for any individual in the long run, whether a job or other postsecondary options, is going to be employment."[3]

The 1986 Louis Harris survey of disabled Americans indicates their lives have improved in the last decade. Yet 66 percent of disabled people between ages sixteen and sixty-four do not work. Only one in four work full time, and another 10 percent work part time. Young blacks, a group often singled out because of their high level of unemployment, are much more likely to be working than are disabled Americans. An ICD (International Center for the Disabled) survey says, "It is in the area of work, even more than social life . . . that disability excludes people most from mainstream American life. Americans below retirement age, who do not work, live somewhat apart from the mainstream of life in this country. Unemployment excludes them from many of the common experiences known by most Americans."[4]

THE CARL D. PERKINS ACT

As the parent of a disabled adult, I am pleased with the changing perspective toward disabilities, as with the passage of the Americans with Disabilities Act, and the TV depiction of working disabled people (Benny on NBC's *L.A. Law*). Another boost to independence for disabled people is the Carl Perkins Vocational Education Act of 1984 (PL 98-524), which requires school districts to provide disabled students with many more services than in the past, including vocational evaluation, counseling, and career development planning, plus services to aid the transition from vocational training to a job. Under this law, "special needs students" are those with a disability or are disadvantaged or who know limited English.

In 1990, the Perkins Act was amended by PL 101-392. The new amendment changed the name of the act to the Carl D. Perkins Vocational and Applied Technology Education Act. The purpose of this new law is to make the United States more competitive in a world economy. Resources will be used to improve educational programs needed for a technologically advanced society. This law expands the term "special populations" to include people with disabilities, those who are economically and educationally disadvantaged, such as migrant children, those with limited English, people who participate in programs to eliminate sex bias, and those in correctional institutions. The Perkins Act and IDEA support full vocational education opportunities for youth with disabilities.

New laws say a disabled person must not be hired on the basis of his or her disabilities but valued for what he or she *can* do. The ADA, in particular, removes barriers that previously kept disabled people from working, namely, public transportation and access to public buildings.

SECTION 504 AND THE ADA PROHIBIT DISCRIMINATION

The public law that made an impact on the welfare of people with disabilities was Section 504 of the Rehabilitation Act of 1973 (PL 93-112). Section 504 makes it illegal to discriminate against handicapped individuals in any program or activity receiving federal funds. Section 504 prohibits discrimination in employment practices, including recruitment, hiring and rehiring, promotion, tenure, layoff, compensation, job assignments, leave, fringe benefits, training, and employer-sponsored activities.

The Americans with Disabilities Act expands Section 504. ADA gives the same rights to people with disabilities as federal laws gave to blacks and women in the 1960s and 1970s. The ADA prohibits firms with more than twenty-five employees from discrimination in hiring or promoting employees with mental or physical disabilities. It prohibits discriminatory job tests. The ADA goes a step further than Section 504 in saying that an employer cannot discriminate against an individual because of the known disability of someone else with whom the individual associates. This can include family, friends, and people who provide care for persons with disabilities.

There are conditions to the meaning of handicap or disability. A physical or mental problem is not classified as a disability unless (1) it is severe enough to hamper one or more of the major life functions, (2) a record exists of the impairment, or (3) a person is regarded as having the impairment. Major life functions are caring for oneself, performing manual tasks, walking, standing, hearing, speaking, breathing, learning, and working. The ADA expands the definition of disability to a condition that impairs a "major life activity" and includes such conditions, diseases, and infections as orthopedic, visual, speech, and hearing impairments, cerebral palsy, epilepsy, muscular dystrophy, multiple sclerosis, HIV (the AIDS virus), cancer, heart disease, diabetes, mental retardation, emotional illness, and specific learning disabilities. Also protected are severe burn victims who, because of disfigurement, are viewed by others as having an impairment that substantially limits some major life activities, such as working or eating in a restaurant, and are discriminated against on that basis.

The ADA says employers may not discriminate against persons with disabilities in hiring or promotion if the person is otherwise qualified for the job. One goal of Section 504 and the ADA is to make work available or accessible. Some areas of the employment building may need changes, or perhaps the disabled person's work area could be moved to a better location.

The law does not expect physical changes for the sake of hiring a disabled worker to cause *undue hardship* on an employer. Employers with twenty-five or more employees must comply with ADA requirements by July 26, 1992. Employers with fifteen to twenty-four employees must comply by July 26, 1994. Employers with fewer than fifteen employees are not covered by ADA.

The employment section of the ADA does not protect against discrimination of employees of private membership clubs and religious organizations or of employees who engage in illegal use of drugs and alcohol. People with a contagious disease or infection may be excluded by an employer if they pose a direct threat to the health and safety of other employees.

The ADA requires new buses to have lifts for wheelchairs. Six years from the passage of ADA, large over-the-road bus companies must have accessible buses. Small over-the-road bus lines must have accessible coaches in seven years. New bus and rail terminals must be accessible. One rail car per train must be accessible by July 26, 1995. Amtrak stations must be accessible by July 26, 2010.

At present, the steep steps and narrow double doors of an old post office near where we live are inaccessible to anyone suffering from no more than a sore knee. The ADA says new buildings must be accessible to wheelchairs. As of January 26, 1992, public facilities, such as restaurants, hotels, theaters, stores, libraries, museums, day-care centers, shopping malls, doctors' offices, banks, office buildings, and private social service agencies, must serve people with disabilities. Restaurants are encouraged to remove barriers to wheelchairs and offer menus in braille or have a person read the menu to people with vision impairments. Telephone companies serving the general public must offer telephone relay services to people who use TDD.

SECTION 504, THE ADA, AND HIGHER EDUCATION

In earlier chapters we talked about children's rights in public education and about safeguards for parents. (Section 504 applies to preschool, elementary, secondary, vocational, and adult education.) What does Section 504 say about freedom from educational discrimination after high school? The law refers to this period as postsecondary.

Universities and other institutions cannot discriminate against disabled people through student recruitment, admissions to a college, or the way they treat a disabled person already enrolled. Colleges cannot make handicapped quotas. That is, a college cannot impose a limit on the number of disabled students it will accept.

Admissions tests must be adjusted so they do not discriminate against a disabled person. The results of these tests should indicate a student's skills and not point out the disabilities.

A college or university does not have to make all classrooms available to physically disabled students, but classes needed by disabled students should be rescheduled in accessible buildings or made available in other ways. Programs must be offered in the most integrated setting appropriate.

If an enrolled student's disabilities affect his hearing, seeing, speaking, or writing, teaching aids must be provided. A student with vision impairments may take a guide dog to class. Teaching aids include taped texts, tape-recorded lectures, interpreters, readers, and modified classroom equipment. A college or university has the freedom to select specific aids or services, as long as they are effective. However, such aids or services should be chosen in consultation with the students who will use them.

Colleges and universities are making an effort to help high school students with learning disabilities experience college success. Through an eight-week program at Ohio's Kent State University (first conducted in June 1991), students live in residence halls and take a math or reading development course and one physical education elective. Individual and small group tutoring is provided daily. The program familiarizes students with study skills, time management, academic grading, group counseling, and university facilities. Any freshman student admitted to Kent State with a learning disability documentation validated by the Kent State Disabled Student Services can apply.

At Kent State, a prospective learning disabled student must submit to the Department of Disabled Student Services evidence that indicates a discrepancy score of two or more between intellectual ability and achievement in one or more of these areas: basic reading skills, reading comprehension, math calculation and reasoning, written expression, oral expression, and listening comprehension.

Instructors can facilitate the instruction process for LD students in a number of ways:

- Instructors can hand out a syllabus or course outline at least four to six weeks before the beginning of class.
- An instructor can use a chalkboard or overhead projector to outline lecture material, reading what is written on previously prepared transparencies.
- An instructor can give assignments in writing as well as orally and provide time during office hours for individual discussion of assignments and questions about lectures.

- An instructor can provide study guides and study questions.
- A student with symptoms of dysgraphia (an inability to write well) can be allowed to take oral instead of written tests.
- Other strategies to help LD college students include readers for objective exams, and allowing a student to take an exam in a separate room with a proctor.
- LD students may continue to have problems taking lecture notes. An instructor can give permission for another student to take notes for an LD student. An instructor can avoid using complex sentence structures in composing exam questions.

Students who acknowledged their learning problems during or before their secondary years usually know which classroom strategies were helpful. They have practiced self-advocacy. To further ease the transition, LD students can contact the college disabled students department months ahead of enrollment. They can familiarize themselves with the campus and college services. They can ask to meet other students with learning disorders to find out how they did it.

Disabled students must receive the same health services as other students. They should have access to the college infirmary or clinic. Their disability should not separate them unnecessarily from regular physical education. They must have equal access to housing at the same cost available to others, equal access to financial assistance, and nondiscriminatory career counseling and placement services.

As these children become adults, they should know (their parents should tell them) that no employer can refuse to hire them because of a disability. If they call to ask about a job, an employer may not ask if they are disabled. A prospective employer may, however, ask if a person can perform certain tasks related to the job. If the employer asks your child to take a physical exam, this exam must be a requirement for all those applying for the same job.

TECHNICAL SCHOOL OPPORTUNITIES

Is your child interested in a private technical or trade school? If so, you should watch out for private school counselors who recruit students on commission rather than student aptitude. In other words, an employment counselor may be a salesperson.

Be wary of instant placement claims. Some technical schools place "Help wanted" ads, but when they say "Immediate Openings," they mean *school* openings, not job openings. Watch for "special connections," celebrity instructors, talent tests, discount enrollments, or bait-and-switch enrollment techniques. Some trade schools tell prospective students that a necessary course for employment is filled, but other courses are still open, for which they are eligible.

Ask about the length and expense of training. If technical schools teach specific skills for employment, the practical needs of local employees should influence course content. The purpose is to help a young person qualify for a job. Tutoring for ongoing reading and math problems should be incorporated in technical or trade schools if disabled people are accepted into their courses.

To obtain the paper *Young Adults with Learning Disabilities and Other Special Needs: Guide for Selecting Postsecondary Transition Programs*, write or call HEATH Resource Center. See Resources, p. 253. HEATH will also send you these free resource papers:

- *Computers, Disability, and Postsecondary Education*
- *Education for Employment: A Guide to Postsecondary Vocational Education for Students with Disabilities*
- *Resources for Adults with Learning Disabilities*
- *Vocational Rehabilitation Services—A Postsecondary Consumer's Guide*

For more information and to obtain the booklet *Adults with Disabilities, How to Get Your GED*, and to receive the booklet about adult learning disabilities, contact the GED testing Service (Special Testing), One Dupont Circle, Suite 20-B, Washington, D.C. 20036-1163, (202) 939-9490.

Edith Bunker said, "Archie doesn't know how to worry without getting upset." Parents of disabled kids know what she meant. We have children who need more of our ingenuity in searching for resources. Even with support, learning disabled young people carry a legacy of high school into adulthood. Children who repeatedly failed elementary and secondary subjects do not have healthy opinions of themselves. Add peer ridicule and ostracism and life becomes painful.

SCHOOL SUCCESS HELPS SELF-ESTEEM

School is a general nightmare for students five years behind in reading and spelling. It is nearly impossible to convince such students that they are not "dumb" unless steps are taken to find a program—public, private, or tutoring—in which they can succeed part of the time and they are not seriously penalized by their disabilities. Dr. Paul H. Wender says in *The Hyperactive Child, Adolescent, and Adult: Attention Deficit Disorder Through the Lifespan* that our self-esteem is formed on the basis of other people's responses to us. An ADD boy realizes daily what he is up against. His low opinion of himself is not neurotic but rational:

> He is failing at school, with his peers and with his parents. He fails in all the important areas of a child's life. He feels he is dumb, lazy, disobedient, and unlikable because that is the way his world regards him.
>
> Obviously anything that can help the child change his behavior will prevent him from suffering the consequences of that behavior. Although a child may eventually outgrow the physiological and temperamental problems, the psychological problems may persist. He will have learned—and not forgotten—patterns of psychological maladjustment. On the other hand, if the physiological problems and symptoms can be kept in check until he outgrows them, he will avoid many bad experiences and grow up more easily. He will be better at school and have better relationships with his family and friends. He will not suffer severe consequences from his attention deficit disorder. Many ADD children can now be helped to achieve this major goal.[5]

About the only thing that reassures children with learning disorders, and begins to change their self-image, is actually experiencing success in learning to read and write and spell. Even young kids are not fooled by pat answers or pats on the head when they feel miserable about learning. Young persons' esteem begins a swing upward when they *know* they are improving, when they can read or do math even a little. Learning disabled persons begin to improve when they feel there is hope. In his book for educators, *How to Write an I.E.P.*, John Arena said students begin to feel better about themselves even after short goals are accomplished. "For example, 'Look, Tony, first of all we're going to work on having you be able to write your first and last name in cursive, OK?' " Then comes the second objective when Tony learns to write his address, city, state, and zip code. Arena said, "This is why breaking tasks into small manageable components, such as name first before address, leads to a success-oriented program." The idea is to help Tony gain small successes that have some meaning, that is, Tony realizes this skill will eventually help him find a part-time job.[6]

In addition to this, a child's relationship with his or her family, friends, and teachers has a major impact on his or her improvement, on the ability to concentrate even for short periods. Small successes are cumulative. A little progress in reading can make a difference in vocational gains. When a child with learning disorders is identified early and has a supportive family, a reasonably healthy self-image, and correct remediation, the prognosis for the future is good.

SOCIAL ACCEPTANCE—HOW FAMILIES CAN HELP

As learning disabilities become publicized, many adults are beginning to understand the basis of their inability to comprehend reading materials or follow through on written instructions. Some continue through high school, valiantly keeping their heads above academic waters, thinking of themselves as generally inept. With vocational assessments they learn they are not weak or dumb but struggling with reading and math disabilities.

A teenage boy or young man may understand he has learning disorders, but he still worries about social acceptance. The job problems he encounters, in fact, may be more social than skill-related. His social discrepancies may be clear to teachers and parents but not to the general public.

You can strengthen your young daughter's employment skills by helping her evaluate her behavior in social situations. Does she talk too loudly or too much? Does she interrupt? Does she express her viewpoint too often instead of listening? Is her dialogue a monologue?

Talk it out without hurting her feelings. Counsel her about impulsive decisions. Teach her to think before speaking, wait before acting. Talk about the amount of space she should leave between herself and another person during a conversation. She can shake hands when introduced to a man or a woman. Explain that conversational skills apply to everyone, not just people with disabilities. She can't use swear words or "with it" expressions in talking with adults or reveal personal or family business. She should not talk to strangers on the bus or the elevator, only with business people, such as clerks in stores. She can learn to pay a compliment, "You look nice," instead of "That's a foxy dress." Impaired judgment means she cannot afford the luxury of getting carried away. We don't want to dampen our children's spirits so they are afraid to say anything, but they need to think through responses in getting along with fellow workers and vocational trainers.

Darlene Cunningham says students with disabilities need social skills as much as work skills. She says many students lack the maturity accompanying their job skills. Their behavior is sometimes inappropriate and they may have problems interacting with peers on the job. She says as partners, parents can help work on social and job skills at home. "Consistency is important in learning these skills. In addition, children are greatly helped by an earlier start on employment, either through job site visits to see people at work, or through exposure to volunteering."

You can help your child get a head start on humor with family "inside" jokes and gentle kidding. Life is easier for people who recognize the ridiculous. Maybe your child needs to learn how to tell jokes. Who else can listen to a joke three times over but a parent? If necessary, teach your child an off-color joke (but let's not get carried away here). Then explain when to tell it, that he or she can tell his or her friend Rodney or Sheila but not Grandpa. With humor that is neither deprecating nor cruel, you teach your child to "take it." Ridicule is deflected when the object of the joke isn't bothered. On the other hand, humor at the expense of a disabled young person teaches hostility.

Young people with perceptual problems may display inappropriate behavior in new situations if they are confused or afraid. In addition to "rehearsing" now and then, you continue to explain to your older child what is going to take place or what you *think* is going to happen.

PRACTICAL HELP FOR JOB HUNTS

In what other ways can a young adult prepare for work or for job hunting? If filling out forms is trying for typical kids, it is dreadful for students with impaired reading and writing skills. Help your child prepare for job interviews with a "data sheet," which he or she carries at all times, for filling out applications with the correct information and spelling.

He or she needs to list everything (or you print or type it for him or her): full name, address, telephone, birth data, birthplace, weight and height, Social Security number, previous addresses and dates he lived there, high school graduation date, all previous employment and volunteer experience, plus addresses and phone numbers. Write out parents' or guardians' full names, mother's maiden name, teachers and friends who are references, their addresses and phone numbers. Some applications require a brief medical history, including immunizations. Help your child practice writing some of the information, particularly if he or she has trouble with printing or cursive.

EMPLOYMENT PROSPECTS FOR WOMEN WITH DISABILITIES

Are job training and employment prospects any better for boys than for girls? Discrepancies certainly exist in opportunities for both men and women with disabilities. Recent reports on special education students show that in the first year after high school, disabled males are more likely than females to be employed, to be employed full-time, and to remain employed full time during the next two or three years. In addition to this, all of the women students with disabilities were employed in unskilled jobs. The 1986 Louis Harris report said most unemployed disabled people depend on government benefits or insurance payments, and 40 percent receive no benefits at all. The latter are mostly women who depend on someone else for support.

Studies indicate that three out of four disabled women are neither working nor looking for work. Only one woman in five in the working-age disabled population works. But of those who work full time, disabled women earn almost as much as do nondisabled women. It appears that women who overcome discrimination on the basis of disability, sex, and other factors tend to do quite well in the labor market.

Parents of young women with disabilities wonder what they can do to create a better climate for employment and eliminate serious barriers to independence. For a more complete discussion of male and female roles, societal expectations and independence for women, write NICHCY. (See Resources on p. 253). Ask for *News Digest* No. 14, October 1990, "Having a Daughter with a Disability: Is it Different for Girls?"

In 1984 I was astonished to see a Levi's commercial featuring a young man "popping wheelies" in a wheelchair. Television has contributed greatly to the national image of disabled people in normal environments. We may never know how much we owe these advertising and programming visionaries. Until recently, disabled (especially retarded) people were not shown at all, or were shown as objects of pity or charity. National perceptions of retarded people are improving, as with Chris Burke, a young man with Down syndrome who plays Corky in ABC's *Life Goes On*. The attorneys who employ Benny on *L.A. Law* often behave like parents, supporting and counseling Benny through trouble and occasionally butting in when he could have handled the situation by himself.

EMPLOYMENT AND PEOPLE WITH MENTAL RETARDATION

What are the employment prospects for people with mental retardation? Much improved over the past twenty years. Darlene Cunningham says employment may be easier for people with mental retardation than those with learning disabilities because professionals have more experience and expertise in addressing the needs of people with mental retardation.

We are discarding our previous ideas about persons with retardation. People with retardation differ as much among themselves in their abilities and limitations as other people do. There is no sharp distinction between normal and below normal adult functioning, in fact. People with retardation are not equally impaired at all levels of functioning; they are proficient in some ways and deficient in others. Not all retarded persons are good at repetitious jobs, for instance. Some are, some are not, depending on functioning and maturity. However, their overall capabilities fall short of what is expected for people of their age and experience. Mental retardation should not be confused with mental illness or emotional problems, although people with retardation can have emotional problems just like everybody else.

What job opportunities are suitable for persons with retardation? Qualified mentally retarded people have been successfully employed as stock clerks, sales clerks, office clerks, couriers, messengers, mail carriers, domestics, nurses' aides, attendants, busboys, dishwashers, ushers, porters, plant maintenance, staff packers and assemblers, inspectors, and various kinds of federal workers.

Retarded adults without behavior problems are usually enthusiastic workers because they are motivated, but fear and timidity can hinder their success. How can prospective employers relate to employees with retardation?

• Talk to a retarded person as you would to anyone else but be more specific. Avoid abstract thinking and demonstrate what should be done. Show and tell but don't talk down to the person.

• Show a retarded person where things are—the time clock, lockers, rest rooms, cafeteria, drinking fountain, supply room, and other areas. Don't rush and make sure he or she understands.

• Take extra care to explain about working hours, proper clothes for the job, the workstation, and rate of pay. Be sure the retarded employee knows whom to report to everyday and where to go to catch the bus or other transportation.

• Ask questions now and then to make sure the person understands the routine. For example, ask him or her to explain a job or to show you where he or she works at various times during the day.

• Introduce the retarded employee to his co-workers, and if possible select one person who is available to answer questions and provide extra help. Shyness will fade as the retarded person gets acquainted and gains confidence. Let the person know that he or she belongs to the work family, but don't force after-hours friendships.

• Offer to help when new situations or problems arise. As time passes, make every effort to understand the retarded person's strengths and weaknesses as an individual.

• In locating an employee to help a new retarded person, try to find someone comfortable with retardation. These people are not difficult to find, particularly in social service agencies and hospitals. Many times they have personal experience with difference if they grew up with a retarded brother, sister, or cousin.

In any workplace, rules change and decisions are handed down in regard to everyone. Make sure employees with retardation are aware of these changes. If they can't read well, they will miss that sign posted in the lobby. They probably won't know the starting time has been changed from 9:00 A.M. to 8:30 A.M. because they don't socialize in cliques or company groups. It is only fair that they receive information afforded other workers. A retarded individual who is treated fairly and with dignity can become an outstanding and loyal employee.

Darlene Cunningham says what is needed is an earlier orientation of students to work instead of waiting for graduation or a training program to end. She says kids need early input into employment plus involvement in business activities.

Cunningham believes the ADA is going to make a difference for people with disabilities, but much depends on how employers are approached. She adds, "We can't say to employers, 'You have to comply—you must hire these people with disabilities.' Through partnerships we can offer training and provide employers incentives for hiring people with disabilities."

Chapter 8

YOU ARE THE EXPERT

When Todd's brother was in elementary school, he came home one day and said another child told him the cause of Down syndrome.

"And what is it?" I asked.

"Down syndrome is caused by a mother eating cottage cheese and beans when she is pregnant." That afternoon we drove to the library to look up chromosomes.

We rely on the truth. Our kids need correct information about everything: disabilities, how to make change from a dollar, prejudices and biases, sexual abuse, the Persian Gulf, and whatever else they ask about. No one expects you to be a fount of knowledge, but you and your children can search for answers together.

You need information about yourself; you need to know that your inner experience in rearing a child with a handicapping condition is not the same as five years ago and will change five years down the road. We see what we can. Then we see more. Fred Rogers, creator and host of *Mister Rogers' Neighborhood*, says few parents come to parenting without ambivalence, and there are some days we'd like to be free of the responsibility. "How much harder it must be . . . for parents whose newborn child is clearly going to need a great deal of extra care and attention, or for parents whose once healthy and flourishing child suddenly develops these extra needs." Rogers further says, "There's certainly no way parents *should* feel about this or any other sad or difficult situation that comes with raising children. In fact, the beginning of our being able to cope with anything is in our acknowledging the feelings we *do* have and accepting them as part of being human."[1] Rogers says the way a handicapped child feels about himself and how siblings feel, is related to parents' feelings.

Feeling good about your child gives you hope. This means someday you may need to superimpose your faith in your child when he or she is criticized or at least critically evaluated. You ask, "But how can I feel good about a person who is so behind other kids, can't pay attention in class worth a hill of beans and causes trouble on the bus?" By working with professionals to help your child compensate for his impairments, and by not constantly comparing your child with neighborhood kids or with cousins.

We were crushed in the early years when a pediatric neurologist told us that Todd was minimally brain damaged. Our school evaluation team said he would need a special class and speech therapy. The relatives asked when he was going to learn to mind (if ever) and the dentist said he had tongue thrust.

At the same time, I noticed a handsome little boy with a contagious laugh who charmed his teachers by complimenting them on their pretty dresses when he wanted to get out of work. I saw a boy developing a good sense of humor when he had only one neighborhood friend. I saw a child who refused to give up learning to ride a bicycle, to swim, and to be a regular person. I appreciated a YMCA worker who saw his good qualities and told me, "This is a terrific kid."

Everyone is vulnerable about something, and some of us are more wounded that our child is disabled. An experience of this magnitude cannot take place in a vacuum. Seymour B. Sarason and John Doris say a diagnosis is

> . . . a series of actions and checks taking place over time, and not infrequently, involving interventions and treatments that give a more secure base to diagnosis. Similarly, diagnosis and treatment of the social–interpersonal context is an ongoing process that should not terminate when the mother and infant leave the hospital, to be

resumed at the first office or hospital visit, or to be changed as a function of telephone calls from parent to physician. After all, from the moment the family leaves the hospital the quality and quantity of interactions within that social unit take on a fateful and changing character that is far from predictable. And what is at stake is no less than the direction of the diagnosis of the change in the lives of three interrelated human beings. The sad fact is that the diagnosis of the social–interpersonal context is almost never carried out in the sustained, painstaking, probing manner that characterized the diagnosis of the infant's condition . . . we know amazingly little in these instances of what goes on, less because so much is going on and more because our conceptions and practices are inappropriately neglectful of the issues.[2]

Rearing a child with special needs requires creativity and unusual responsibilities. By unusual, I mean strategies not often faced by parents of nonhandicapped children. When Todd was a teenager, my friend Linda wanted to know if Todd could act as a part-time companion to her son who has spina bifida.

My first response was incredulity. In view of Todd's confusion in carrying out simple jobs, I could not see him caring for a child with physical disabilities. I also felt Linda had little comprehension of Todd's limitations.

She persisted until I agreed to give it a try. For almost ten years Todd was a part-time companion to Linda's son. The first day Todd walked five blocks to her house, however, I was so worried if he could find it, I slid along behind him, hiding behind trees.

Leaping from tree to tree is minor compared to what other parents have done. Yet most parents who carry out extraordinary measures for their own child and in behalf of all children with special needs (such as sitting on boards of mental retardation, school committees, and parent groups, acting as advocates for new parents) do not like to hear they are doing anything out of the ordinary. Linda has spoken to many medical groups about the social and medical aspects of spina bifida. She took her son rafting on the Colorado River.

COMPASSIONATE TALK ABOUT THE DISABILITIES

There is irony in the birth of any disabled child, no matter how slight the impairment. I deeply regret Todd will not be able to enjoy reading as much as I have. For years I thought I could fix his dyslexia with access to intense therapies. All that helped some. As an adult he reads slowly and with difficulty. One day when we were reading he asked, "Have you been sorry?"

"What do you mean?"

"Have you been sorry you had me?"

How could I answer? Our emotional investment in this child has been great. He has changed and improved our lives in unexpected ways. It would be easy to gloss over this question, to pretend he didn't ask it. Talking about his place in society produces anxiety in both of us. To avoid social issues would do him a disservice, however, and produce a conflict he might not be able to handle after I am gone. And I told him the truth, that I was only sorry he has this problem, that he and his brother are the most wonderful people we know.

Which brings us to a sensitive issue in living with differences: explaining your child's disabilities when he or she is teased, ridiculed, or chosen last for the team. Even with the impetus on mainstreaming, we cannot believe these scenarios are not going to occur. Dr. Peggy Finston says we can't change the circumstances, but we can help our child blow off steam. We can listen and avoid the three pitfalls of telling the child it doesn't hurt, giving advice about what he or she should do about it, or directly criticizing the other kids and their parents.[3]

Talk is important for a child with learning problems who cannot perform athletically or academically as efficiently as other children. (We say "efficiently" because we continue to look for ways they can perform.) A child with physical disabilities needs a clear account as much as a child with retardation or learning disabilities. If your son is quite different from peers in regular classes, he is aware of these differences too. If other children call him names, he wonders if they are true. He needs to know that naming a disability is not the same as knowing the whole person. He needs to know the disability is no one's fault, certainly not his.

If disability is not the whole person, how much normality can we expect from our children? In other words, where does the disability leave off and the child begin? Perhaps we can tell when we notice that they are using their personality, even their impairments to manipulate us and other family members and friends. Wait a minute! Do I mean this sweet-faced, curly-headed handicapped girl is twisting my meaning to get what she wants? Sure she is. All children regardless of their attributes learn early what makes us mad or glad and how to get our attention.

As children grow and mature you continue to be the expert on their learning patterns and feelings. You learn the perimeters of their personal safety zone; you learn that they need safe ways to vent, not a person on which to vent. After Virginia's learning disabled son put his fist through the family room wall, she bought him a punching bag.

LEARN ABOUT YOUR CHILD'S SCHOOL

Your expertise includes learning about your son or daughter's school. When you join school committees or volunteer to be a room mother (or father) you get more than cookie baking practice. By going to school and mingling with other parents and school personnel, you find out what's going on. You discover how teachers perform, their impact on the class and on the school itself.

You listen to the general attitude of neighborhood parents. Are they enthusiastic about school staff? Are neighborhood groups of parents always meeting to complain about a school incident or the lack of services? Evaluate their behavior. Are complaints valid? Are they part of a clique?

How do administrators react to complaints? Do they search for satisfactory ways to solve them? Does everyone work together in problem solving?

What is the economic condition of the school district? This is a tough issue because nearly all school districts in the country have financial deficits of one kind or another. Is the school district efficient in using money, volunteer help, teacher talents? Does your community continue to defeat school levies? How does your local newspaper comment on these issues?

What is the school's general appearance? Are hallways well lighted? Are examples of the children's work attractively displayed? Is the school clean? By all means, check out the rest rooms.

How does your daughter feel when she comes home from school? Is she satisfied with her school day? Is she jumpy, nervous, or hostile? Is she sullen or enthusiastic about her day? Does she talk about her friends and teachers?

The following questions (adapted from *Help Your Child in School* by Bernard Percy, (©) 1980, Prentice-Hall Inc., Englewood Cliffs, NJ 07632) apply to special-needs students in regular classrooms.

Does the teacher know the subject matter? Is he or she prepared in terms of knowing and presenting materials in a clear, understandable way?

How ready is this teacher to handle a variety of students' responses and needs? Does he or she handle classroom enthusiasm well? When many hands fly up, can he or she cope? What does the teacher do when children show inappropriate behavior during a teaching situation?

How much evidence is there of children's successes, gains, and accomplishments? Is everyone's work displayed?

Are the children at ease when they actively participate with the teacher in classroom activities? What is the class mood (fearful, relaxed, active, passive, happy, angry, good morale)?

How respectful, helpful, and cooperative are the children with each other? How much interaction among the children is allowed and motivated by the teacher?

How well has the teacher instilled in the class a sense of respect that he/she is the teacher? Do the children understand their responsibilities to the teacher, themselves, and other children? When children approach the teacher or yell out questions when they are supposed to be listening, how does the teacher respond? With anger or with purpose as to what the children should do?

Is the teacher receptive to the varied and fascinating ways of little children? One mother said that her son's class was asked to draw a picture of running water. When the mother attended Open House, there on the wall (amid waterfalls and rivers) was her son's drawing of their toilet. If the teacher handled the incident with fairness and sensitivity, then that teacher understands children and has a sense of humor. He or she is also a teacher not locked into standard answers.

Fewer parents volunteer at school these days. The obvious reason is that both parents work and have less time. Your contributions are sorely needed and very appreciated. Perhaps you can build a piece of equipment for the class. You might want to join a planning committee. Of course you attend all conferences on behalf of your child. Your involvement tells the teacher you care about what is going on.

Why learn all you can about PL 94-142 and other laws? In 1988, at a spring meeting of the Akron (Ohio) Area Association for Children and Adults with Learning Disabilities, one parent said her child's IEP was written three years in advance. Another said she had never attended an IEP meeting. (As we mentioned in Chapter 2, the IEP update and meeting is not every two years or three years, but every year.) In *The Misunderstood Child: A Guide for Parents of Learning Disabled Children*, Dr. Larry B. Silver stresses parent involvement. "Whichever program your child or adolescent goes into, remember that no matter how sincere and cooperative the school may be, your concerns are greater. Keep informed. Monitor what is done. Don't be afraid to ask if the trainer is trained and certified in special education. If the school does not plan occasional conferences to give progress reports, request one, and then request others at reasonable intervals. If you have not heard from the school by early spring about planning for next year's placement, call and ask for a meeting."[4]

Your interest in your child's education means you know *when* to become involved. In some communities, groups of parents make it a practice to "lobby" the school. They lobby for new playground equipment even when there are no available funds. They demand innovative math programs culled from recent news magazines. These groups enjoy the power struggle. They have more reunions than the Whiffenpoofs. Use your common sense to separate the important from the whimsical. When your child has special needs, this kind of affiliation can damage your credibility.

ADVOCACY IS NOT AGGRESSION

As your child's expert advocate you need to know the school is applying resources toward optimal learning experiences. In *One Miracle at a Time*, authors Irving R. Dickman and Dr. Sol Gordon say most parents are reluctant to stand up to bureaucracies because they confuse assertiveness with aggressiveness.

"Parents are often surprised to discover that advocacy can be studied and mastered, that assertiveness is less a matter of temperament than of techniques and skills that can be learned and taught. More parents . . . do need some help in learning how to be assertive effectively, and many parent and disability groups are now providing assertiveness training for parents."[5]

Confrontation is inefficient and usually alienates the people who provide the most education. Meaningful interaction is the tool by which parents and schools avoid confrontation. The federal regulations ask, "What is the role of the parents at an IEP meeting?"

"The parents of a handicapped child are expected to be equal participants along with school personnel, in developing, reviewing, and revising the child's IEP. This is an active role in which the parents participate in the discussions about the child's need for special education and related services, and join with other participants in deciding what services the agency [school] will provide to the child." The regulations add that a national survey conducted under contract with the Department of Education indicates most IEPs are signed by parents. Also, "An IEP signed by the parents is one way to indicate that the parents approved the child's special education program."[6]

PARENT GROUPS UNDERSTAND

From the beginning you need written information about your child's specific disabilities. Professionals who work with your child may not know where help is found. If this happens, call an information hotline. Ask for a parent support group whose children have similar problems. Call this number, and ask to talk to parents of an older child.

Become an active and valued member of your support group. As a long-time member of the ACLD (now LDA), I discovered the value of parent knowhow. Many parents attend just one or two meetings. Others show up for powerhouse speakers. A last group of parents attend whenever possible, ask questions, and talk with other parents. They are the ones who benefit from worthwhile information and emotional support. The father of one dyslexic boy commented, "Some of the speakers here have been terrific. Others are hogwash. So why do I keep coming back to this group? If I don't hear something meaningful from the speaker, I get it from another parent—some knowledge, a bit of insight. Sometimes it helps to know other parents have the same problems."

Another advantage of groups is in the ability of older members to inform new ones which community specialists (doctors, psychologists, speech therapists, tutors) can help with specific disabilities. They know which professionals genuinely care about special-needs kids. These parents are not timid about privately endorsing helpful services.

KEEP TRACK OF VALUABLE RECORDS

With the first phone call you make, the first trip to see any specialist, you want to begin an information file. Not only are records important now, but they take on added value after the school years when a child is preparing for college or vocational training. The following suggestions are based on an Academic Therapy parent brochure, "Safeguard those Valuable Papers."

Purchase an accordion-type folder with at least ten pockets, and label each pocket. Make sure that on dated material, the year is included.

Pocket labels include:

- official records, including birth certificates, Social Security card, diplomas, certificates of all kinds, and fingerprints, if available
- report cards from every school your child attended, including informal reports and comments, and reports from summer camps and summer schools
- correspondence, including copies of letters you wrote and all correspondence received about your child
- medical records, including test results, diagnoses, plus names of diagnosticians, and where tests were done (hospital, clinic), also immunizations and illnesses
- psychological test results (After psychological tests are done, a conference is held between parent and professional. What is said during this conference can be as important as test results. Keep the notes you took in this pocket.)
- visual and/or auditory test results (separate or added to psychological)
- work samples, including the early years, such as kindergarten (These development samples are as important as tests.)
- photographs and school pictures
- out-of-pocket items (Whenever you take out a piece of information, record not only what piece was pulled out but

when and to whom it was given. This pocket can contain a pad and pencil on which to record removal and return of documents.)

- telephone conversations (This includes a record and the general substance of conversations with professionals about your child.)

The last item is especially important because telephone conversations fade away. If you cannot write down the substance immediately, perhaps a few points can be put on tape and transcribed later. If you are inclined, purchase a receiver device at an electronics store, attach it to your phone and tape recorder, and tape calls pertaining to education and therapy. Be aware, however, that a possible violation of local, state, or federal laws may exist. If in doubt, check with an attorney or call the office of your local or county prosecutor.

This pocket in your folder can also include blank copies of work sheets for contacts made to possible sources of help and their addresses.

SAMPLE RECORD-KEEPING WORK SHEET

Person or agency I talked to and address _____
Name of contact person _____
Date called _____ Phone # _____
Results of discussion: _____
_____
_____
Action taken (if any) _____

It is not a good idea to loan original documents and records, but it is easy to photocopy them. If something is not returned or lost, you have the original.

Include another sheet on which you write down the schools

and camps your child attended and names of teachers, counselors, and principals. You may think you'll never forget school personnel, but memory fades when school ends.

Keep the accordion folder in a safe place. Fireproof boxes are available at hardware stores.

Professionals respond positively to a parent who can produce background information for the detailed forms that seem to be necessary for each new school or clinic. Not only will you have information at your fingertips but you also make it accurate. No more guesswork. No more long, exasperating searches through clinical or school files. It's never too late to start a record system.

WHY DO PARENTS AND PROFESSIONALS CLASH?

It is nearly impossible to know ahead of time which teachers, teacher aides, related service people, or coaches will feel compassion toward your child. Your feelings play an important part in how you approach professionals, however. When parents realize their child is afflicted, they pass through stages of adjustment similar to anyone who has experienced a profound loss. It is normal to be shaken. To believe your reaction could be otherwise is unrealistic. Did any parent ever want a disabled child? Bette M. Ross asks an important question about parent and professional relationships in *Our Special Child: A Guide to Successful Parenting of Handicapped Children*: Why is it that schools and parents often see each other as antagonists? Because both feel so deeply about the children. "Tempers flare and professionals clash with parents not because they are unfeeling or careless, but because in the fields of service to the disabled child—to any children—each professional is so deeply involved, cares so deeply as a parent or a teacher or a doctor and is so deeply dedicated to the betterment of the one child or the many like him that honest differences of opinion regarding training or treatment often meet on the sharp edge of hostility."[7]

Someday you may discover the ability of a professional to influence your feelings about your child. Through your contact with diagnostic specialists, you may have discovered that some cannot accept disagreement about your child's therapy or education. Not all professionals are intolerant of disagreement, of course, and all of us play a part in creating or healing attitudinal barriers. Nevertheless, some professionals may view your questioning attitude as a lack of acceptance of the handicap. Most parents understand full well their children's limitations, especially as they grow older. You convey your viewpoints without rancor, but you are always entitled to an opinion.

Unless you explain, professionals may be unaware of troubling family dynamics. In their recent book, *Ordinary Families, Special Children: A Systems Approach to Childhood Disability*, Drs. Milton Seligman and Rosalyn Darling say when families are seen outside of their situation in a school, clinic, or treatment center, the cause of their problems is more likely to be seen as within the family. "When the family's situation is not completely understood, parents' neurotic symptoms may be attributed to their inability to cope with the disabled child rather than to some external cause . . . such symptoms are as likely to result from lack of social support or community resources as from the child's disability. Parents are expected to *accept* and *adjust* to their situation, and the professional role is perceived as one of helping parents cope. This view assumes the family's situation cannot or should not be changed."[8]

Sometimes the situation *can* be changed, say the authors. The child can be placed in a better program or provided respite care. Financial aid may be available. They add that a community's lack of resources to ease parent burdens is not the parents' fault. And learning to cope may not be a more appropriate response than bringing about change.

Coping families look for worthwhile help and positive reinforcement when they have a need for it, and they recognize their own unique stresses, such as caring for a toddler with orthopedic problems or managing the behavior of a child with characteristics of autism. Finding new services can be painful for parents whose children's disorders are reflected in their behavior. It is almost masochistic for a mother to sit for an hour in a doctor's waiting room with an obstreperous, retarded child, under the scrutiny of four or five other mothers.

Time is dear when children are young and one of them has special needs, when you frequently see professionals for purposes of early intervention and education. Use your parenting expertise in locating specialists receptive to special problems of handicapped individuals and their families.

PROFESSIONALS CAN EASE PARENT STRESS

Kathleen has been taking Robert to early intervention programs for more than a year. Robert, born with symptoms of cerebral palsy, is making good progress. His strength and coordination have improved, and he is beginning to say a few words. What's more, Kathleen is a positive influence on mothers involved with the children's hospital intervention programs and with a parent–support group. Kathleen has been a sort of ad hoc person in charge of acquiring community speakers.

One afternoon, after the parents had left and staff cleaned up the refreshments, Kathleen took the social worker, Helen, aside and told her she wouldn't be coming to the program or chairing the support group nor would Robert receive his ongoing therapy.

Helen was dismayed. "How can you consider taking Robert out of the program? He's making wonderful progress and you have helped us so much."

Kathleen was blunt. "Because Robert and I have no other life," she said, eyes brimming over. "I want us to act like other families that take vacations or just do regular things like going to the park or even Disney World. My husband and I talked it over; we've about had it with 'special.'"

Disabled children do need more care, as infants needing

special feedings or medications or as hyperactive toddlers. I was probably my strongest (and thinnest) when Todd was three and four years old. We spent our days chugging from one end of the house to the other, Todd on a roll except when napping and I in pursuit while carrying a ten-pound baby on one hip. I didn't need a bench press. I could have whipped bears.

At the same time, we were saddened by Todd's ongoing evaluations, the growing recognition of his serious delay. We would take walks on warm summer evenings, the baby in his stroller, Todd walking beside us. I studied the houses we passed and asked myself why those families were better than we were and wondered how we could be more like them.

We were also stressed by conflicting professional opinions and duplicate testing. Todd was given hospital neurological evaluations at age four and again at seven because school personnel asked for another test before reading his file. When I asked how tests compared, they replied they had no idea he had already been tested.

A basic fact: We can help parents by making a few simple changes. Nearly all parents of young disabled children would and will suffer fewer strains from the early years if:

- Diagnostic and therapeutic services are readily available without searching and without hassles.
- Parents are not sole coordinators of community services or required to sort overlapping services.
- Overly busy parents do not take on organizational tasks better left to specialists.
- Agencies, including schools, could investigate resources for parents whose income is too high for community services. Health plans may include psychiatric counseling but rarely private tutoring. Families may not be able to afford specialized dental care if their company health plan doesn't cover it or they have no health benefits. We hope these troubling scenarios are somewhat ameliorated with the use of the IFSP.

FIRST, WE ARE A FAMILY

With many professionals seeing our child, and not always under optimal circumstances, how do we feel good about our-selves as parents? By considering our needs. When was the last time you took a day off to have fun as a family, when parents saw a movie without the kids, took time to stuff pictures into your family album? When child care, therapy, and/or educational inter-vention become hindrances instead of helps, we take time to make a list. We decide what activities and involvements we need, which are irrelevant or wasteful, which ones we need to maintain healthy family interaction, and how we plan to reschedule.

When Todd and his brother were young, we frequently drove past an enchanting miniature golf course. "Can we stop for a while today, Mom? Can we play golf today, huh? Can we, please?"

"No, your father has to eat early. I have to cook dinner. I'm tired and the laundry isn't done yet." (Besides, the whole idea of playing miniature golf wears me out.)

One day, to my sons' surprise, I drove into the golf course and we played. And that wasn't the last time.

Foremost we are a family, whether we are a one- or two-parent unit. We begin to feel better about our circumstances when we take time to be *us*. So what if most of those golf balls flew into the parking lot? So what if the laundry molders on the basement floor, if dinner is late because it took two hours to play the course?

We feel good about ourselves by recognizing our unique stresses and strengths. Does it matter how we feel? Yes, because our belief in ourselves is directly related to our child's self-esteem and faith in his family. We are enabled as parents when we realize how much we have learned, knowledge encompassing every aspect of our child's life. We are empowered as parents when we realize what a good job we are doing and how much our child has gained because of our efforts.

We begin to feel better when we realize that this is not a perfect world, that other people are not always going to react positively to a child with a hearing impairment or to our family the way we expect, certainly not the way we want. Some friends and relatives are extraordinarily wonderful, some are Monday-morning quarterbacks, and a few will hurt us. The way we choose to counteract makes the difference in our feelings and those of our children.

A healthy way to counteract is to eliminate your vision of doing everything right. How did the idea get started that parents of disabled individuals should make the best informed decisions, that they should make fewer mistakes than other parents? Dale E. Galloway wrote in *Rebuild Your Life: How to Survive a Crisis* that many people suffer from a sense of unworthiness because their lives do not measure up to their ideals. He says the emotional cost of being unwilling to accept anything less than perfect is very high.

Galloway says acceptance means you stop fighting the inevitable. "Let's face it. There are some things you cannot change. You cannot change the weather. You cannot change the tick of the clock. You cannot change the past. You cannot change another person against his or her will. You cannot change what is right and what is wrong. . . . There is nothing in this world that can happen to you but with God's help, and with a positive attitude, you can come out on top."[9]

Almost daily the media reports treatments for all types of disabilities. Some treatments are viable, others ineffective. (At one time caffeine was said to reduce hyperactivity—if a child could drink many cups of coffee a day.) What matters is what treatments help individual children. Consider your pocketbook too. The strongest gains are made when you and your child's educators and medical–psychological specialists combine resources to make school productive. Adjustment to a child's disability does not mean total acceptance of all ideas and therapies. Acceptance includes a thoughtful evaluation.

PARENTS' RIGHTS NOT MENTIONED IN LAWS

As concerned guardians, we read and study. We talk with other parents. We filter the significant from the frivolous. The following are basic rights of parents not mentioned in PL 94-142, taken from a 1981 *Perceptions* newsletter. You have a right to:

- hope and work for some improvement in your child's functioning and learning
- understand everything explained to you
- be present when important decisions about your child are being discussed
- expect people to view your disabled child as a child first with the same basic needs as any other child
- air your worries without criticism or intimidation
- say "I don't know" or "I don't understand"
- receive encouragement in the difficult job of rearing your child
- search for adequate professional advice periodically as needed[10]

It is your child's right to put in a regular school day. Unless he or she has limited stamina or serious behavior problems that impair functioning in regular settings (for which he or she receives educational services at home or in a hospital), your child should be going to school all day. Your child should not be subject to a shortened school day or a very long one because of bus schedules.

Some final thoughts about productive meetings, whether they are annual IEPs or general meetings. Attendees need to stick to the topic, which is your child's placement or IEP, math skills, behavior at school or vocational training, and how everyone is combining resources to help. Nothing is accomplished by discussing a school levy or characteristics of disabled children in general.

Go into meetings with your facts straight—personal notes or printed literature or letters from professionals who know your child. Be specific with requests. Rather than saying "My child isn't learning this year," say "My child cannot read his/her fourth grade material," or "My child doesn't understand his/her assigned math problems, even with help at home." Rather than

"We want more speech therapy" say "We believe another half hour of speech therapy a week would give William the boost he needs to function better in class and get along with other children."

The meeting should last long enough to target important issues and remediation. If attendees rise to leave or indicate they are adjourning before your concerns have been addressed satisfactorily, you stay seated and ask to continue the discussion. (As we mentioned in chapter 2 about the IEP, you should bring up your major concerns early in the meeting.) Another option, if some attendees must leave, is to request *in writing at this meeting* another meeting in a month or so and list specific people you want to be present.

Dress up for meetings. Wear a suit or a dignified dress. Look as if you are attending a meeting of the board of trustees or applying for a bank loan.

Parents of disabled children who push for change or improvement have been told they are too emotionally involved for the objectivity required in educational planning. Yes, you feel involved. Your emotional involvement is nothing more than the conventional savvy of parenting that fuels your child's growth. Emotional involvement means you care.

Parents of disabled children have been told that other students in the school will suffer educationally if money is spent on disabled children's needs. The truth is, if schools must cut back, nondisabled as well as disabled children must be deprived equally. Each student must receive the same amount granted another.

In 1980, David L. Trott, a legal advocate for handicapped children, reported, "In truth, many school systems do *not* have enough money in the budget for educational services needed by handicapped children. Inflation has driven costs higher and higher. Resistance to tax increases is strong everywhere.

"The average amount spent to educate each child in the school system must also be spent on each handicapped child. [This figure is defined in the Public Law 94-142 regulations, and is referred to as the 'average per pupil expenditure.'] The money must come from state or local sources."[11]

Since 1985, states have been required to provide information to the U.S. Department of Education on the kinds of improvements needed in special education programs and services. According to the 1990 Twelfth Annual Report to Congress on the Implementation of the Education of the Handicapped Act, nearly every state said improvements are needed in instructional programs for handicapped children. Specific areas are:

• Effective programs for students with specific disabilities; deaf/blind students and those with severe mental retardation, serious emotional disturbance, and learning disabilities.

• A more integrated team approach between special education and regular teachers, psychologists, and social workers.

• Personnel; thirty states called for the hiring of more teachers to reduce class sizes and staff new programs. A general shortage of certified teachers and aides, particularly those qualified to teach students with severe handicaps, including serious emotional handicaps, was noted across the states. States with high percentages of students with limited English proficiency mentioned a need for bilingual staff.

• Transition services; thirty states expressed concern about vocational education and student transition to postsecondary experiences. Program improvements are needed in work–study options, job counseling, skill development, career awareness, and vocational training. *States are concerned that students move on to appropriate postsecondary experiences by acquiring transferable skills needed for adult independence.*

Now you see why the average per pupil expenditure is a selling point for your participation in IEP planning, in requesting essential services. School is your child's primary resource in becoming a functioning adult in the American mainstream.

Do you resist special education involvement because you think everyone else knows more than you do or you will make mistakes? Educational involvement is like life. Life means getting involved and making mistakes because no one is perfect—not a parent, an educator, or any other service provider.

Ten years from now your children's teachers, speech therapists, and camp counselors won't remember you; you probably won't remember them either. But your children will know you were there for them during their education years.

Chapter 9

PARENT AND SCHOOL
A Winning Combination

Public Law 94-142 has been a leader in encouraging parent–teacher working relationships. When you and your child's special education teacher(s) talk to each other honestly, respect each other's special problems (his or hers at school and yours at home), and try to coordinate strategies, your child will make gains. The same philosophy applies to regular teachers, guidance counselors, speech therapists, tutors, and volunteers—anyone who works with your child.

How can you contribute to a successful education team? As noted earlier, one step at a time. Jot down questions and concerns before meetings. What skills did your child gain over the summer? Do you notice improved verbal skills or better balance?

When you meet with teachers in the fall, share anything the teacher is not aware of or mentioned on the IEP. Have you moved? Did your child's neighborhood friend move away? Did you get a new pet? Does chocolate make your daughter sick? Did she attend summer camp or summer school? Does she have a new brother or sister? Any of these can change school performance.

How else can you contribute to your education team? Volunteering helps your child directly. When you volunteer, you free the teacher *for* individual attention and *from* extraneous classroom duties. You can help with recess and playground duty or work in a resource room or library. You can share a hobby, such as ceramics or archery. You can share your job with your child's classroom or school. If you are unavailable weekdays, you can contribute scrap materials, egg cartons, empty paper towel rolls, anything teachers use for projects.

Most teachers teach because they enjoy it. They impart valuable knowledge, and they are rewarded by contributing coping skills to growing minds. Special education teachers, in particular, genuinely like kids with special needs. Of course they get frustrated just like parents, and they suffer for kids who have trouble with school. Teachers fully appreciate what parent–teacher interaction can do for a child with special learning needs. A veteran elementary teacher says if there is one thing teachers want, it is more parent interest.

A FIRST DIAGNOSIS IS DIFFICULT

A note for teachers: Be cautious of first-time IEP meetings held after evaluation results are presented to parents. Parents may have already suspected beforehand but may have only recently been informed that their child has an impairment. The situation is somewhat different from one in which parents have known about their child's disabilities since his or her birth.

Parents struggling to keep their composure are still assimilating a powerful revelation. You can be assured they are not really participating. Gretchen, a teacher and director of special education in Summit County, Ohio, says parents of children with learning disorders go through the same grief process "a little later" than parents of children with other types of disabilities. Gretchen says although the term "learning disability" is vague, she tries to tell parents new to learning disabilities that LD students are average or above average in intelligence and in their natural ability. She says to parents, "We are going to help your child compensate for his disability. This does not mean he isn't going to succeed. He may have to work a bit harder in some areas and very hard in other areas to gain skills other folks come by naturally."

"Everyone has disabilities," says Gretchen. "Some of us develop strategies to overcome spelling problems, for instance. In special education we help an LD child develop strategies to use his abilities."

Gretchen says parents become more comfortable with special education after children are in the program for a while and parents begin to see progress. "Still, it's a shock to be told one's first grader is learning disabled."[1]

Susan Duffy says in *Acceptance Is Only the First Battle* that developmental assessments are hard on everyone. "Even when a child has been involved with early-intervention services . . . the periodic evaluations of the child's progress are hard on parents. No matter that the parents have seen even great progress in their child, developmental tests are normed on regular kids and the handicapped child is always going to be behind in comparison. Parents may be able to ignore these comparisons in their daily routine, but the day that test results are discussed is almost always a tough one and professionals need to be aware of this."[2]

Adjustment is ongoing, but if teachers sense a troubling situation with parents, perhaps they can schedule another meeting to be held in two or three weeks. Call the parents and ask how they are doing. Let them talk about it.

Do teachers wonder why some parents never come back? Parents of children with disabilities may not attend conferences for various reasons, including child-care burdens, work schedules, and the like, but it does make a difference how you greet them. "How nice to see you" is better than "Boy am I glad to see *you*."

Say something positive about the child. A compliment breaks ground for dialogue. Does the child have an attractive smile? Ask the parents what their child likes and dislikes (play, food, pets, neighborhood pals). Parents continue to need someone to share their concerns. Friends and relatives may not relate to their unique situation, but teachers and other staff members can fill this need. Sensitive areas of parents' feelings are usually sidestepped by all parties because no one wants to cause pain or feel it. But parents are helped by professionals who acknowledge their frustration by saying, "It's OK to feel upset that your child's tests came out the way they did," or "Feeling angry about this situation is natural, but these evaluations can help us treat your child." A younger parent can be helped by a list of books and magazine articles about the disability or by a referral to local parent groups.

TEACHERS AND PARENTS STAY IN TOUCH

How can parents stay in touch with educators without wearing out the telephone? The mother and teachers of a child with autism can use a daily notebook with ideas about learning and behavior at home, on the bus, and at school. You can purchase a gym bag (preferably one with inside compartments) for your child's lunch, homework, and teachers' notes (papers tend to get lost from open folders). You and the teachers can tape-record messages to each other. You can establish the best time to talk with teachers on the phone.

For eight years Cindy, a teacher in Ashland, Ohio, has taught children with severe behavior handicaps. Cindy says she uses a behavior modification program known as "PEP," or Positive Education Program. "In the fall I send a letter to parents explaining the program, and I encourage parents to take a part in our morning circle group. I explain to parents that my job is not to cure their child, but to help him develop coping skills to return to mainstreamed classes."[3] Through the school year Cindy uses weekly progress reports to communicate with parents about a child's behavior.

When Heather, who has Down syndrome, was integrated into regular school environments, the only real problem she had was with an impatient lunchroom attendant. Heather's mother and teacher visited the attendant together to explain that Heather was still learning school routines, and to work on a lunchroom plan.

When you see a problem, start first with the problem. Talk to teachers first about school concerns, not to other parents about the teacher. Generally deal with the teacher first, the special education supervisor next, then the school psychologist, then the principal, and after that the superintendent. You will be more effective if you follow the chain of administration rather than going over a teacher's head.

What if you are truly upset about something that happened at school? Unless your child is in danger on the playground or bus or elsewhere, cool off a day or two before phoning or writing. Give the school a day's notice if you want to visit the classroom to ensure your child is there instead of out for an assembly or other reason. You should be allowed to visit the class a day or two after your request.

Sometimes you wonder when to step into or stay out of a troublesome school situation. We step in when we determine that our child lacks the resources to solve the problem alone.

At age fourteen Jim still had plenty of learning and school problems. Although he had made progress academically, he felt isolated from kids in regular classes. Jim's saving activity was long-distance track.

One day Jim told his parents that he planned to quit the track team because two other students from the LD resource room were interrupting his runs and harassing and roughing him up.

Jim's parents did not advise him to quit, run away, or fight. Instead, the three of them took the problem to Jim's teacher, who arranged a meeting with a school counselor and the parents of the two other students. Jim and his parents explained the situation. The students were counseled and the harassment ended.

STRATEGIES FOR STUDENTS WITH ADD AND SIMILAR NEEDS

What can parents do if their children have mild learning problems and/or ADD, but their deficits are not severe enough and their behavior has not deteriorated enough to warrant special education? They think the children are better off in regular classes anyway.

When children suffer in regular classes, their teacher wants interventions as much as parents. Ellen Frasca, an educational consultant at the Ohio Division of Special Education in Columbus, Ohio, says a lot of kids with ADD do fine with accommodations in regular classrooms. She says, "As long as the teacher knows the child and his idiosyncracies and behavior, what works and what helps, the more the teacher can help."[4]

The parents' input is invaluable here—to help the teacher understand their children's learning patterns and personality, what works and what helps. Parents can explain to school personnel that their children may need to move through school at a slower pace, may require more personal supervision. They may need modified textbooks or extra materials. They may learn better in small groups or with one-to-one instruction. Perhaps children with learning disabilities and/or attention deficits will work better in individual classroom carrels. They may need behavior modification to build a longer attention span, shorter assignments with more frequent breaks, and activities to enhance self-esteem. A student with an attention deficit disorder needs clear behavior guidelines and positive feedback without harsh discipline. Such a student also needs physical activities for relief between study times.

A medical–physiological condition hinders the learning of students with ADD, says Nancy Berla, editor and information specialist at the National Committee for Citizens in Education. "An ADD student is similar to a child with a chronic illness. The child has normal intelligence, but still needs accommodations in regular classes. Parents of ADD students I talk with understand their child needs accommodations, but parents do not want the child labeled as handicapped for the same reasons as parents of a child with a chronic illness do not want a label."[5]

If your child is not adapting to regular education, another strategy is to ask the teacher to write a description of your child's school and educational problems. Take these assessments to your family doctor or pediatrician. These data will help the doctor make a diagnosis of ADD and may, in turn, lead to school interventions without using special education.

Ellen Frasca says parents should use caution in how they approach teachers to share resources and information. Instead of saying "You need to try this because it will help my child," parents can approach the teacher in a sharing frame that says we're all trying to help this child. "I have found something that's helpful and maybe you'll find it helpful too."

Frasca says it has been her experience that when a child is identified with a problem such as ADD, for instance, parents look for any information they can use. Sharing information helps the teacher, especially if the strategy is effective and can be used with other children. Frasca says, "Parents can find information at regional resource centers about how teachers can handle children with ADD. Even a flyer or a two-page article can help and is better than expecting a teacher to find out on her own. Teachers have so much to accomplish, that searching for information is just one more thing to worry about." She says parents can hand the teacher a good article or a booklet that's not lengthy, but provides some good tips. Then parents can talk with the teacher about the individual child's situation.

Ellen Frasca says parents should not rule out special education if a child is having other problems such as achievement deficits, in addition to the attention disorder. "If the child displays problems beyond ADD, the rule of thumb is to evaluate the child. If medication turns things around dramatically, then that child is not a candidate for special services. When medication makes a difference, however, but the child is *still* struggling and *not* making it in the classroom, then something else is going on such as a learning disability." Frasca says the multifactored evaluation should not be overused, but should neither be ruled out in order to locate the problem.

In another situation, your child does not qualify for special services but struggles in regular classes. You feel ambivalent about his or her teacher, and now you discover that he or she is going to have the same teacher next year. What is best for your child? A new teacher or a familiar one?

Talk with the teacher. You can approach the topic with tact. The teacher may realize that your child would be more comfortable with a change in school environment. In *How to Parent So Children Will Learn*, Dr. Sylvia B. Rimm advises, "If your child has had a negative past school year, you should informally investigate whether you, as parents, can recommend or select a teacher for your child. Schools vary a great deal in their policies about honoring parent requests for teachers. . . . You aren't likely to be able to specifically select a teacher, but many schools will permit you to suggest the teacher that you would like for your child. . . . In some schools, the child's teacher may make a recommendation for the following year. In that case you may want to discuss with the teacher your preference for the following year. Again, the teacher won't be able to provide a guarantee, but it may be worthwhile for you to initiate the discussion."[6]

On the other hand, if your child has made great strides this year, and you realize he or she and the teacher are compatible and make a good team, you probably want to encourage this learning surge. Arrange a meeting to discuss continuing with the teacher. Todd had the same LD teacher for three straight years because we requested her, although she and Todd transferred to another school building.

HOW TEACHERS ENCOURAGE PARENT COOPERATION

Most parents welcome an evaluation to clear the way for special services, if needed, or to locate alternate strategies, if a child's learning deficits are not severe enough for special education. But what can educators do when parents refuse testing, if parents appear to ignore warning signs of learning problems or a reading disability?

In some cases a teacher, special education supervisor, or school psychologist can help parents assimilate facts about learning disorders. Dismissing parents as not accepting a child's differences will not hasten adjustment. Parents may believe assessments are needed, but family members are saying, "This child is normal, you simply can't handle him," or "Why are you trying to find something wrong with this child?"

Parents may, in fact, be gathering strength to go ahead with assessments in spite of family opposition and their own ambivalence. In this case, teachers can help parents prepare an explanation of learning disabilities and/or ADD.

Gretchen says parents have refused initial testing for special services because they thought the school was "jumping the gun," and tests weren't needed. She adds, "In some cases the parents were right. In other situations, we watch the child for a year to see if tests are needed."

Gretchen welcomes the input from parents who do not sign an IEP right away because they want to show it to friends, doctors, and other people who know the child. "Parents have refused to sign because they were not comfortable with the IEP, and they wanted more or less educational services." Gretchen says when it comes to children's needs, none of us has the right answer all the time.

POSITIVE REINFORCEMENT FOR KIDS = LEARNING

Many LD and ADD children for whom school is so difficult develop an attitude that they cannot succeed. Even without an IEP, you and the teacher can work out a behavior plan of positive home-to-school tactics. What methods you use depend on your child's personality and learning styles. You and the teacher focus on rewarding good behavior, effort, and persistence rather than grades.

Depending on your child's impairments, and whether or not an IEP is in place, he or she needs the maximum in services to distill the best from his or her school years. This is the tenor of PL 94-142, that parents and teachers coordinate information to enhance learning and reduce a child's frustrations. You request change when you believe change is needed. It never hurts to ask, but it may hurt more in the long run not to ask. If you feel your child needs more than one hour a week of specific services, you request a change in amount of services be added to the IEP. Perhaps your child has been seeing a psychologist for attention and behavior problems or you are consulting a counselor about how to control him or her. You can request that behavior modification strategies be added to the IEP. You can request an extension of occupational therapy or physical therapy into next year. You can request a modified physical education program to lessen your child's frustrations. As your child becomes more integrated in regular environments, you work with the teacher and learning specialists in locating appropriate mainstreamed classes.

Gretchen says, "When parents ask for more related services, we look at how the child is progressing. Has the child improved with what he receives? Do parents think he is not progressing enough? Although some requests are not reasonable, we nearly always try to go along with parents' requests."

EMOTIONAL PROBLEMS AND LEARNING DISORDER SYMPTOMS

What can you do if your child shows emotional problems in addition to learning problems? Dr. Larry B. Silver says (about LD children in particular, but the same thought can apply to children with other disabilities), "The emotional problems are due to the stresses your child experiences. The first goal is to minimize these stresses. Often, once the school recognizes his or her learning disabilities and sets up a program to help, once you rethink your relationship based on your new knowledge, and once, if needed, medication is used, the emotional problems minimize or disappear."[7]

With some children, emotional problems do not disappear. Many with hyperactivity, attention disorders, and/or learning disorders do not pay attention or sit still in class for more than four minutes, not because they don't want to but because they cannot. These are the children who were kicked out of Saturday recreation programs and library story hour. They suffer from low self-esteem as a result of society's reaction to symptoms of learning disorders.

These problems require continued communication with the teacher, school psychologist, and special education supervisor to formulate classroom changes, diet changes (if necessary), and self-esteem enhancers to help your child in regular or special education classes. If your child is troubled, do not let the school address his or her problems as solely emotional disturbances when help for learning or attention disorders is what he or she needs most.

Cindy encourages family counseling. She says some parents use counseling and others do not, depending on the circumstances. "Some parents are discouraged with private counselors. Others say parents should keep looking until they find a counselor who can help. Many parents can't afford counseling and others aren't interested, but I have seen dramatic results when counseling was used. Some of the children benefit from group counseling with the school guidance counselor."

Cindy says special education is not the only answer for children's behavior handicaps. Some of her parents are involved with school or community parent support programs. She says, "These parents welcome support because they are frightened by their children's behavior. Parent groups are a great help, especially for parents with acting-out children. The behavior modification strategies we use are most effective when parents coordinate strategies at home."

How do you locate the right therapist? Primarily, you want to find out if the therapist is compatible with disabled children and with their parents. Ask other parents, teachers, and the family doctor about their knowledge of a particular therapist. Perhaps you met a therapist at your support group. Some counselors participate in conferences and panels sponsored by disability organizations. You'll want to talk on the phone or meet the therapist (not the secretary) to determine how he or she relates to disabled children. A therapist should understand the social stresses of children with attention disorders and/or learning disabilities. Does he or she understand the psychological repercussions of teenagers with spina bifida, for instance? Be open with the therapist. Explain family stresses.

Dr. Harold Lubin, a psychiatrist specializing in the treatment of learning disabled children, wrote in *Perceptions*, "The stresses of the learning disability traumatize the child just as any other form of stress would. An LD child's ineffectual defense mechanisms range over the entire spectrum of neuroses as they would with any other psychological trauma."

Dr. Lubin says it is perfectly proper to ask if the doctor understands learning problems. "You can [also] tell how important the therapist considers the organic aspects of the learning disabled child's problem by whether . . . he does a modified neurological examination in the search for 'soft signs.' If he is not qualified to do a neurological, the therapist should at least refer the child to a practitioner who is able to perform that service for him. [It is assumed that the therapist is of high enough caliber that he will not accept the diagnosis without confirming the fact that the child has a learning disability through his own examination.]"[8] Dr. Lubin says distance and fees are two other considerations for families, so that your stress is not increased by this therapy.

KIDS, PARENTS, AND HOMEWORK

Homework takes on new dimensions when children have learning problems. Should you work with your child on homework? Kids with learning problems are so different from each other and parent–child relationships so varied, it is impossible to pass judgment on this sensitive question. Memory deficits and poor penmanship contribute to school troubles for children with learning problems. A teacher's oral directions sound garbled. An LD student can't remember to read the assigned pages, answer questions about them, or comprehend the correct method for completing a page of math problems. What's more, the student can't copy an assignment from the board or write fast enough to get it all down. It's much easier to tell parents there is no homework rather than admit the instructions were too difficult to understand. If your child suffers from perception and organizational deficits, ask the teacher to write out homework assignments for him or her, or provide a paper to copy, or go over assignments to see what he or she is missing.

How much work can your child do at home? How much can you help? When Todd was in elementary school, I read with him and helped him with some homework, but I had no patience for spelling. When Todd, who is an auditory learner, took regular high school American history, we worked out a plan with his teacher to read aloud the texts, and he took the tests orally too. This plan worked well for Todd because he has trouble with proper names (although Todd's father said he learned more than he ever wanted to know about the labor leader, Samuel Gompers).

Nevertheless, if you help your child with homework, you stop at first pressure-cooker feelings. "But knowing the way my daughter avoids homework, should I just let her fail?" you ask. Here is one method of doing homework.

In *Making the Words Stand Still*, Donald E. Lyman suggests to parents not to teach their children their homework, or do it for them, or teach them parts of it but to do it with them. "As you do it he does it. You have one piece of paper and he has another. In the case of math, you do the problem step by step on your paper and he does it step by step on his paper. Don't say, 'Now try one all by yourself.' If he tells you that he'd like to do a problem by himself or that he can finish the assignment by himself, let him. If he gets some wrong answers, don't go back and teach him those problems, just keep going on but slow down your pace."[9]

If children can do homework alone, they need a private place free of distraction, such as wild wallpaper, colorful posters, television, and siblings. They should be comfortable. Allow breaks and snacks. Let them sprawl on a couch or the floor if they want to. To some students music is useful in drowning out household noise, while to others it is a distraction.

All homework is not created equal. A sheet of work that takes Kathy, an average student, thirty minutes takes your son two hours, if he endures to the end, and he will most likely quit long before that. Learning disabled students, in particular, are creative in avoiding unattainable homework. This sensitive area requires teacher communication and methods to break homework into smaller units, if necessary. They work for five minutes and then rest or receive a reward. They work for another five minutes, and so on. The goal is to learn, not to finish one page at the expense of your patience and the children's frustration and anger. Coercion is ineffective. Children will not learn math if you deny them soccer practice.

Your child needs a united front about schoolwork. If you disagree with teachers—if you think the homework has little value or there is too much of it—don't share this view with your child. Explain that you are looking for another way to help with the homework. Then schedule a three-way meeting—you, your child, and the teacher. Or schedule a meeting with teachers and/or the special education supervisor. Explain to educators that your child needs alternative strategies to overcome this hurdle.

Many LD students find decent grades hard to come by. Your child's grades should not be reduced because of absenteeism, tardiness, or behavior outside of academic endeavors.

Look for a tutor. A good tutor relieves you from this singular stress and gives you and your children the freedom to enjoy each other. Yes, tutors *are* expensive. Perhaps you can locate a college student majoring in special education or elementary education. Call the special education department of colleges and universities in your area. Ask your local parent group. Perhaps you and another parent can tutor each other's child. Do you know a high school student in your neighborhood who would tutor for a nominal fee?

Ask the teacher if he knows any tutors in the area. Explain that you are unable to help your child with homework and you need to find someone who can. Todd made the strongest gains the years that his tutor and teacher coordinated his classroom materials and worked with us at home to strengthen his skills.

Interview potential tutors. Ask about their training in teaching reading and math, their experience with children who have mental retardation, learning disabilities, or other impairments. Do they understand that kids with poor school experiences can be defensive or difficult to work with, at least in the beginning?

The prospect of using a tutor should not hang over children's heads. ("Better do your homework or we'll get you a tutor," etc.) Children need to regard their tutor as a means of learning and improving in school.

Last, find out when school tests and evaluations are carried out. Talk with your children before tests. They are entitled to know what is going on. Listen to their concerns. Try to structure your home before tests so that the children are rested and have had a good breakfast. It is not a good idea to plan or attend highly stimulating events (family reunions, movies) the day before evaluations.

AN OPTIONAL READING PROGRAM

Some parents have time and an inclination to help their child academically. Do you want to take a few minutes a day to help your child with reading? Here is an easy-to-use technique that cuts across all areas of special education. Since 1962, when R. G. Heckelman, Ph.D. introduced the Neurological Impress Method (N.I.M.), it has been used by thousands of teachers and parents. The N.I.M. does not require special materials, it does not overwhelm parents, and it combines seeing/hearing/speaking for simultaneous learning.

The N.I.M. is an effective home method because no special training is required and the cost involved is negligible. All you need is reading material at the proper level for your child. Dr. Heckelman recommends you start at two or three grade levels below the child's actual grade level. The material can be borrowed from the school or checked out at the local library.

Don't be misled by the simplicity of the N.I.M. It works! And it is particularly effective in the one-to-one setting of parent and child. Only fifteen minutes a day (on consecutive days) for a period of eight to twelve hours is required. Generally, positive results will occur at about the fourth hour of instruction. (If no gains have been noted by this time, there may be other interfering difficulties that are limiting the child's progress with N.I.M.)

Seat the child slightly in front of you so that your voice is close to the child's ear. Dr. Heckelman recommends that the parent sit on the right side of the child.

From the very first session, you and the child will read the same material out loud together. It is generally advisable in the beginning sessions that you read a little louder and slightly faster than the child. Initially, the child may complain that he or she cannot keep up with you, but urge him or her to continue and ignore any mistakes. An alternative is to slow down slightly to a more comfortable speed for the youngster. By rereading lines or paragraphs several times together before going on to more reading material, this discomfort on the part of the child is quickly overcome, and you will find that you and he/she will establish a comfortable rhythm in a very short time. In most cases, only two or three minutes of repetition is sufficient.

Very little preliminary instruction is necessary before the reading begins. The child is told not to think of reading since we are training him/her to slide his/her eyes across the paper. *At no time is the reading corrected.* As you and the child read together, move your finger simultaneously under the spoken words in a smooth continuous fashion at precisely the same speed and flow as the verbal reading. This gives the child a clear target, keeps the eyes from straying all over the page, and helps establish left–right progression.

If it is desired, the child may later take over the finger function. If you notice any difficulty, reach out and place your hand on your child's finger and guide it to a smooth, flowing movement. Pay particular attention to the end of a line, where the finger should move rapidly back to where the new line begins. It is common for people not to move their fingers back rapidly enough (something like a typewriter carriage returning to position at the end of a line).

Be sure that your voice and fingers are synchronized. Very good readers tend to look ahead and run their finger ahead of where their voice is. In using N.I.M., it is absolutely essential that the finger movements, voice, and words all be synchronized.

Not only should you absolutely avoid correcting the child's misreading of words, but at no time during the session should you stop and ask questions about word recognition or comprehension. The major concern is with style of reading rather than accuracy.

Usually, by the time it is apparent that children need some remedial reading, they have accumulated a number of poor reading habits and eye movements and have lost confidence, all of which produce inefficient reading patterns. They are apt to read word by word, and often that is accompanied by the body rocking back and forth as they try to force recognition and comprehension of each word as it comes along. One of the most important aspects of the N.I.M., as far as you are concerned, is to forget conventional reading approaches you may have heard of and think more in terms of exposing your child to a correct reading process.

Even after the child's reading has speeded up considerably, word recognition will probably improve somewhat more slowly. Word recognition can lag behind the functional reading process by a year to a year and a half. Not to worry! Once your child has begun to read newspapers and magazines at home voluntarily and has gained confidence in this new skill, he or she will make rapid strides in word recognition.

"Pacing" is another extremely important aspect of the N.I.M. Pacing means that the material should be periodically speeded up, and the youngster is literally dragged to higher rates of speed in the reading process. This is done only for a few minutes at a time but probably should become a part of every reading session.

The material used is of great importance to the success of the N.I.M. As mentioned earlier, it is suggested that the child be started on material that is two or three grade levels below the child's actual grade level. But care must be taken not to spend too much time at the lower levels of the child's reading ability. Over-exposure to difficult words is far more important that underexposure.

One of the reasons for the success of the N.I.M. seems to be the enormous exposure readers have to words. An ordinary session of N.I.M. reading, for fifteen minutes, will run as high as 2000 words! It is not at all uncommon in elementary-level books to range from ten to twenty pages of reading material in one session. Too little exposure is more detrimental than too much. There have been no instances reported where tremendous amounts of exposure to material have been harmful to any child.

A Word of Caution

In using the N.I.M. method, you must take care not to try to push your child beyond his or her intelligence expectancy grade level. For example, children who have approximately 100 IQ and are in the fifth grade are assumed to be able to read up to the fifth-grade level. Many times this grade level can be achieved within about eight to twelve hours of the N.I.M. if the children have started at the third-grade level. If you continue on with the N.I.M. after expectancy has been achieved, very little additional gain is to be expected. However, if you wish to spend a few hours of instructional time experimenting to make certain the child has reached his/her optimum level, this may be well justified. It will not harm the child if you are sure not to press for results beyond his/her capacity.

Make It an Adventure!

The attitude of the parent is going to make or break the success of the reading sessions. Your approach should be cheerful but businesslike—for example, "Okay, we are going to read for fifteen minutes. I've been looking forward to it all day." Tune out any negative signals you may receive from the child. Simply get out the materials, sit down on the couch, and pat the place next to where you wish the child to sit. The sessions are so short and so undemanding, we can promise that the child will cooperate, especially when he/she begins to notice signs of improvement in his/her reading—and he/she *will* notice.

Don't stint on praise—but keep it honest. A pat on the head accompanied by, "Wow! You were great today," will do much to keep the level of enthusiasm high.

Do not allow interruptions. This is your time with your child for a specific purpose, and your child is not going to take it seriously if you bound up to take a telephone call or answer the door. Have another adult or a sibling posted to handle interference during these important fifteen minutes.

Scheduling the reading session at the same time and in the same place every day not only helps to bring organization and structure to the commitment but places a value on it. "This is the time when Johnny and I read together, but I can see you in fifteen minutes."

It should be carefully noted that not all parents are capable of working with their child on an academic level. Very simply, some parents work extremely well with their children—others find it a frustrating, exasperating experience. If you are one of the latter, waste no time on feelings of guilt—we cannot all be all things to our children. (You're probably terrific in a number of other parent–child activities.)

YOUR CHILD SUCCEEDS ONE DAY AT A TIME

You can help your daughter with schoolwork, but you worry about her lack of survival skills and her poor public behavior. You wonder where to begin. "We have so little time together and she needs so much. Besides, what can I do with a child who is impulsive and plain out of control?" you ask.

Start simple—one day at a time. Take a walk, go on a picnic, plant beans in the garden, bicycle, wash the car, cook a frozen vegetable, rake the grass, play miniature golf, shop for groceries, or practice dialing the phone.

Purchase an inexpensive pocket calculator. Take it to the store, and let her keep track of the total. Did she make a mistake? Drop the calculator? Relax and start over. Eventually you can show her how to reset a clock radio or phone in a catalog order. You set a learning example when you garden, go fishing, read for fun, or work with ceramics. When your child asks about a word or phrase or historical incident, you can look it up together.

Have you heard that kids with disabilities are more comfortable with structure? Structure is the same as routine. In structured homes, meals are eaten and chores are done at regular times. Homework begins at a regular time and bedtime is 9:00, 10:00, or whatever is established. Be realistic about TV schedules. Do you think a child, with or without learning disorders, is going to do homework while you are watching TV? You are flexible, but weeknights are more successful and easier for everyone in a structured environment.

Reward good behavior as much as you dish out consequences for broken rules. Your daughter needs to hear she is a good person in spite of her inability to always follow directions or use appropriate behavior in public. Help her find words to express herself, which is preferable to acting out and tantrums. Ask yourself, "What does my child want to happen as a result of the way she is acting?"

Do not give out more than one or two instructions at a time. Get close and make eye contact before you tell your son to do something. Keep your voice low and slow. Say what you need to say, but say it once—clearly—completely—firmly—calmly. If you tell him to "sweep the porch," he may not know how to begin. If a task seems too hard, break it down into smaller parts and teach each part separately. Teaching him part by part—one job at a time—how to clean his room, dust, vacuum, make the bed, pick up clothes, shovel snow, is a gradual process requiring a small part of your day.

Reason with your children without teasing, ridicule, or sarcasm. We were helped considerably by stock phrases Sally L. Smith listed for parents and teachers in her 1979 book *No Easy Answers: The Learning Disabled Child* published by the National Institute of Mental Health, U.S. Department of Health, Education, and Welfare. Here are some:

"That's not appropriate behavior. It does not fit the situation. This is the appropriate behavior. Let's try it."

"When you're frustrated, it helps to tell us about it and then we can help you deal with it."

"Slow down now. Organize your thoughts. We have time."

"Stop. Think. What are we going to do first?"

"You are just going to have to try to accept my word that you are making progress. You will see it for yourself soon."[10]

Adjust your own perspective to a certain amount of chaos. It is easier to expect improvement than perfection. Sorrow is not the result of spilled milk or broken dishes but of hurtful words that follow.

What else can you do to encourage learning? Use the library. Many larger libraries are like free community centers with video and audiotape departments, travel films, outside band concerts, kids' activities, and craft demonstrations.

Read to your child. Read together. Let your daughter read what she wants to read, even if it's cartoons, funny papers, and stories below her reading level. Help her find short books about dogs or horses—whatever interests her. Let her pick out a library videotape as well as books, a strategy that adds excitement to the experience.

Subscribe to adult and kid magazines. Watch TV news with your kids, and comment on news. Comment on the commentators.

You can cut down on stresses by eliminating unnecessary activities in your own life and hanging onto things that reward you. When your child has disabilities, you need to be involved at school. You also need your workout at the gym twice a week, but your local civic organization has asked you to chair the annual Christmas dinner-dance for five hundred members. Your child will not be in school forever. Perhaps someone else can chair the dinner-dance, and you can continue your workouts.

Although it is normal to be never wholly comfortable with special education, you stimulate progress by working positively with teachers. Teachers who want to improve your child's learning experiences are receptive to how you *think* the child learns, even when you aren't sure. The more you share your child—your child's personality, abilities, needs, and dreams—with school staff, the more effective your child's education during these critical years will be.

The mother of a disabled young adult talked about her concern for the future. "I have a vivid memory of something that happened years ago at a parent support meeting. Most of the parents had young children, as we did. We were always discussing how to manage weekends and playtime. After a while, an older couple stood up and said we should be thinking about the future—when our children left school. They talked about their daughter, in her early twenties, who sat home and could find no work."

With the passage of ADA, the Americans with Disabilities Act, our society is going through a learning process of assimilating disabled people into regular settings. ADA means our institutions of business, entertainment, higher education, and government are focusing on what disabled people *can do*.

This is both easier and tougher on parents and kids. From now on, persons with disabilities will have fewer limitations foisted on them. Our goal is to smooth their passage into a regular society.

Chapter 10

POSTSCRIPT ON PARTNERSHIPS

Considering the urgency in rearing children with disabilities, how do parents and professionals become partners? There is more to consider in using nontypical medical, psychological, and educational interventions. How do parents and professionals cooperate to enrich early intervention and later academic remediation? By remembering that families by necessity focus on how their child affects them *today*, in addition to wondering about this child's future. And by remembering that professionals, even those with special kids of their own, need to address long-range plans for *one* disabled child, plus what works for all kids with similar needs. Parents of disabled children and all those who interact with them should look beyond a typical family experience in addressing the needs of families, whether those needs are born out of hospital diagnosis, diagnostic clinic, or the first months of public school. They begin from the premise that parents are the primary caregivers for a child with disabilities.

In *Support for Caregiving Families: Enabling Positive Adaptation to Disability*, Frank and Sandra Warren say the role of parents is obvious. "Their participation should be pervasive, limited only by the express will of their adult son or daughter in areas involving personal choice. . . .

"The role of parents in creating and maintaining quality services is essentially one of creating order out of chaos, or creating an arrangement . . . that serves particular family needs. What may appear to be chaos is, in reality, a multitude of orders created by others to serve a multiplicity of purposes, almost none of which neatly mesh with the needs of a particular family. Parents of children who are not handicapped may expect to find the order of things somewhat amenable to their family needs. But parents of children who have any one of a great variety of labels attached to them such as mental retardation, autism, cerebral palsy, and epilepsy, have already begun to understand that the order of things is much more chaotic, ill-fitting, and not arranged in the best interest of their family or of their child in particular."[1]

Parents of children with disabilities share an experience of getting to know professionals in several fields. Some specialists contribute to chaos. Others help us create order and strengthen our resolve to provide our child with the best services possible.

One thing is clear. We hear too much about what parents and professionals do *to* each other. How can parents and professionals work together without a metaphor of confrontation? What roles can parents and specialists play to smooth the child's passage through identification, special education, and related services? How are parents empowered and enabled to make the right choices through the early years and beyond?

WHAT DO PARENTS WANT?

Professionals often ask what young parents want. In the early days of a diagnosis or discovery of a disabling condition in a child parents rarely know what they want. It is later, when emotions and reactions set in, that they begin to realize needs and formulate plans. Primary parent needs are respect, helpful information, worthwhile time with professionals, and support to maintain family life.

How can support that sounds easy be so difficult? Because parents and specialists are participating in a volatile human experience, the shock and sadness attendant in treating a child with disabilities.

Support is difficult because parents new to disability feel helpless. Diagnosis is so outside their experience, they have no idea what to do next. The authors of *Early Services for Children with Special Needs: Transactions for Family Support* say, "Almost universally, the parents of at-risk and disabled children express, early in their experience, a sense of powerlessness in the face of their child's special condition. A habit of deferring to professionals for everything can easily develop in response to this sense of powerlessness. Such deference can be not only flattering to professionals, but justified in the belief that it is taking some load of decision making from already burdened parents."[2]

Support is difficult because of an urgent need to coordinate services offered by agencies and schools. Support is also difficult because parent esteem plays an enormous role in how parents and extended family nurture a handicapped child after they leave the hospital or school-based diagnosis.

In December 1984, Ann Oster described her experience as the parent of an infant with developmental problems in a keynote address for a Washington, D.C. conference on "Comprehensive Approaches to Disabled and At-Risk Infants, Toddlers and Their Families":

> Five and a half years ago, when my son Nicholas was born prematurely, I felt more hostage than partner to a gang of powerful professionals who sustained his life and taught me the rules of a strange new variety of motherhood. I didn't question their competence in treating any of us: my husband and I needed to believe that someone had wisdom in this situation that had spun our lives out of control and made us wonder who we were and whether we were any good. The individuals stand out who helped me begin rebuilding a sense that I was worth something: the nurse who sat and talked with me when she had time, and loaned me a nursing text when I was frustrated by my ignorance; the child life teacher who asked how I was doing and then sat down to listen as I told her; the physical therapist who celebrated Nick for what he *could* do instead of defining him by his disabilities.
>
> But so many of our contacts with professionals were frustrating or destructive to our self-esteem. We were given very little informa-

tion and our skills training consisted more of prohibitions than positive action. So we became expert at handwashing and technical jargon about blood gasses and electrolytes. Instead of being instructed about how to deal with Nick's developmental immaturity, we were encouraged to play the strange nursery game of pretending he was a normal baby. One day I asked a nurse how this experience affected mothers and babies in the long run. She told me that a few mothers were abusive, but most were just a bit overprotective. This was scant preparation for the blast of my own emotions over the next two years or so.[3]

Ann Oster and other professionals say what parents know, that the cumulative impact of childhood disability on families is profound. Professionals who care for at-risk babies and present parents with diagnosed infants and children *must* appreciate families' needs and respect the magnitude of their task. As families rebuild their lives, professionals should help them in ways that increase their strength and build on self-esteem.

If parental esteem and respect foster healthful environments for disabled children, what hard-won knowledge contributes to healthy adjustment for parents?

PARENTS WANT SENSITIVE, SUPPORTIVE INFORMATION

I remember only two items from Todd's diagnosis: the term "minimal brain dysfunction" and the orange-brown pattern of the hospital room draperies.

When a child is born or diagnosed with a disability, parents need a sensitive, basic informational packet about the child's type of disability. If the child is an infant, the packet explains what parents can expect from PL 99-457 and hospital and community interventions. The underlying packet message says, "We know this is difficult, but we can help you." If the disability is discovered or occurs later, parents are given a similar packet with a fuller explanation of federal and state education laws.

Professionals who are relatively sure a child is going to have developmental problems should not withhold information from parents or wait for another professional to tell them. In addition to this, parents should receive diagnostic information about retardation, hearing or vision impairment, Down syndrome, learning disability, autism, etc., in a private office, not over the phone, in the lobby or hallway, or standing next to the child's bed, unless the child is an infant and the physician is explaining the disability to parents.

Professionals begin and end meetings on a positive note, avoiding absolute predictions or negative value judgments based on IQ or ability. When children are severely impaired, parents know they are not going to college. Parents of mildly impaired children realize their children are not relating to school or learning to read, are emotionally disturbed or socially immature.

As Ann Oster says, it helps to define children more for their abilities than their disabilities. Positive introductory statements, "I can tell you are working with John. His articulation (lunchroom behavior . . . following classroom instructions) has improved" or "Susan looked pretty this morning in her pink jacket," can help a parent relax and lead to finding solutions to serious dilemmas.

Todd had a teacher who began conferences with, "He works so slowly." Not knowing how to respond, I sat silently waiting for the discussion to continue. Although this professional was probably trying to address Todd's learning style, the conferences that year were unproductive. Instead of interacting with teachers who worked daily with Todd and with related service persons who improved his speech, I worried about the degree of Todd's slowness. (How slow do they mean? Too slow to work, to drive a car? Too slow to relate to normal people when he grows up? Do they mean too slow for this class?) And a last thought that I should have expressed—that Todd was trying and working, albeit slowly. Like other parents overwhelmed by the specialness of remediation, I was afraid to ask how we could work to adapt Todd's working speed to class materials.

A professional introduction, "We asked you to come in because John is quite honestly creating havoc in the hallways and yesterday he opened the emergency exit on the school bus," may accurately describe John, but provoke already distressed parents. First, John's parents are placed on the defensive, which means they argue or say little while waiting for the meeting to end. Two, unless their esteem is strong enough to withstand the assault, they may not return.

How much better to begin the conference in a sharing frame in which all parties deal from John's strengths and abilities, then explore alternative strategies to help John improve his behavior.

Parents have a lot to think about, much of it unapparent to professionals in a single encounter. Elizabeth Webster says in *Counseling with Parents of Handicapped Children: Guidelines for Improving Communication*, "While sharing concerns common to all parents, those whose children are handicapped also have different concerns, just by virtue of having to provide for a child who is different. It is a hurtful thing to have a handicapped child; it is also confusing . . . parents of children with handicaps have different strains imposed by having to provide for their children's special treatment or education. For example, many parents have children with dental problems, but parents of children with cleft palates may have particular difficulty in locating dentists and providing for regular and usually extensive dental help. As another example all parents want their children to develop motor skills, but the parent of a child with cerebral palsy usually must seek special treatment to help the child develop motorically."[4] Dr. Webster adds that the desire of parents for their children's education can lead to a series of disappointments and frustrations for parents of children with learning disabilities.

Martha Ziegler, parent of a girl with autism, says she was asked in the early years, "Mrs. Ziegler, what do you see as the long-term prognosis for your daughter?" She says she never knew what to answer, and still does not know what answer was expected.

She says how much more helpful it would have been if specialists had gone about helping Mrs. Ziegler and her husband frame a context for future planning with meaningful questions:

What kind of life do we hope our daughter will have?

Where do we want to see her live?

What kind of work do we want to help her plan for?

What skills will she need in order to have friends and a social life?

What should we be doing now to get ready for that life we wish for her?

How can we prepare her for a life of meaningful choices?

How can we help her achieve a maximum amount of control over her own life?

What can we as a family do to promote healthy self-esteem in our daughter as she grows up?[5]

These are hope-affirming plans involving parents as experts. They demonstrate a professional need for parents to enter into decision making. They recognize the parents as prime movers in all aspects of a child's development.

DEFINING PARENTS AS EQUAL PARTNERS

After diagnosis or identification, professionals support parents' self-confidence by encouraging parents to be equal partners in the care and nurture of the child. Martha Ziegler says professionals can support mothers by allowing them to be present during therapy, testing, or other sessions with the young child. "In case of doubt about her presence, the mother should be welcomed. Such a policy conveys a message to the mother that she plays an important role with the child, and that she is a partner who can be expected to contribute valuable input and can be relied upon to carry out any follow-up activities that may be indicated by the session."[6]

Parents need listening professional partners. Many new parents read extensively about the disability. Studying materials about a disability is one way of coping, of trying to feel they are regaining control. Professionals can listen nonjudgmentally to parents' ideas, even when terminology is mispronounced or misunderstood. Professionals do not say "Forget that and listen to what I am saying about muscle tone."

Professionals allow parents to use technical terminology from other disciplines. The pediatrician is not turned off by parents' use of testing words and phrases they heard from the school psychologist. Professionals can assist parents in preparing material about the child for a specialist in another discipline. A teacher says, "I understand you have an appointment with Dr. Smith about changing Bobby's medication. Would you like for me to write a paragraph about Bobby's improved reading skills (or problems with afternoon fatigue, difficulty with math, acting out on the playground)?"

How do professionals gain information about disabilities and family dynamics? With care and sensitivity in how their approach affects parents. Linda and her son agreed to take part in an interdisciplinary symposium about spina bifida. She said, "They sat us on a little stage with professionals grouped around us asking questions. All we needed was a spotlight. There were no introductions, so afterwards I went around and introduced myself and asked everyone his name. The next day a hospital secretary called and asked if I wanted to come in for 'counseling.' "

Parents are not made to feel like textbooks in professional education. Families respond positively to a sharing frame that says: "Together we can combine resources to help your child. Let's exchange information about your child, his or her medical problems, school and family life, and how he or she is getting along in the neighborhood."

FROM IDENTIFICATION THROUGH THE SCHOOL YEARS

We eliminate the negative. In the long term, we parents gain more information from parents with positive attitudes than those in constant enmity with schools. Parents enter school meetings with a willingness to cooperate. At the same time, they are entitled to their viewpoints about how the child is learning.

Small kindnesses foster respect. Parents show up on time. They call if they can't make it. If professionals cannot attend or they know they are going to be delayed, someone contacts parents to schedule another meeting. All professionals actively engaged with the child make every effort to attend meetings so parents do not feel only part of their child's needs are addressed. Consequently, parents are not forced to ask for another meeting in order to reach everyone concerned with the child's education.

School meetings of all kinds were originally based on the premise that mothers could attend during school hours. With both parents working, different strategies are needed to make IEP meetings accessible. In order to increase parent participation, meetings can be scheduled in parents' homes, in neighborhood churches, synagogues, or community centers, by arranging parents' transportation through community volunteer groups, or using school funds to defray the cost of public transportation. Child-care problems can be minimized by conducting meetings in locations with access to a playroom or playground or by using community volunteer helpers for child care. IEP meetings can be held early in the morning, late in the afternoon, evenings, over the lunch hour, or on Saturday mornings.

If only one parent can attend an educational or IEP meeting, professionals can write an information sheet about the child's progress and school lessons (in addition to the IEP copy). An "info paper" gives a parent something substantial to share with the other parent or family support person. This is another reason for a full explanation of the IEP. It's difficult to remember everything four hours later when the phone is ringing and your toddler is tossing spaghetti at the dog.

We focus on the present. It serves no purpose to tell parents that advanced therapeutic techniques will help children ten years down the road when in ten years one's child with spina bifida will be twenty. Better to target parent–professional interventions to this year.

We exchange ideas about special education programs and related services. Parents who ask questions are not challenging professional expertise but wonder how techniques apply to their child. "If therapy (speech, physical, or homework) involves me, will I have time to do it, and will Susie cooperate?" Parents do not always follow through because they did not understand what the therapist or teacher was talking about. Parents may not follow through if the efficacy of a treatment is unclear, if home-based interventions interfere with family life.

After Todd began taking Ritalin®, I read an alarming but erroneous newspaper account that said children who took methylphenidate had delayed puberty, if they reached it at all. Parents who ask how medications (Ritalin® and Cylert®, for example), are going to affect their child are not challenging the prescription. It is normal to wonder how giving one's child a pill twice daily is going to affect him or her in the long run.

Professionals cannot avoid using special education terminology in meetings but are careful to explain technical terms. Parents should speak up. For too long I said nothing and consequently learned nothing about "encoding" and "norms."

Professionals avoid telling parents they are emotionally involved. Instead, they are genuinely interested in parents' goals for the child. Goals might be unrealistic from lack of accurate information, not from parent resistance to the disability. Professionals provide printed material about community resources for specific disabilities. They help parents use resources efficiently so family–community life is not sacrificed for a child with disabilities.

Professionals can be careful to talk with both parents and not address discussions to one parent, whether or not that parent is interacting. Everyone listens and is genuinely interested instead of regarding the meeting as "Let's do it and we're out of here."

In IEP discussions, we exercise caution with "appropriate," a fundamental work in PL 94-142. For parents new to special education terminology, appropriate can mean almost anything, from suited to one's child to suited to available school resources. Therefore, when parents request related services or want to change special services, let's not say the requests are inappropriate. Richard P. Holland says "appropriateness" refers to the unique requirements of the individual child. Appropriateness is determined within the LEA (local school), and education choices are suited to each student based on his/her needs.[7]

IEPs and other conferences are draining for parents, only because they resurrect the discomfort of knowing one's child is not like other kids. Momentary disappointment at test results, worries about the future—we would put these feelings aside if we could.

BEHAVIOR MANAGEMENT BEGINS HERE

But it's conference time and we are discussing Karen's math homework. (Karen was so furious at the teasing she received on the school bus yesterday, she tossed another girl's purse out the window.) Academic and vocational discussions are important, but parents with children in the early grades are justifiably concerned with the moment. Children's social interaction affects the strata of their school career, from bus rides to playgrounds. Hyperactivity and emotional lability are just two characteristics of learning disorders. Interacting parties can remember that a consistently impulsive, acting-out child is not necessarily learning. These are kids who run amuck through stores and restaurants. (Children without disabilities run amuck for other reasons.) When school personnel tell parents, "I simply can't handle your child," they close windows to parent–professional interventions. Parents also want to control their children, especially at school, if they only knew how.

Professionals can refer parents to a community professional (psychologist, psychiatric social worker) who specializes in behavior modification. Professionals nearly always know where ethical, competent professionals can be found, but parents do not, especially if they are new to special education. Professionals can share referral knowledge with parents.

In addition to this, it is vital for parents to utilize professional advice without taking offense at suggestions for behavior modification. Behavior management is the norm in school situations involving paying attention and following instructions. If neither school personnel nor family can control a child, they search together for an outside professional who can help.

The purpose of intervention is to modify teaching so children can learn. Everyone tries to follow through on suggestions as much as possible. Parents work with teachers and related service persons who, in turn, carry out goals written on the IEP. But neither parents nor professionals are to blame if periodic evaluations indicate the child isn't progressing. Blame is counterproductive to the child's immediate needs. Better to meet and discuss further strategies.

Teachers face the stark truth that regardless of how much effort you put into a child's IEP, or how positively you approach them, some parents are not going to participate. You have not failed these parents or their children. Some circumstances are beyond your control, although you can continue to reach the child.

PROFESSIONALS COMMUNICATE

Professionals communicate with each other, especially in regard to medication. Drs. Raymond J. Dembinski and August J. Mauser wrote in *Perceptions*, "Since the field of learning disabilities . . . involves many professionals from different fields, it is strongly urged that more than 'lip service' or token communication between professionals be made. . . . Educators and not just parents should be communicating with physicians regarding behavior changes. . . . [Parents] can recommend that the physician call the teacher to explain the desired and adverse reactions to a particular medication. Parents may indicate to the physician that the teacher has their permission to contact the doctor regarding the use and effects of medication."[8]

Parents expect IEP goals to be followed, but you can be pragmatic about how much is accomplished. You take into consideration that professionals are trying to fit everything, including paperwork, into a fourteen-hour day. Have faith in educators' teaching styles and responsibility to curriculum. Observe your child's classroom with an open mind. What looks to you like a nonproductive activity about environmental recycling may be an exercise in counting and communication skills.

Professionals say volatile parents tend to lose credibility. As a parent, you can resolve to keep your cool through meetings, regardless of who says what, including, "We can't offer you this service because we don't have the money." You politely point out that PL 94-142 requires schools to locate necessary services for a disabled child if the school receives federal funds. You add, "We feel money spent now on providing Robby with _____ as listed in his IEP will in the future make him less financially dependent on state and local supports."

CHILDREN BENEFIT FROM A PARENT–PROFESSIONAL TEAM

Gretchen says anger is alienating but good things happen when parents and teachers come into conferences thinking of themselves as a team. She says, "Too often parents are overwhelmed by special education. They feel their input can't make a difference because special ed is somehow 'different' from regular education. Other parents come in feeling, 'I'm not going to get what I want today, so I have to fight.'"

"How much better when parents and teachers develop a sense of trust in each other, when *both* sides come to conferences thinking, 'We are *one* for this child. Let's decide as a team how to get the most for him.'"

Gretchen adds there are many reasons why a parent comes in with a chip on his or her shoulder. Sometimes a parent is having a hard time dealing with the fact that the child has special needs. Sometimes it's parent or teacher personality. "On the other hand, teachers and directors of special education need to recognize that parents are experts on their children. Professionals may know about education and curriculum, but a parent knows her child. We need to look at what is needed for each child, what is going to make him successful. We balance this concept with the fact that every child in the school system could benefit from a one-on-one approach."

The use of parent support meetings to belittle school districts and teachers is not practical. Instead, parents use support groups to discuss common strategies to help teachers and related service persons effectively teach disabled children in self-contained units, pull-out remediation, or regular settings. Parents support teachers who are trying to increase a child's self-esteem and accelerate learning.

Parents can suggest helpful strategies that are not going to burden teachers financially by taking money out of their pockets or interfere with teaching the rest of the class. Teachers are grateful when parents recognize their constraints in terms of class size, plus an ongoing responsibility for documentation.

Parents can beware of pixie dust: quick-fix programs and private therapies that rob you of money and time and faith in your personal judgment. Most probably won't hurt your child, but they won't help much either. Virginia Carr, an education instructor at Auburn University in Alabama, wrote in a *Perceptions* newsletter that parents should never be so intimidated by a professional that they cannot ask directly about his/her background or training. Teachers should not hesitate to ask over the phone about a psychologist or private therapist's credentials, expertise, and knowledge with disabled children. Carr says, "Remember, parents of exceptional children are easy prey to charlatans and quick cure artists. Avoid private programs which use 'hard sell' tactics to encourage you to enroll your child. Steer clear of programs which use tactics that make you feel guilty for daring to deny your child the opportunity to participate. Those are cheap shots which should signal you to seek help elsewhere."[9]

Professional reliability is fundamental to early evaluations and therapy, relieves a chaotic lifestyle, and prevents parent cynicism. A father says he took off a day from work to take his young son into a children's hospital for tests. He signed the yellow pad and waited an hour only to be told, "Oh, tests aren't being done today."

The authors of *Acceptance Is Only the First Battle* wrote, "We probably understand the nature of medical emergencies better than most people, but when we are left sitting in medical waiting rooms without any attempt to discover whether rescheduling would be a better option or whether we might have errands we could be running during the delay, we become angry and frustrated. It is difficult to transport some of our children, difficult to find baby sitters for them if it is one of our other children who needs attention. And most of us work. The time we miss by sitting in waiting rooms means less money we have to pay the bills."[10]

Community agencies cooperate, not compete. I have attended meetings where representatives of a local agency spent upward of fifteen minutes maligning another agency. This wastes time and does nothing to enhance the future of children with disabilities. Community agency differences should not include parents. Parents—young or more experienced—unencumbered by MRDD (mental retardation–developmental disability) strikes or funding disputes, are more efficient as parents.

HOW DO WE HELP PARENTS OF NEWLY DIAGNOSED CHILDREN?

In the beginning new parents cope by receiving support and information. If friends are backing away, if one's family remains silent and embarrassed at the prospect of an impairment, parents' healing begins when professionals acknowledge the change in parents' lives. Healing begins when someone says to parents, "We are here for you and we understand."

In a recent book about helping families, authors Carl Dunst, Carol Trivette, and Angela Deal say families are enabled when professional help begins "where the family is, beginning with things that are important to the family unit and individual family members." Professionals work within family strengths or help families acquire new ones. Help is effective when decision making focuses on parents and when help does not interfere with a family's culture or social network. The authors say help for families is likely to be harmful if it reinforces negative feelings of self-esteem.[11]

"The dilemma that professionals get themselves into when working with families is thinking about things as right or wrong, black or white, night or day," say the authors. "Anytime a professional thinks about things in an either–or fashion, sooner or later the professional will see him or herself as right and the family as wrong and try to convince or even coerce the family into doing what the help giver considers appropriate or right. We describe such situations as *oppositional encounters*."[12]

The key to success in parent–professional interaction is confidence that parents, most often mothers, are making a difference. Instead of agonizing if her child is doing this or that because she is doing something right or wrong, a mother is empowered to help her child because she knows how, because she and professionals share decisions and responsibilities. Medical and educational goals are complex when one's child is different, and neither parent nor professional has a monopoly on the truth.

Earlier we mentioned parents having to orchestrate appointments, transportation/parking, and child care. Many families need the benefits of two incomes, even after their disabled child is born. Parent help is effective when the costs do not outweigh the benefits in terms of money or family resources. Today, an adequate IFSP implemented through PL 99-457 should include provisions for respite for a mother who stays home with her at-risk baby or for families who need two incomes to pay the mortgage and maintain family life.

YOUR CHILD AND ACCEPTING PROFESSIONALS

After identifying a child's special needs, parents need to monitor their search for professionals: physicians, psychologists, tutors, physical therapists, who welcome children with special needs. Specialists differ in their orientation toward handicapping conditions. Parents can inquire tactfully which professionals are accepting. Professionals who want to foster healing relationships with families of disabled children need to assess their attitudes concerning disabilities. When professionals preface their talks to parent–support groups, for instance, by announcing they have no disabled children of their own, parents do not interpret the same message. The professional may mean he or she does not understand parents' unique problems as parents. Parents may construe the statement to mean the professional did not (or could not) produce a disabled child. Susan Duffy says, "For parents of the child born with an obvious handicap, it is the manner in which the aftermath of the announcement is handled that really counts. Let's face it, there are doctors who just don't see much value in the lives of children born with particular handicaps. They don't like them, they don't want them in their waiting rooms and they wouldn't do their best to save the child's life in an emergency. I believe parents' lives would be much easier if these doctors would just come right out, say what they think, and direct parents to a doctor who is sympathetic and *does* see value in the child's life. Families of handicapped children need pediatricians who are allies, not sources of further frustration."[13]

An appreciation of varied abilities is what contributes to our passing laws such as PL 94-142 and the ADA. Accepting differences is perhaps 90 percent attitudinal contributing to 100 percent societal. Social stigma in our society is beginning to change, say the authors of *Meeting the Challenge of Disability or Chronic Illness— A Family Guide.* "Persons with disability and chronic illness are becoming a more visible and vocal minority. They are speaking up for their own rights. More and more, they are being looked on as people who are valuable, equal, contributing members of our society. Still, some professionals practicing today might not yet have lost some of the earlier views about disability or chronic illness. The fear of confronting professionals who will stigmatize you is real, particularly if you are poor, a member of a minority, or have less assertive communication skills. . . . There are other professionals available who believe in the strengths and potential of all your family members."[14]

Professionals who employ nurses, secretaries, and other staff sensitive to problems of families with disabled children enhance a supportive environment. Parents treated ignominiously by support personnel may not be receptive to the most caring physician or psychologist.

Professionals are not expected to solve parents' problems or be marital counselors, but they can listen to explanations of family life, problems with finances, neighbors or siblings. They can schedule a longer appointment, especially if parents ask for one. When a parent verbalizes a troubling situation, that situation may be the most consuming event in the parent's life at the moment, perhaps more critical to the child's well-being than the prescription, IEP, or psychological assessment.

Although disability awareness has increased, professionals who work with families still see examples of rejection and abuse. They are rightly concerned about this treatment of handicapped children. Yet, from a parent's perspective, do professionals know that the parent of a mentally handicapped child can go almost indefinitely without hearing a positive comment about his or her child or his/her parenting skills? Parents routinely see specialists who offer suggestions and medicine and schedule surgery, all in the context of problems. Among family and friends, few praise parents for their extraordinary efforts or compliment them on their child's progress. In time, a parent internalizes the world's opinion of her child, and if her suffering needs expression, the child is a handy target.

PARENTS NEED MORE THAN PRESCRIPTIONS

Parents learn about advocacy from parents' groups and books such as this one. Parents learn about their rights under new laws, but they rarely know *how* to advocate, *how* to take charge of services, *how* to take care of a fragile baby or manage education for a special-needs child, until someone shows them. When parents are discovering the disability, when all they ever wanted was a simple life with their children, the process is overwhelming. Therefore, no parent question or behavior is inappropriate, even when parents appear to feel nothing.

Vulnerable parents take professional assessments to heart. When a mother makes her monthly trip to see each specialist, she needs more than prescriptions. She needs professionals willing to consider her child's potential. She needs freedom of expression and a modicum of encouragement. The mother of a child with Crouzon's syndrome (skull and facial anomaly) says, "I would encourage specialists to tell parents once in a while that they are doing a good job. My child's pediatrician has been especially sensitive to my need to hear it. It is so easy to believe one's child is or isn't doing something because of something you are doing or not doing. Being told you are doing a good job is a wonderful source of strength."

Thirty years ago my eighth-grade student, Thomas, was overactive in the extreme and could not attend to tasks more than a couple of minutes. From the early grades, his teachers had struggled to find clues for his total inability to process the written word. We reasoned it couldn't be the mother and father, who were responsible, caring parents. Thomas himself—attractive, sweet natured, blue eyed, and freckled—was showing signs of becoming a class clown. In the teacher's lounge we wondered if Thomas was sick in some way. Could he have a brain tumor?

Now I think Thomas showed classic symptoms of learning disabilities and ADD. He could neither read nor write. He missed verbal cues. He lost his book bag and his jacket. Other children scorned his weak social skills.

But I remember how hard he tried. During late afternoons Thomas tried to read and copy the simple words and sentences I gave him. He sat at his desk (for as long as he could) and applied every brain cell he could muster until drops of sweat appeared on his face. Sometimes he cried.

Why did he try? Because he had parents and a school faculty who loved him and refused to fault him for his trouble. I say trouble because none of us realized it was a serious disability.

Now I believe without evaluations and special education, Todd would have been Thomas. Because of special education and related services Todd received from first grade on, he learned to read enough to decipher a driving manual and pass the driver's test. Today he can read most signs, parts of newspapers and magazines—enough to function in a print-oriented society.

Was Todd labeled in order to remediate his learning disabilities? Yes, he needed a category in order to be taught, but he is not labeled now as he matures and becomes independent.

Did Todd suffer the stigma of special education and special classes? Maybe, but his stigma would have been worse, his humiliation profound from trying to compete and conform to regular class work. To put it another way, the payoffs exceeded the inconvenience.

Did we as parents always agree with the school district and employ the correct procedures in working with school professionals? Did we consistently keep our cool? No, but we learned through the years which strategies helped the school help Todd, when to compromise and when to stand our ground. More important, we could not have learned any of this without being there.

Did we as parents suffer knowing our oldest child was not like other kids and required special education and special classes? At first. Later we assimilated the knowledge as one part of our lives as parents. It hasn't been easy. Counselor/writer Leo Buscaglia says the anguish related to our child's differences is real indeed, and normal. "Everyone, to some extent, knows these feelings, often experienced early in life and continued on . . . throughout all periods of development. We want to be somewhat the same as others. We fear being labeled *oddballs* or *weird*. We know that obvious physical and mental differences are often seen as such. We feel the desire to hide these differences but are powerless to do so. We feel guilty about our inadequacy and inability to deal with differences. As behavior, this is *very understandable*."[15]

With integration of disabled children, and with disabled and nondisabled children in the same classes, children who receive special services do not feel as different as they once did. Special education is not a brand but the means to a better life for children with disabilities when parents and educators create partnerships. I hope the Thomases of today can benefit from partnerships, from trust, and from the correct educational interventions in order to become functioning adults.

Chapter 11

ONE DAY AT A TIME

In a 1987 talk in Toledo, Ohio, to parents and professionals who work with disabled children, counselor and vocational consultant Dr. William Timmerman said parents are pulled several ways. Society wants them to make their children independent. Yet there is a tremendous pressure on mothers to develop an emotional attachment and on parents to overcompensate for a cruel world. Another problem is SSI (supplemental security income), which helps a disabled person but often keeps him attached to parents. Dr. Timmerman said parents should learn all they can about SSI. A disabled person can work without losing SSI or Medicare health benefits, for instance.[1]

Preparing our children for the future includes three important components. *One* is an appraisal of what a disabled young person can do in light of his or her abilities and how he or she has compensated during his/her growing up years. *Two* is a pragmatic view of what your community can offer in employment opportunities for disabled people in industry and recreation or service or health care facilities, such as hotels and hospitals. How large is your community? How broad is the employment base and what is the economic climate? Does it make sense for your child to train as a child-care aide when aide jobs are scarce and child-care jobs are filled by nondisabled, experienced child-care workers? Is it realistic for your child to learn silk screening when you live in an area with no silk-screening opportunities?

Three, young people with disabilities need new opportunities and a great deal of encouragement to become as self-sufficient as possible. They need to experience various jobs as they grow and mature. Your nineteen-year-old may be able to handle a job that was unsuitable at age seventeen, for instance. Young people need help with life tasks that nondisabled kids seem to learn effortlessly. They need to practice self-advocacy, that is, learning to speak up for themselves in employment and community situations.

A friend refers to the teen years (about fifteen up) as the paper-bag age. They can't drive but they don't want to be seen with you, so you drive around with a paper bag over your head. "Let us out a block from the house, Mom. We'll be fine."

Kids with special problems are not much different although the paper-bag age is going to last longer. Special kids are going to rant just as loudly about curfews and hanging out at the mall, but they don't need what they want any more than kids with better resources need what they want. Special kids need more guidance in making healthy choices, however.

When is a young person ready for independence? How long do we wait? At the risk of contradicting ourselves, we believe you can help your child prepare, but if you wait until he/she is ready, he or she will probably never move into an apartment, group home, or other arrangement. Todd has lived alone for several years, and he still isn't ready. We work on it together.

REALISTIC EXPECTATIONS LEAD TO INDEPENDENCE

The HEATH Resource Center publication *Young Adults with Learning Disabilities and Other Special Needs* says professionals think it is crucial for parents to have realistic expectations. "Parents' goals for sons or daughters should be based on a clear understanding of the young person's capabilities in order to capitalize on positive motivation. It is important to guide choices toward successful experiences rather than activities which lead to disappointment or failure. This is especially difficult in families where parents and other siblings are high achievers who enjoy and expect high levels of academic, business, and social success.

"Contrary to what many parents have been told, the way this young adult learns cannot be radically transformed or eliminated by training, although maturity will bring many abilities into focus. In other words, the patterns [which some call deficiencies] will not be entirely outgrown, but they are manageable."[2]

Parents are sometimes seen as overprotective when they intervene for their young disabled child. Conversely, your friends and family may not understand when you allow your young son to try something new and fall flat on his face. This goes with the territory, folks. The HEATH paper says, "Parents who pull back and allow the process of growth and experimentation to occur find that young people can accept the lessons from life which they learn from false starts, even if the lessons are painful. They sometimes accept 'the real world' more readily than having their parents tell them 'what might happen.' It is also true that you have to be willing to let go even when you receive overt or subtle criticism from the extended family and well-meaning friends."[3]

Naturally you have mixed feelings about the degree of independence. What can your daughter do for herself? How much should you do for her? Has she learned how to get around town on the bus? Can she walk to the store, shop, and keep track of money? Does she know how to write checks against her bank account? Can she drive yet? If so, is she responsible enough to drive your car?

If your son lives by himself, how much control should you, the parent, exert over independent living? Translated, this means a touchy matter of visiting his apartment. How much do you do for him while you are there? How much interaction do you have with a group home? And an issue that should not concern you, "What do friends and relatives think about this? Do they think we're trying to get rid of him?" No, particularly if you enlist their help, and you explain the family's goals for independence. You tell them that independence is not abandonment, but gradually letting go with love and support.

WHEN YOUR CHILD NEEDS YOU—PART THREE

One of the hardest jobs for parents of disabled children is letting go. We have seen their suffering in a larger society. It is entirely possible your child has been the target of occasional impatience, avoidance, and discrimination. It is normal to want to protect him/her as long as you can.

As much as you know this young daughter, her moods, joys, and sense of humor, it is still hard to know how much independence she can tolerate. It hurts to watch a disabled child labor to master a skill. Some of her attempts will differ from the way you taught her. Washing clothes, for example: How many kids, disabled or not, stuff unseparated clothes into the washing machine and forget the detergent? The key to success is trying as opposed to not trying. As with nondisabled children, you guide her into independence, with small tasks gradually becoming more demanding. When tasks are too difficult, you can always back off and try again later.

You can fight some of his battles along the way, such as monitoring the IEP and insisting on vocational and educational rights. But most battles of independent living children will win by themselves, and this is where you come in. What battles do we mean? Beginning with shoelaces when they are small, we progress to washing dishes, setting the table, using a microwave, learning to press one's shirt, mowing grass, taking one's coat to the cleaners before it becomes odoriferous, using public transportation, or learning to find one's way by bicycle.

Other skills are driving, if possible (more adults with mental retardation are learning to drive), choosing food at the grocery store or in a restaurant, scheduling and keeping appointments, and handling emergency situations.

Children can learn *some* things—to compensate—depending

on their abilities, not disabilities. In spite of coordinated efforts of Todd's high school special education teachers, his tutor, and his parents, he cannot balance a checkbook. He needs help with personal business, such as paying bills. But he has his own apartment and he does laundry. He recycles newspapers. He shops for groceries and scoffs at us for shopping at another supermarket. He has strong opinions about politics and other matters, including our life-style, "I don't care much for your socks."

And he works. He works in a restaurant after vocational rehabilitation in preparing for work. How did Todd adjust to vocational rehabilitation and on-the-job training? Initially, not well. He disliked it at first, but he went. Not that we are paragons of parental patience, but we learned to listen to his emotional pain about being learning disabled and dyslexic.

One way to smooth the passage to independence is to help children find a skill or an interest, even if it takes years. This may seem incongruous for children who are so alienated from peers they can't fit in anywhere. No child exists, however, who doesn't have the capacity for doing something—from planting bean seeds to playing checkers. Todd's temporary claim to fame was cross-country track. Other students have succeeded with stamp or sports card collections, checkers and chess clubs, caring for pets, bowling, and working backstage for the drama department. Did we hear chess? Some LD students succeed at chess in spite of impaired perceptions in other areas.

Sometimes negative forces hit hard and kids with learning disorders are injured in spirit if not physically. When children hurt, parents hurt too. Should they ignore peer abuse, fight back, run away? Should you intervene or let them handle difficult situations alone? I believe parents intervene when children are not old enough or mature enough to deal with it. Parents intervene if abuse is truly demeaning, if there is danger of physical abuse, or no other action is undertaken in the neighborhood or at school.

Your child can feel successful and needed at home. Household jobs should be divided so one child does not feel more or less needed than another (or picked on, depending on one's perspective). Although children with learning problems need more guidance in carrying out chores, they can contribute. Parents succeed when one sibling says to the other, "You don't have it so bad. Yesterday *she* made me sweep the driveway after I cleaned my room."

Children with attention and learning disorders are notoriously difficult to live with. They are impulsive and excitable, and they break things. Your lamp shades look like forty miles of bad road. The mother of a very active eight-year-old said she can never take her son to her sister's house because of all the "china and glass sitting around on low tables."

Your children don't want to hurt you. They want to please you, not break things or accidentally tear things or forget instructions. They want to fit in the family. They want mutual, reciprocated love from a more or less relaxed parent. Until they are older and more settled, you can kid-proof your house. Your child can learn photography with a really cheap camera. You put away your antique bud vase and store the good drinking glasses Aunt Emily gave you. If Aunt Emily asks where they are, tell her the truth, that you are waiting for "later."

Kids with learning problems are impulsive, emotional, and unsteady in social relationships. Before they relate to the wrong people, you have talked about drugs. You discuss that sniffing solvents and like substances can be fatal. Alcohol leads to trouble they don't need. Early on you locked up your handguns or, better yet, got rid of them.

Don't be surprised if your child becomes independent in ways you think are inappropriate, i.e., "off the wall." Young adults with different perceptions typically operate on the periphery of the mainstream. Their adult friends and interests may be outside your life-style but totally right for them. How "outside" do we mean? Do his friends wear black-leather jackets and tie bandannas around their heads? Does she attend every Star Trek convention in the city? Like Todd, your child may even adopt a new religious denomination. As long as he and his friends aren't wearing those

205

bandannas over their noses and breaking the law or engaging in dangerous promiscuous behavior, does it matter?

These young adults will eventually have to take care of their health needs—everything from cleaning a scrape and applying a bandage to talking with their doctor. Earlier we talked about locating a primary care physician of young children. When your child is young, you phone ahead to determine a doctor's receptiveness to an impaired person. But now your child is twenty and you're still calling. How long do we intervene on behalf of an impaired person? Through the teens? Into adulthood?

We intervene when it is obvious our child can't handle the situation. Children with severe intellectual impairments cannot speak for themselves, but young adults with moderate to mild retardation and learning disabilities can learn partial or more self-advocacy.

Depending on the circumstances, you may need to investigate the acceptance of medical specialists toward young adults with handicaps. A doctor or dentist who understands children's difficult speech and has treated their illnesses regularly since childhood is not the same as a new specialist taking on an adult with severe or even mild disabilities. Don't take the word of a receptionist—ask to speak to the specialist.

Perhaps at first you can intervene for your young adult and he or she can handle the rest. I recently asked an allergist if he is comfortable seeing people with mild learning problems. I explained that Todd is perceptively impaired, that he cannot understand long instructions or fast explanations, and that he may ask questions about information the doctor already discussed. I explained that Todd will probably forget a number of verbal instructions about medication, for example, but he can follow written or typed instructions.

Most doctors won't object if you explain ahead of time. You don't want to shortchange your child's capacity to communicate with health care providers. On the other hand, because people with learning disorders do not necessarily *appear* impaired, a professional may be impatient with what he or she thinks is inattention.

Eventually these young adults are going to have to assert themselves in dealing with medical people in local clinics, even hospital emergency rooms. Children can be taught (using role playing or rehearsing) to politely ask a doctor to repeat what they misunderstood or they can ask the nurse how to take a medication.

HOW TO AVOID THE "CATCH-UP" SYNDROME

More than 10 percent of all school-age children have special needs. They have disabilities or emotional disturbance or they are gifted. Between 1976 and 1977 and between 1988 and 1989, the number of learning disabled students in public schools increased by 152 percent. Changes are needed by which students with mild learning disabilities are identified without damaging their self-esteem. Young children who struggle and continue to fall behind educationally or are held back one or two years before they qualify for services may be persuaded initially that the practice is worthwhile. Later they know they are failing, as do their parents and peers.

How much better to offer special services to children in their early years when their difficulties are not so apparent, when failure is not the criteria for implementing appropriate services. In 1989, Joan Wiswall, a Minnesota teacher and 1984 LDA educator of the year, asked in an *LDA Newsbriefs* why children have to fail, that is, experience the severe discrepancy on standardized tests before they can receive help "If a student exhibits a severe discrepancy, by the time he/she is identified—at the end of the second or third grade—the child not only has the stress of the special education program but must try to keep up with the regular, grade level instruction. They have the *catch up* syndrome all through their school careers. They graduate from high school with minimal skills for post high school studies or to obtain self-supporting employment."[4]

In the summer of 1985, staff members at the National Committee for Citizens in Education (NCCE) reported that many states have tightened eligibility criteria for learning disabled children, and parents are told their children cannot receive special services. In addition, parents report that learning disabled children are placed in classrooms with students who are mentally retarded, emotionally disturbed, or behavior disordered rather than given substantial help for learning disabilities. In other cases, parents say tests reveal their child needs special help for learning disorders, but instead of being given a special class or tutoring, the child is retained.

In *The Misunderstood Child*, Dr. Larry B. Silver says about retention: "I hope we have passed the point where children who do not learn well enough are routinely kept back in school. Repeating a grade may be appropriate for some children, but it should not be implemented until enough studies have been done to understand why a child is not learning. A child with a learning disability who is kept back, but who gets no additional help, may do no better the second time. Do not let the authorities at your school force your child to repeat a grade unless they have done an evaluation, unless they know why he or she did do poorly, and unless they have specific rationale for such an action. Even then, the school should consider moving the child on, but with special help, rather than keeping her or him back."[5]

OHIO IATS ASSIST STUDENTS IN REGULAR PLACEMENTS

What else can schools do to remediate mildly disabled learners on their way to adulthood? How can they encourage positive learning experiences for marginally impaired children at risk in the classroom? A number of schools are intervening for children with learning problems who do not quality for special education. Several Ohio school districts are using Intervention Assistance Teams (IAT) to help children with ADD and others who fall through diagnostic cracks.

An IAT is a problem-solving group; it assists regular teachers in helping at-risk children before they are referred to special education or given multifactored evaluations. Each school uses the same basic approach. The IAT process begins when a teacher realizes a student has an academic or behavioral problem. If the teacher cannot solve the problem using classroom interventions, he or she refers the problem to the building principal, who calls a conference. Core team members can include the principal, assistant principal, referring teacher, former teachers, school psychologist, special education teacher, reading teacher, guidance counselor, speech/language therapist, and parents.

Education consultant Ellen Frasca says the idea is to help kids who don't qualify for special services but definitely need help from regular education. Ohio principals using IATs have found that students benefit academically when teachers share ideas and strategies. Intervention Assistance Teams also encourage mainstreaming of disabled students into regular classes and reduce the number of students inappropriately referred to special education.

Other states, using different wordings, are beginning to use this concept. A prereferral or assessment team helps teachers improve the learning and behavior of students in regular classes, and students with mild disabilities remain in regular education.

Marge Goldberg, codirector of the PACER Center in Minneapolis, says all education problems are not the responsibility of special education, but education has a responsibility to all children. Children with disabilities should receive special services, but when a student in regular education is having learning difficulties, regular education should be called upon to give him or her extra help.[6]

Early services are better utilized to *save* a student when problems appear, not years later when they are serious enough to warrant special education. If your child is not learning and benefitting from regular education, but the school says he or she does not qualify for special education, the next step is to initiate evaluations and an appropriate placement.

Again, call your local LDA, appropriate parent group, or community hotline for information about tests through private psychologists, clinics, the nearest SERRC center, parent training center, or state equivalent.

SPECIAL EDUCATION AND STUDENTS WITH SOCIAL MALADJUSTMENTS

We mentioned that children with social maladjustments are not included for the purpose of special educational services. The federal definition of "seriously emotionally disturbed" excludes students whose behaviors indicate social maladjustments rather than emotional disturbance.

As we entered the 1990s, circumstances for children changed dramatically. In view of the adverse conditions many children endure—upheavals ranging from frequent moves and blending families to poverty and living in homeless shelters—it becomes increasingly difficult to tell the difference between children who are socially maladjusted and those who are emotionally disturbed. Does SED or "severely emotionally disturbed" mean a child does not adjust to peers and teachers because he acts out and refuses to follow school practices? Is another child socially maladjusted because he belongs to an irresponsible peer group? What about a child with mild learning problems whose parents are divorcing or a young recent immigrant who is teased on the bus for the way she dresses? What about a child who lives in a homeless shelter and frequently cries in the classroom? Which child needs special education for emotional disturbance?

Special educators C. Michael Nelson and Robert B. Rutherford, Jr. believe that excluding socially maladjusted children from the federal definition is unfounded plus unsupported by research, scholarly opinion, or good professional practice. Drs.

Nelson and Rutherford say there are no reliable tests to distinguish SED from social maladjustment. "In our view, the problem
of delivering effective services to troubled youth supersedes that
of differentially diagnosing an adolescent as emotionally disturbed or socially maladjusted. The time spent in attempts at
differential diagnosis seldom results in more effective treatment,
and the label resulting from this process may allow school personnel to abrogate responsibility by claiming that socially maladjusted youth do not qualify for 'special' educational provisions or
program modifications."[7]

Where is the line between emotional and social disturbance?
Studies indicate social maladjustment is a significant and usually
a long-time handicapping condition in many people from childhood to adulthood.

We realize how much schools are expected to do, with some
tasks outside teacher–school responsibility. But we think it is
logical to assume that kids with emotional and social maladjustments carry similar burdens adapting to school routines. Drs.
Nelson and Rutherford recommend two strategies for kids with
social maladaptions who fall through educational cracks. First,
schools need to identify and intervene for pupils who are at risk
for emotional or behavioral problems early in their school careers.
Second, the federal definition of SED (seriously emotionally disturbed) should be revised to include socially maladjusted children.[8]

According to professionals at the Ohio Division of Special
Education in Columbus, social maladjustment has never been
defined and is not defined in PL 94-142, although some school
districts have tried to define it to exclude children who are unruly
or those involved with the courts. In addition, some states have
tried to declassify children identified as having a conduct disorder
in order to exclude them from special education services.

In Ohio the emphasis is on the meaning of the law, which says
a child must display one or more of five characteristics describing
SBH (severe behavior handicaps)—before he or she is classified as
seriously emotionally disturbed:

- an inability to learn that cannot be explained by intellectual, sensory, or health factors
- inability to relate to peers and teachers
- inappropriate behaviors
- general depression or unhappiness
- extreme personal and school-related fears

If a child's behavior or emotions seriously affect educational performance, the child can be both socially maladjusted and severely behavior handicapped and thus receive services. Ohio school districts serve approximately 70 percent of children referred to as conduct disordered.

The Ohio education consultants feel much attention is directed to redefining social maladjustment, time better spent analyzing the system for delivering services to children rather than to child identification. In addition, they ask if we need to create a handicap category for every need that arises. If we continue to identify every child with problems as needing special education services, we could eventually eliminate general education altogether. The current special education system reinforces the tendency of making children different and apart from other kids. Perhaps a restructuring is needed to begin looking at education as more inclusive and to provide services to the general educator so that kids don't have to be labeled as different.

This is another benefit of the Intervention Assistance Teams concept used in Ohio elementary and secondary schools. IATs help teachers intervene for students with academic–behavior problems who are not identified as needing special education services. They implement assistance for all at-risk students with similar school problems.[9]

SPECIAL SERVICES FOR GIFTED AND TALENTED STUDENTS?

In recent years, concern has increased for adequate educational services for gifted and talented students. Parents have played an active role in encouraging school districts to plan and implement programs for these children. In 1972 Sidney Marland, the U.S. Commissioner of Education, created the Office of the Gifted and Talented, an agency responsible for locating funds for school programs and gathering information about gifted children. In 1974, Public Law 93-380 (the elementary and secondary amendments) resulted in the Special Projects Act, which provides funds to the Office of the Gifted and Talented.

Who are the gifted and talented? They are children in the top 3 to 5 percent of the school population who show achievement and potential ability in general intellectual ability, talent in visual and performing arts, and psychomotor ability. Their characteristics include early use of advanced vocabulary, a keen observation and curiosity, retention of a variety of information, and intense concentration. They understand complex concepts, perceive relationships, and think through abstractions. They employ critical thinking skills and self-criticism.

Sandra Berger, information specialist with the ERIC Clearinghouse on Handicapped and Gifted Children in Reston, Virginia, says the Sidney Marland report demonstrated to Congress that gifted and talented children require services beyond those normally provided by regular school programs.

Berger says being gifted is not thought of as a handicapping condition, however, and PL 94-142 does not apply to gifted children's needs. She adds, "There are notes in the *Federal Register* indicating that gifted children require differentiated services. This does not mean that 94-142 can be used as a lever for the gifted and talented."[10]

Sandra Berger says the needs of gifted students can be addressed through other avenues. Some children are both gifted and handicapped, such as children who are gifted and learning disabled or gifted and physically disabled. There are gifted, bilingual children.

States have different ways of providing for gifted and talented students. Some states require nothing, others require support services, and still others define these children as "exceptional" and provide for testing and placement in appropriate classes. Some states, while not including the gifted under special education, have chosen to use components of PL 94-142, such as the IEP, in educating gifted and talented students. Forty-five states refer to gifted and talented students in their education laws or allocate extra money for educational programs. Seventeen states (Alabama, Alaska, Arizona, Florida, Georgia, Kansas, Louisiana, Nevada, New Jersey, New Mexico, North Carolina, Oklahoma, Pennsylvania, South Dakota, Tennessee, Virginia, and West Virginia) require services for gifted students.

If you feel your gifted child needs more appropriate services, contact your state education agency to see what special services can be acquired through PL 95-561, the Gifted and Talented Children's Act of 1978, or special programs.

RESOURCES FOR YOUNG ADULTS WITH PERCEPTUAL DISORDERS

As we enter a period of faltering national resources, it is increasingly necessary to identify and assist every young adult with marginal learning and attention disorders.

Over the past twenty years, names for learning disorders or school handicaps have varied, from hyperkinesis, motor problems, minimal brain dysfunction, the awkward child, and specific learning disabilities to the more recent terms, ADD (attention deficit disorder), ADHD (attention deficit hyperactivity disorder), and SDD (specific developmental disorder).

Learning disabilities are physiological: A person has trouble taking in, retrieving, and sending messages through the senses. The LDA and PL 94-142 regard learning disabled children as having normal or above normal intelligence, but who suffer from disabilities of perception and coordination. Learning disabled people have problems learning *how* to learn, especially in regular classes (without modifications). They have trouble with language, and they can be clumsy and uncoordinated.

Early identification and special services have been paramount in improving the school careers of many children with school handicaps. A recent analysis of letters to NICHCY found that learning disabilities was the handicapping category most frequently inquired about, and, in fact, it was the topic of concern more than twice as often as the category that ranked second.

Special education is available to students diagnosed as learning disabled. Although ADHD children exhibit academic performance problems, most are not eligible for placement in learning disability programs.

What is the outcome for students with learning and attention disorders? Does an LD or ADD diagnosis indicate a propensity toward criminality? Does a learning disability or an attention deficit hyperactivity disorder cause adolescent delinquency? No, a learning disability or ADD does *not* cause delinquency *per se* in children with school handicaps, but years of damage to self-esteem contribute to antisocial attitudes.

Many young adults with learning disorders lack accurate perceptions of other people's behavior. Ansel is an example. From his early years Ansel worried about school rules. In fifth grade Ansel listened to teachers tell students how they were expected to take care of books and personal belongings, follow instructions for using the library and going to the cafeteria, plus getting everywhere on time.

Ansel arrived home in a panic. "I'll never be able to do it. I didn't know what he was talking about. I can't remember all this stuff. I'm never going back!"

Two years later Ansel's brother, William, studied his sheet of fifth grade instructions. He recognized a list of rules handed out to students year after year. He had no trouble towing the school-social line and he knew instinctively one infraction would not seriously damage his academic career.

People with learning disorders have more trouble than most filtering nuance. They take rules literally. They take blanket statements personally. Their perceptions of how people behave can be largely black and white. As a young adult, Ansel continues to take information at face value. He watches the evening news and wonders how a local councilman (discussed at length by his parents) can make a statement one month and retract it the next. When Ansel's superintendent at work announced to the shop employees they "had better clean up their act," in other words improve productivity or the company was in danger of closing for six months, Ansel was traumatized. He could not visualize a worried superintendent taking out his frustrations on one branch of the business.

An ability to select and sort needed information is known by various terms—information processing, perception, organization, comprehension, or a combination of terms—varies from person to person, and affects social skills needed for adulthood.

Most sources on learning disorders mention social integration as particularly difficult for young people with learning–perceptual disorders. By this time (postpuberty but prematurity) parents and teachers have an idea which hurdles a disabled young adult can conquer with ease and which are boulder-sized bumps in the road. Most employers, fellow workers, and bank tellers do not understand the idiosyncrasies of LD/ADD people, however. Persons with impaired perceptions may ask inappropriate questions if they ask any at all. They have trouble getting their jobs done at work. They avoid reading signs if they have never made sense. Because of processing problems, they may not arrive on time, read a road map, or distinguish east from south.

Individual differences can be extreme. The same learning disordered person who can program a VCR into next Tuesday cannot remember more than two spoken directions. Another person may fail dismally in language areas but succeed in music or art. Not all LD and/or dyslexic people have social problems, however, and many adapt well to their environments.

Individuals with these types of characteristics are particularly stressed by academic formats. Classroom routines are incomprehensible. They cannot concentrate on a filmstrip nor do they hear everything the instructor is saying. Although they have no hearing acuity problems, "Line up at the door" sounds to them like "Left on the floor."

In work situations, persons with impaired perceptions react

badly to "hurry up." They emotionally overload to pressure.
Without early identification and remediation, they may believe
their struggles with society are caused by low intelligence or
weakness, a perspective that paralyzes their desire to improve.
The mother of a learning disabled adult says his continuing
employment problems are caused by his unwillingness to talk.
"He is so afraid of ridicule, he won't talk much although he talks
plenty at home," she says.

Perceptually impaired, learning disabled adults may continue to display these residues of childhood disorders:

- They have vision problems, including an inability to use
  eyes together; misreading beginnings, endings, or middles
  of words; an inability to understand the material, even with
  increased study time. Eyestrain can cause red, watery eyes
  or headaches.
- LD people sometimes produce vocal sounds (to help them
  associate sounds with written words) while they are reading, writing, or listening.
- In writing they substitute letters, erase frequently, rewrite,
  and cross out words.
- They are confused by sequential order; they confuse days of
  the week and months of the year. They are vague about
  time.
- Perceptually impaired persons may not be able to effectively apply new learning to basic experiences.
- They have a low level of frustration. LD adults can be easily
  frustrated by their inability to integrate sensory functions,
  and repeated frustration leads to a poor self-image.
- A metabolism imbalance can result in inconsistent behavior,
  nervousness, tired feelings, and short attention span.

In terms of employment, LD people are often more severely
challenged than people with retardation. Vocational trainers say it
takes longer to train adults who cannot follow a series of tasks to
change a tire or clean a machine, a discrepancy that shows up in
carelessness.

We need to be realistic about the characteristics of learning disabilities and attention disorders that can be challenged by training programs. A disabled person who trains in a factory job may be highly distracted by shouted instructions and clanging machinery. A young person with symptoms of dyslexia may have a natural bent for electronics, but frustrated by fine print training manuals. A disabled young man can work in the same job for months or years and gradually improve his skills and behavior at work. Although he compensates, he will not be able to overcome residues of learning disorders. Allen, a young man with learning disabilities, quit his job working with heavy machinery because of "all the stuff that went with it," meaning reading and writing.

Jack is an example of fitting a learning disabled person with a job he can handle. Jack, who is a skilled, responsible driver, is employed as a courier. He delivers interbusiness memos. He also drives people who have lost their driver's licenses usually because of DUI (driving under the influence), back and forth to their jobs.

Todd has the perceptual impairments characteristic of learning disabled individuals, which means he cannot reason on a par with people his age. Although Todd's adult compensations are nothing short of fantastic and he does not appear disabled at first meeting, he remains limited. Consequently, he is treated as normal in some circles, then censured for continuing problems by those who do not understand learning disabilities. One example was his two-year search for employment after high school graduation. (A two-year job search is not unheard of for adults with learning disabilities. Before they give up, many spend years looking for adaptable work. Much depends on the severity of the learning disability.) On one occasion a potential employer instructed Todd to rewrite a messy job application, not realizing he had already spent two hours on it. But after we typed up the application for him, he was told to fill it out again himself. This application was also rejected. At another place, Todd took an applicant "literacy" test, which he summarily failed.

It is no mystery why independence is so difficult to master for Todd and other people with gaps in understanding and learning.

Before Todd could drive, he tried to walk through the "drive-through" at the bank only to be told walk-throughs are not allowed because they are dangerous. This meant Todd had to wait for a free day when he could walk into the bank or sign over his check to us to be cashed.

One of the first times Todd drove through the drive-through, the cashier (who probably noticed his penmanship) refused to cash his check, although Todd had an account there and by this time a bank cash card. Todd's father later intervened via a discussion about civil rights with the bank's assistant manager.

I was waiting in the car the day Todd tried to pay for a Natatorium (community exercise club) membership. I wondered what was taking so long. At the front desk I overheard the clerk tell Todd, "We can let you use the facility now even though we need to see a cash card for your mother's check. But when you come back tomorrow, either bring cash or this check with a cash card or other proof of identification although we still need to see a proof of banking where this check was written."

"What?"

Perceptually impaired people often have poor opinions of themselves, especially if they were constantly told to "try harder." Young adults with more troubling problems may combine frustrations with emotional illness, a by-product of painful experience. When they are stressed and tired, their clumsiness increases or their speech slurs, a physiological condition that can lead police to think they have been drinking or are on drugs when they are not.

Todd's rather professorial appearance by no means indicates he is cured of learning disorders or that his comprehension of social and work nuances is going to approach normalcy. Todd improves daily, but his adult experiences and responses to society are not going to be as whole as people with intact neurological systems.

Compensating for adult learning disabilities is not the same as a cure. Mildly impaired adults need insight into their strengths in order to buffer ongoing threats to their self-image and to accept them more fully into the mainstream. They need information to help them read other people's body language and facial expressions. Like Ansel, they need help to interpret the larger picture. When we determine, socially and educationally, to enhance the abilities of children with learning problems and school handicaps during their early struggles, when we replace educational and vocational doctrine with reason, we eliminate the debilitating hostility that leads to failure.

PARENTS CAN OFFSET NEGATIVE FORCES

What can you as parents do to offset negative forces of ADD and LD that cause your child to suffer when most of society does not recognize or understand the symptoms?

You can read and learn all you can about characteristics of learning problems and determine where your child fits in. Are his/her learning deficits mild or is he or she tested daily by severe perceptual impairments? How is your child adjusting to school and the neighborhood? Is he/she shy and withdrawn or beginning to act out? Is your child an auditory or a visual learner? Does he/she need practice on how to follow more than one verbal instruction? You can make a game of following directions, simple for children, more sophisticated for teens.

You can help your child understand that he is a fine person who happens to have a disability, but you, he and his teachers are finding ways he can achieve and compensate.

You are the expert parent of a child with disabilities. Becoming a parent of this child with special needs did not change you from being an excellent parent to a poor one. Your parenting may be labor intensive, but it is also a blend of frustration, love, and laughter. There is nothing you cannot overcome with insight into your feelings and faith in yourself as a parent. You gain strength from each other and from others who understand your child.

This is the role of support groups, really any group of parents who can say, "We have been there," or "We *are* there." Try to find a parent group willing to share feelings and where fathers are welcome. Most parents who attend support groups go there looking for practical guidance for day-to-day living. They appreciate speakers, but they *need* to know how to control an impulsive child or how to get him/her to sleep through the night. They want to learn how to explain Down syndrome or cerebral palsy to grandparents or a ten-year-old brother.

Share your fears and joys. Ask other parents what words and phrases they use to talk with friends, family, school personnel, and other professionals about their children. Tell parents in your group about your child's progress, no matter how small. Listen to other parents. Tell them they are doing fine, and their efforts will bear fruit.

We hear that parents directly contribute to children's self-esteem. Yet we feel helpless knowing our child's budding self-image is shaped by experiences we rarely hear about. As your child interacts with a wider circle of people at school and in the community, your control lessens. You are not the sole determiner of your child's successes, failures, or life-style, yet your child's positive self-image begins with your understanding of undesirable behavior resulting from stresses of disability.

Eventually we become what we think about. Our thinking determines our self-image, in turn, our feelings and behavior. Your self-respect should have nothing to do with your child's participation in special education. Nor is your esteem borne by the lack of accomplishments or achievements of your children. Each of us is a respected person in his own right. *Your* self-esteem results from being a good parent and from your willingness to see that your child receives an appropriate education.

KNOWLEDGE IS POWER

As for doing too much or not enough, I believe if parents must err, "overparenting" is a better stance than waiting for something to happen. No one is going to care about your child as much as you. No one else can be the catalyst for educational change as successfully as you.

Good things happen for children on a day-to-day basis. Growth is rarely dramatic or overnight. Teachers who make a difference need your support. When your child makes significant, even gradual progress because of a teacher, tutor, or therapist, write a letter of appreciation to your principal or superintendent. Tell professionals how much growth you notice, and how much you appreciate their work.

As specified in education law, the best IDEAs for all children occur when schools and parents cooperate and communicate to the best of their ability. Marge Goldberg says, "Knowledge is power. A well-informed parent can help others help his child."

We have a certain perspective on our children's achievements, but we can never tell how they are going to turn out in regard to values we cherish: charity, tolerance, and personal consideration for others. Like other children, the ones with disabilities take their parents as models while they search for individuality. Children with disabilities are always more like typical children than unlike them.

Sometimes in special parenting we cannot help but wonder what our child would have become. We remember the agony of realizing the disability, how much plain sweat we expended in rearing the child. This is the self-doubt mentioned but rarely delineated by other parents and professionals because of the pain in asking. Is parenting the child worth it? Have we done too much or not enough? When other people see our child, do they realize how hard we have all worked? And the hardest question of all— has it been worth it?

One day we look into our child's eyes and see images of ancestors, gifts forever suppressed, the person he might have been were he not disabled. We rejoice in his successes, yet we cannot help but wonder if things had been different.

Does it matter what you have done for your child, that the simple fact of his/her being has changed you? It matters a lot.

Other people will rarely notice your child's successes, but you delight in the ones who do. What matters is that you congratulate yourself and your efforts on behalf of your child, and he/she appreciates you.

In *When All You've Ever Wanted Isn't Enough*, Harold S. Kushner asks if it makes a difference how we live. He says in a secular society, it seems only deeds have values, and so people are worthwhile only if they do things. "Did you win or did you lose? Did you make it happen or did you fail? Did you show a profit or a deficit?"

Rabbi Kushner says that when we cannot measure people by God's standards, we can only evaluate them by human standards. "But if people see only what is visible, measurable, God sees into the heart. He not only forgives our failures, He sees successes where no one else does, not even we ourselves. Only God can give us credit for the angry words we did not speak, the temptations we resisted, the patience and gentleness little noticed and long forgotten by those around us. Just being human gives us a certain value in His eyes, and trying to live with integrity makes us successful before Him. . . . I prefer to believe that God sees us so clearly that He knows better than anyone else our wounds and sorrows, the scars on our hearts from having wanted to do more and do better and being told by the world that we never would."[11]

Yes, rearing the child is worth the effort—the heartache you put into it. If a child is a label, the label is love.

REFERENCES

Introduction

1. Terry Jarvis and Tannis Jarvis, *You Are Not Alone* (London, Ontario, Canada: T. P. Jarvis, April 1984), pp. 4, 10.
2. Margaret Burley, "Advocating for Independence," keynote address (Toledo, OH: Toledo Society for the Handicapped, 4 April 1987).
3. Albert Shanker, *Public Law 94-142: Prospects and Problems*, **Exceptional Parent** vol. 10, no. 4 (August 1980), p. 51.
4, 5. H. Rutherford Turnbull III, *Free Appropriate Public Education: The Law and the Education of Children with Disabilities* (Denver: Love, 1986), pp. 240, 243–244.
6, 7. Interview with Frank E. New, Director, Division of Special Education, Ohio Department of Education, Worthington, Ohio, 1 July 1991.

Chapter 1
Who Benefits from Special Education?

1. "Education," *Code of Federal Regulations (CFR)*: Title 34 (Washington, D.C.: Office of Federal Register, 1 July 1990), Subpart C, §300.342 When individualized education programs must be in effect, pp. 37–38.
2. 34 *CFR*, Subpart A, §300.5 Handicapped children, p. 13.
3. Rhona C. Hartman, *ADD Sometimes Overlaps, but ≠ LD*, **Information from HEATH** vol. 6, no. 2 (May 1987), pp. 5–6.
4. Rosalyn Simon, *Minority Issues in Special Education: A Portrait of the Future*, **News Digest** no. 9 (1987), p. 4.
5. 34 *CFR*, Subpart C, §300.342 When individualized education programs must be in effect, pp. 37–38.

6. *Preschool Regulations Now Open for Public Comment*, **The Pacer Advocate** vol. 7, no. 4 (December 1987), p. 2.

7. Seymour B. Sarason and John Doris, *Educational Handicap, Public Policy, and Social History: A Broadened Perspective on Mental Retardation* (New York: Free Press, 1979), p. 363.

8. Frances Dwyer McCaffrey and Thomas Fish, *Profiles of the Other Child: A Sibling Guide for Parents* (Columbus, OH: OSU/Nisonger Center, n.d.), p. 5.

Chapter 2
A Personal Program

1. *Questions Parents Often Ask about Special Education Services and Public Law 94-142* (Washington, D.C.: National Information Center for Children and Youth with Handicaps, September 1988), p. 3.

2. 34 *CFR*, Subpart E—Procedural Safeguards, §300.503 Independent educational evaluation, p. 48.

3. 34 *CFR*, Subpart E—Procedural Safeguards, §300.532 Evaluation procedures, p. 52.

4. Margaret Burley, Toledo, Ohio, 4 April 1987.

5. 34 *CFR*, Pt. 300, Appendix C, p. 91.

6. Betty Binkard, *What's Wrong with This?* **Pacesetter** (May 1986), pp. 2, 5.

7. Charlotte Des Jardins, *How to Get Services by Being Assertive* (Chicago: Coordinating Council for Handicapped Children, 1980), p. 46.

8. Jon Skaalen, *Parents May Seek Change in Child's Placement at Any Time, OSEP Says*, **The Pacer Advocate** vol. 9, no. 3 (30 April 1990), p. 4.

9. *Education of the Handicapped Amendments of 1990 (P.L. 101-476): Summary of Major Changes in Parts A Through H of the Act* (Washington, D.C.: National Association of State Directors of Special Education, October 1990), p. 2.

10. Irving R. Dickman with Sol Gordon, *One Miracle at a Time: How to Get Help for Your Disabled Child—From the Experience of Other Parents* (New York: Simon and Schuster, 1985), p. 264.

11. Oliver Leon Hurley, *Implications of PL 99-457 for Preparation of Preschool Personnel*, in **Policy Implementation & PL 99-457: Planning for Young Children with Special Needs,** James J. Gallagher, Pascal L. Trohanis, and Richard M. Clifford, eds. (Baltimore: Paul H. Brookes), p. 139.

12, 13. Sue Walter, *Public Awareness for Early Intervention Should Be a Family Affair*, **Early Intervention** vol. 5, issue 2 (March 1991), pp. 6–7.

14. Suzanne Ripley, *A Parent's Guide to Doctors, Disabilities, and the Family* (Washington, D.C.: National Information Center for Children and Youth with Handicaps, vol. 1, no. 2, May 1990), pp. 3–4.

15. John Gliedman and William Roth, *The Unexpected Minority: Handicapped Children in America* (New York: Harcourt Brace Jovanovich, 1980), p. 145.

Chapter 3
When Your Child Needs Extra Help

1. Larry B. Silver, *The Misunderstood Child: A Guide for Parents of Learning Disabled Children* (New York: McGraw-Hill, 1984), p. 133.
2. Peggy Finston, *Parenting Plus: Raising Children with Special Health Needs* (New York: Dutton, 1990), pp. 51–52.
3. *Parent Participation Vital in IEP,* **Forum** vol. 9, issue 3 (August/September 1991), p. 6.
4. Philip R. Jones, *A Practical Guide to Federal Special Education Law: Understanding and Implementing PL 94-142* (New York: Holt, Rinehart and Winston, 1981), p. 111.
5. Wayne E. Oates, *Your Particular Grief* (Philadelphia: Westminster, 1981), p. 80.
6. Susan Duffy, Kathy McGlynn, Jan Mariska, and Jeannie Murphy, *Acceptance Is Only the First Battle* (Missoula, MT: University of Montana, 1984), p. 27.
7. Betty Lou Kratoville, *The Parents Speak,* in **The Disabled & Their Parents: A Counseling Challenge**, rev. ed., Leo Buscaglia, ed. (Thorofare, NJ: Slack, Inc., 1983), p. 133.

Chapter 4
Mainstreaming: A Regular Life

1. Stanley J. Vitello and Ronald M. Soskin, *Mental Retardation: Its Social and Legal Context* (Englewood Cliffs, NJ: Prentice-Hall, 1985), p. 68.
2. 34 *CFR*, Subpart E, §300.550 (Least Restrictive Environment) General, p. 54.
3. Barbara Hobbs, *What Services Should My Child Be Receiving?* **News Digest** (June 1985), pp. 2–3.
4, 5. Daryl Paul Evans, *The Lives of Mentally Retarded People* (Boulder, CO: Westview Press, 1983), pp. 193–194, 195.
6. Charles R. Callanan, *Since Owen: A Parent-to-Parent Guide for Care of the Disabled Child* (Baltimore: Johns Hopkins University Press, 1990), pp. 295–300.
7. C. Beth Schaffner and Barbara E. Buswell, *Opening Doors: Strategies for Including All Students in Regular Education* (Colorado Springs, CO: PEAK Parent Center, 1991), p. 21.
8. Philip R. Jones, *A Practical Guide to Federal Special Education Law: Understanding and Implementing PL 94-142* (New York: Holt, Rinehart and Winston, 1981), pp. 67, 73.

9. Terrell Dougan, Lyn Isbell, and Patricia Vyas, *We Have Been There: A Guidebook for Families of People with Mental Retardation* (Nashville: Abingdon, 1983), p. 48.

10. Robert Perske, *New Directions for Parents of Persons Who Are Retarded* (Nashville: Abingdon, 1973), p. 30.

11. Richard Elardo and Judith Freund, *How Parental Behavior Can Affect a Child's Social Development*, **Perceptions** vol. 1, no. 5 (November 1978), p. 2.

12. Michael T. Yura and Lawrence Zuckerman, *Raising the Exceptional Child* (New York: Hawthorn Books, 1979), p. 147.

13. Barbara Scheiber, ed., *For Your 'Rights' Notebook. . . .*, **Report from Closer Look** (Winter 1975), p. 5.

Chapter 5
How Laws Protect You

1. Roberta L. Juarez, *The Kindness of Others*, **Transition Link** vol. 1, no. 3 (September–October 1990), p. 1.

2. Alan Gartner and Tom Joe, *Images of the Disabled, Disabling Images* (New York: Praeger, 1987), p. 192.

3. 34 *CFR*, Subpart G, §300.750 Annual report of children served—report requirement, p. 68.

4. Charlotte Des Jardins, letter to author, 7 January 1991.

5. Des Jardins, *How to Prepare for a Due Process Hearing*, in **How to Get Services by Being Assertive** (Chicago: Coordinating Council for Handicapped Children, 1980), p. 52.

6. Leslie Brinegar, *The Problems and Pitfalls in Implementing PL 94-142*, in **Human Advocacy and PL 94-142: The Educator's Roles**, Leo F. Buscaglia, Ph.D., and Eddie H. Williams, eds. (Thorofare, NJ: Charles B. Slack, 1979), p. 32.

7. Gregory White Smith and Steven Naifeh, *What Every Client Needs to Know About Using a Lawyer* (New York: Putnam, 1982), pp. 59–60.

Chapter 6
Keeping Track of Tests and Records

1, 4. *Psychological Testing of Children with Disabilities*, **News Digest** (October 1985), p. 2.

2. Julius Segal and Herbert Yahroes, *A Child's Journey* (New York: McGraw-Hill, 1978), p. 298.

3. A. Lee Parks and Marilyn Rousseau, letter to author, 10 December 1981.

5. Janet Carr, *Family Processes and Parent Involvement*, in **Scientific Studies in Mental Retardation**, John Dobbing, J. A. Clarke, J. A. Corbett, J. Hogg, and R. O. Robinson, eds. (London: Royal Society of Medicine, 1984), p. 450.

6. 34 *CFR*, Subpart E, §300.562 Access rights, p. 57.
7. 34 *CFR*, Subpart E, §300.573 Destruction of information, p. 59.

Chapter 7
Work, Higher Education, and Disabilities

1. Ann R. Davie, *Young Adults with Learning Disabilities and Other Special Needs* (Washington, D.C.: HEATH Resource Center, Fall 1989), p. 1.
2. Dale Brown, *Supervising Adults with Learning Disabilities* (Washington, D.C.: President's Committee on Employment of the Handicapped, 1985), pp. 3–4.
3. Interview with Darlene Cunningham, Columbus, Ohio, 10 June 1991.
4. *The ICD Survey of Disabled Americans* (New York: Louis Harris, March 1986), p. 47.
5. Paul H. Wender, *The Hyperactive Child, Adolescent, and Adult: Attention Deficit Disorder through the Lifespan* (New York: Oxford University Press, 1987), p. 43.
6. John Arena, *How to Write an I.E.P.* (Novato, CA: Academic Therapy, 1989), p. 95.

Chapter 8
You Are the Expert

1. Fred Rogers and Barry Head, *Mister Rogers Talks with Parents* (New York: Berkley Books, 1983), pp. 83–84.
2. Seymour B. Sarason and John Doris, *Educational Handicap, Public Policy, and Social History: A Broadened Perspective on Mental Retardation* (New York: Free Press, 1979), p. 46.
3. Peggy Finston, *Parenting Plus: Raising Children with Special Health Needs* (New York: Dutton, 1990), p. 172.
4. Larry B. Silver, *The Misunderstood Child: A Guide for Parents of Learning Disabled Children* (New York: McGraw-Hill, 1984), p. 127.
5. Irving R. Dickman with Sol Gordon, *One Miracle at a Time: How to Get Help for Your Disabled Child—From the Experience of Other Parents* (New York: Simon and Schuster, 1985), p. 235.
6. 34 *CFR*, Pt. 300, App. C, pp. 84–85.
7. Bette M. Ross, *Our Special Child: A Guide to Successful Parenting of Handicapped Children* (New York: Walker, 1981), p. 104.
8. Milton Seligman and Rosalyn Benjamin Darling, *Ordinary Families, Special Children: A Systems Approach to Childhood Disability* (New York: Guilford, 1989), p. 225.
9. Dale E. Galloway, *Rebuild Your Life: How to Survive a Crisis* (Wheaton, IL: Tyndale House, 1981), pp. 33, 60.
10. Arlene Spiller and Bebe Antell, *Believe in Your Rights Before You Begin*, **Perceptions** vol. 4, no. 1 (May 1981), p. 4.

11. David L. Trott, *What Can You Do If . . . The School System Says: 'We Don't Have the Money'?* **Report from Closer Look** (Spring 1980), pp. 1, 5.

Chapter 9
Parent and School: A Winning Combination

1. Interview with Gretchen Beattie, Hudson, Ohio, 18 July 1991.
2. Susan Duffy, *Parents, Professionals and Conflict*, in **Acceptance Is Only the First Battle**, Susan Duffy, Kathy McGlynn, Jan Mariska, and Jeannie Murphy (Missoula, MT: University of Montana, 1984), p. 40.
3. Interview with Cindy Gilligan, Ashland, Ohio, 25 June 1991.
4. Interviews with Ellen Frasca, Worthington, Ohio, 13 March 1990 and 13 May 1991.
5. Interview with Nancy Berla, Columbia, Maryland, 9 March 1990.
6. Sylvia B. Rimm, *How to Parent So Children Will Learn* (Watertown, WI: Apple, 1990), p. 117.
7. Larry B. Silver, *Attention Deficit Disorders, Booklet for Parents* (n.d.), p. 9.
8. Harold Lubin, *How to Choose the Right Therapist*, **Perceptions** vol. 2, no. 8 (April 1980), pp. 1–2.
9. Donald E. Lyman, *Making the Words Stand Still* (Boston: Houghton Mifflin, 1986), p. 183.
10. Sally L. Smith, *No Easy Answers: The Learning Disabled Child* (Rockville, MD: National Institute of Mental Health, 1978), pp. 125–126.

Chapter 10
Postscript on Partnerships

1. Frank Warren and Sandra Hopfengardner Warren, *The Role of Parents in Creating and Maintaining Quality Family Support Services*, in **Support for Caregiving Families: Enabling Positive Adaptation to Disability**, George H. S. Singer and Larry K. Irvin, eds. (Baltimore: Paul H. Brookes, 1989), pp. 55, 60.
2. Alfred Healy, Patricia D. Keesee, and Barbara S. Smith, *Early Services for Children with Special Needs: Transactions for Family Support*, 2nd ed. (Baltimore: Paul H. Brookes), p. 48.
3. Ann Oster, *Equals in This Partnership: Parents of Disabled and At-Risk Infants and Toddlers Speak to Professionals*, keynote address (Washington, D.C.: National Center for Clinical Infant Programs, December 1984), pp. 27–28.
4. Elizabeth J. Webster, *Counseling with Parents of Handicapped Children: Guidelines for Improving Communication* (Orlando, FL: The Psychological Corporation, 1977), p. 42.
5, 6. Martha Ziegler, *A Parent's Perspective: Implementing PL 99-457*, in **Policy**

Implementation & PL 99-457: Planning for Young Children with Special Needs, James J. Gallagher, Pascal L. Trohanis, and Richard M. Clifford, eds. (Baltimore: Paul H. Brookes, 1989), pp. 87–88, 92.

7. Richard P. Holland, *Clarification of P.L. 94-142 for the Special Educator* (Westerville, OH: LINC Services, Inc., 1980), p. 9.

8. Raymond J. Dembinski and August J. Mauser, *What Parents Want Professionals to Know*, **Perceptions** vol. 2, no. 2 (June 1979), p. 1.

9. Virginia Carr, *It's Time to Get Off the Merry-Go-Round*, **Perceptions** vol. 2, no. 2 (June 1979), p. 2.

10, 13. Susan Duffy, Kathy McGlynn, Jan Mariska, and Jeannie Murphy, *Acceptance Is Only the First Battle* (Missoula, MT: University of Montana, 1984), pp. 25, 39.

11, 12. Carl Dunst, Carol Trivette, and Angela Deal, *Enabling and Empowering Families: Principles and Guidelines for Practice* (Cambridge, MA: Brookline Books, 1988), pp. 37, 61, 63.

14. Lori A. Goldfarb, Mary Jane Brotherson, Jean Ann Summers, and Ann P. Turnbull, *Meeting the Challenge of Disability or Chronic Illness—A Family Guide* (Baltimore: Paul H. Brookes, 1986), p. 51.

15. Leo Buscaglia, *The Disabled & Their Parents: A Counseling Challenge* (Thorofare, NJ: Slack, Inc., 1983 rev. ed.), p. 95.

Chapter 11
One Day at a Time

1. William Timmerman, *Preparing Your Child for Work* (Toledo, OH: Toledo Society for the Handicapped, 4 April 1987).

2, 3. Ann R. Davie, *Young Adults with Learning Disabilities and Other Special Needs* (Washington, D.C.: HEATH Resource Center, Fall 1989), pp. 2, 3.

4. Joan Wiswall, *Why Must They Fail?* **LDA Newsbriefs** vol. 24, no. 5 (September 1989), p. 3.

5. Larry B. Silver, *The Misunderstood Child: A Guide for Parents of Learning Disabled Children* (New York: McGraw-Hill, 1984), p. 104.

6. Interviews with Marge Goldberg, 17 July 1984 and 12 July 1988.

7, 8. C. Michael Nelson and Robert B. Rutherford, Jr., *Troubled Youth in the Public Schools: Emotionally Disturbed or Socially Maladjusted?* in **Understanding Troubled and Troubling Youth**, Peter E. Leone, ed. (Newbury Park, CA: Sage, 1990), pp. 40, 53–54.

9. Interviews with educational consultants at the Ohio Department of Education, Columbus, 20 May 1991.

10. Interview with Sandra Berger, 7 June 1990.

11. Harold S. Kushner, *When All You've Ever Wanted Isn't Enough* (New York: Summit Books, 1986), pp. 186–189.

BIBLIOGRAPHY

"ADD Sometimes Overlaps, but ≠ LD." *Information from HEATH* 6 (May 1987): 5–6.

A Look at Due Process for Parents of Handicapped Children. Columbus, Ohio: Ohio Department of Education, 1984.

Ambler, Lana. "Respite Care: A Gift of Time." *News Digest* 12 (1989): 7.

Anderson, Evelyn. *Parents Can Be the Key . . . To an Appropriate Education for Their Handicapped Child.* Minneapolis: PACER Center, 1981.

Arena, John. *How to Write an I.E.P.* Novato, California: Academic Therapy, 1989.

"A Sampler of Frequently Used Tests." *Perceptions* 2 (October 1979): 3, 5.

Bailey, Donald B., Jr. "Issues and Directions in Preparing Professionals to Work with Young Handicapped Children and Their Families." In *Policy Implementation & PL 99-457: Planning for Young Children with Special Needs.* James J. Gallagher, Pascal L. Trohanis, and Richard M. Clifford, eds. Baltimore: Paul H. Brookes, 1989, p. 103.

Ballard, Joseph, Bruce Ramirez, and Kathy Zantal-Wiener. *Public Law 94-142, Section 54, and Public Law 99-457: Understanding What They Are and Are Not.* Reston, Virginia: Council for Exceptional Children, 1987.

Berla, Nancy. Letter to the author. 15 July 1985.

Binkard, Betty. "What's Wrong with This?" *Pacesetter* May (1986): 2, 5.

Bowe, Frank. *Disabled Women in America.* Washington, D.C.: President's Committee on Employment of the Handicapped, 1984.

Brinegar, Leslie. "The Problems and Pitfalls in Implementing PL 94-142." In *Human Advocacy and PL 94-142: The Educator's Roles.* Leo F. Buscaglia, Ph.D., and Eddie H. Williams, eds. Thorofare, New Jersey: Charles B. Slack, 1979, p. 33.

Brown, Dale. *Supervising Adults with Learning Disabilities.* Washington, D.C.: President's Committee on Employment of the Handicapped, 1985.

Burley, Margaret. "Advocating for Independence." Keynote address. Toledo, Ohio: Toledo Society for the Handicapped, 4 April 1987.

Buscaglia, Leo. *The Disabled & Their Parents: A Counseling Challenge*, rev. ed. Thorofare, New Jersey: Slack, 1983.

Buscaglia, Leo F. and Eddie H. Williams, eds. *Human Advocacy and PL 94-142: The Educator's Roles*. Thorofare, New Jersey: Charles B. Slack, 1979, p. 11.

Callanan, Charles R. *Since Owen: A Parent-to-Parent Guide for Care of the Disabled Child*. Baltimore: Johns Hopkins University Press, 1990.

Carr, Janet. "Family Processes and Parent Involvement." In *Scientific Studies in Mental Retardation*. John Dobbing, J. A. Clarke, J. A. Corbett, J. Hogg, and R. O. Robinson, eds. London: Royal Society of Medicine, 1984, p. 450.

Carr, Virginia. "It's Time to Get Off the Merry-Go-Round." *Perceptions*, 2 (June 1979): 2.

Davie, Ann R. *Young Adults with Learning Disabilities and Other Special Needs*. Washington, D.C.: HEATH Resource Center, Fall 1989.

Dembinski, Raymond J. and August J. Mauser. "What Parents Want Professionals to Know." *Perceptions*, 2 (June 1979): 1.

Des Jardins, Charlotte. *How to Get Services by Being Assertive*. Chicago: Coordinating Council for Handicapped Children, 1980.

Des Jardins, Charlotte. Letter to author. 7 January 1991.

Dickman, Irving R. with Sol Gordon. *One Miracle at a Time: How to Get Help for Your Disabled Child—From the Experience of Other Parents*. New York: Simon and Schuster, 1985.

Disabilities Which Qualify Children and Youth for Special Education Services under the Education of the Handicapped Act (EHA). Washington, D.C.: National Information Center for Children and Youth with Disabilities, 1991.

Disparities Still Exist in Who Gets Special Education. Washington, D.C.: Committee on Education and Labor, House of Representatives of the United States, 1981.

Dougan, Terrell, Lyn Isbell, and Patricia Vyas. *We Have Been There: A Guidebook for Families of People with Mental Retardation*. Nashville: Abingdon, 1983.

Duffy, Susan, Kathy McGlynn, Jan Mariska, and Jeannie Murphy. *Acceptance Is Only the First Battle*. Missoula, Montana: University of Montana, 1984.

Dunst, Carl, Carol Trivette, and Angela Deal. *Enabling and Empowering Families: Principles and Guidelines for Practice*. Cambridge: Brookline Books, 1988.

"Education." *Code of Federal Regulations (CFR)*: Title 34. Washington, D.C.: Office of Federal Register, 1 July 1990.

Education of the Handicapped Amendments of 1990 (P.L. 101-476): Summary of Major Changes in Parts A Through H of the Act. Washington, D.C.: National Association of State Directors of Special Education, October 1990, p. 2.

Elardo, Richard and Judith Freund. "How Parental Behavior Can Affect a Child's Social Development." *Perceptions* 1, 5 (November 1978): 2.

Evans, Daryl Paul. *The Lives of Mentally Retarded People*. Boulder, Colorado: Westview Press, 1983.

"Family Educational Rights and Privacy; Final Regulations." *Federal Register* 2 (11 April 1988): 11944.

Finston, Peggy. *Parenting Plus: Raising Children with Special Health Needs.* New York: Dutton, 1990.

Froschl, Merle, Ellen Rubin, and Barbara Sprung. "Having a Daughter with a Disability: Is It Different for Girls?" *News Digest* 14 (October 1990): 3.

Galloway, Dale E. *Rebuild Your Life: How to Survive a Crisis.* Wheaton, Illinois: Tyndale House, 1981.

Gartner, Alan and Tom Joe. *Images of the Disabled, Disabling Images.* New York: Praeger, 1987.

Gifted Education. Columbia, Maryland: National Committee for Citizens in Education, n.d.

Gliedman, John and William Roth. *The Unexpected Minority: Handicapped Children in America.* New York: Harcourt Brace Jovanovich, 1980.

Goldfarb, Lori A., Mary Jane Brotherson, Jean Ann Summers, and Ann P. Turnbull. *Meeting the Challenge of Disability or Chronic Illness—A Family Guide.* Baltimore: Paul H. Brookes, 1986.

Handbook of Selective Placement of Persons with Physical and Mental Handicaps in Federal Civil Service Employment. Washington, D.C.: Office of Personnel Management, 1981.

Haugland, Barbara and Janet Filer. "Provision of Services for Students with Learning Disabilities." Open letter to prospective students, January 1991.

Healy, Alfred, Patricia D. Keesee, and Barbara S. Smith. *Early Services for Children with Special Needs: Transactions for Family Support.* 2nd ed. Baltimore: Paul H. Brookes.

Hobbs, Barbara. "Alternatives for Community Living." *News Digest* (April 1986): 3.

Hobbs, Barbara. "Introduction." *News Digest* (June 1985): 1.

Hobbs, Barbara. "The Least Restrictive Environment: Knowing One When You See It." *News Digest* 5 (n.d.): 2–3.

Hobbs, Barbara. "What Services Should My Child Be Receiving?" *News Digest* (June 1985): 2–3.

Holland, Richard P. *Clarification of P.L. 94-142 for the Special Educator.* Westerville, Ohio: LINC Services, 1980.

Horne, Richard L. "The Education of Children and Youth with Special Needs: What Do the Laws Say?" *News Digest* 1 (1991): 5, 6, 7, 13.

Hosterman, E. Jean, ed. *Assessment: Special Education Tests, a Handbook for Parents and Professionals.* Minneapolis: PACER Center, 1989.

"How to File a Complaint with the Department of Education under the Family Educational Rights and Privacy Act of 1974" (n.d.)

Hurley, Oliver Leon. "Implications of PL 99-457 for Preparation of Preschool Personnel." In *Policy Implementation & PL 99-457: Planning for Young Children with Special Needs.* James J. Gallagher, Pascal L. Trohanis, and Richard M. Clifford, eds. Baltimore: Paul H. Brookes, p. 139.

The ICD Survey of Disabled Americans. New York: Louis Harris, March 1986.

Intervention Assistance Team Models. Columbus: Ohio Department of Education, 1988.

Jarvis, Terry and Tannis Jarvis. *You Are Not Alone.* London, Ontario, Canada: T. P. Jarvis, April 1984.

Jones, Philip R. *A Practical Guide to Federal Special Education Law: Understanding and Implementing PL 94-142.* New York: Holt, Rinehart and Winston, 1981.

Juarez, Roberta L. "The Kindness of Others." *Transition Link* 1, 3 (September–October 1990): 1.

Kavanagh, James F. and Grace Yeni-Komshian. *Developmental Dyslexia and Related Reading Disorders.* Bethesda: National Institutes of Health, 1980.

Kramer, Saul G. and Ann B. Dorman. *Colleges and Universities: A White Paper on the Americans with Disabilities Act.* New York: Proskauer Rose Goetz & Mendelsohn, 1990.

Kratoville, Betty Lou. "The Parents Speak." In *The Disabled & Their Parents: A Counseling Challenge,* rev. ed. Leo Buscaglia, ed. Thorofare, New Jersey: Slack Inc., 1983.

Kushner, Harold S. *When All You've Ever Wanted Isn't Enough.* New York: Summit Books, 1986.

Laycock, Frank. *Gifted Children.* Glenview, Illinois: Scott Foresman, 1979.

Lubin, Harold. "How to Choose the Right Therapist." *Perceptions* 2, 8 (April 1980): 1–2.

Lyman, Donald E. *Making the Words Stand Still.* Boston: Houghton Mifflin, 1986.

McCaffrey, Frances Dwyer and Thomas Fish. *Profiles of the Other Child: A Sibling Guide for Parents.* Columbus, Ohio: OSU/Nisonger Center, n.d.

Manes, Joseph. *SSI—New Opportunities for Children with Disabilities.* Washington, D.C.: Mental Health Law Project, 1991.

Mangrum, Charles T. II and Stephen S. Strichart. "Services Offered by College Support Programs for Learning Disabled Students." *Transition Summary.* Washington, D.C.: National Information Center for Handicapped Children and Youth, July 1985.

Mays, Francine and Susan Imel. *Adult Learning Disabilities.* Columbus, Ohio: ERIC Overview Fact Sheet 9 (n.d.).

Murray, Charles A. *The Link Between Learning Disabilities and Juvenile Delinquency.* Washington, D.C.: National Institute for Juvenile Justice and Delinquency Prevention, 1976.

Nelson, C. Michael and Robert B. Rutherford, Jr. "Troubled Youth in the Public Schools: Emotionally Disturbed or Socially Maladjusted?" In *Understanding Troubled and Troubling Youth.* Peter E. Leone, ed. Newbury Park, California: Sage, 1990, p. 40.

Oates, Wayne E. *Your Particular Grief.* Philadelphia: Westminster, 1981.

Oster, Ann. *Equals in This Partnership: Parents of Disabled and At-Risk Infants and Toddlers Speak to Professionals.* Keynote address. Washington, D.C.: National Center for Clinical Infant Programs, December 1984.

Parks, A. Lee and Marilyn K. Rousseau. *Mainstreaming Series: The Public Law Supporting Mainstreaming.* Hingham, Massachusetts: Teaching Resources, 1977.

Parks, A. Lee and Marilyn Rousseau. Letter to author. 10 December 1981.

Percy, Bernard. *Help Your Child in School.* Englewood Cliffs, New Jersey: Prentice-Hall, 1980.

Perske, Robert. *New Directions for Parents of Persons Who Are Retarded.* Nashville: Abingdon, 1973.

Phelps, L. Allen, Carolyn Chaplin, and Alice Kelly. "A Parent's Guide to Vocational Education." *News Digest* 8 (1987): 1–2.

"Preschool Regulations Now Open for Public Comment." *The Pacer Advocate* 7, 4 (December 1987): 2.

"Psychological Testing of Children with Disabilities." *News Digest* (October 1985): 2.

Public Law 101-336. 26 July 1990, "Americans with Disabilities Act of 1990." 104 Stat. 327.

Public Law 101-476. 30 October 1990, "Education of the Handicapped Act Amendments of 1990." 104 Stat. 1103.

Questions Parents Often Ask about Special Education Services and Public Law 94-142. Washington, D.C.: National Information Center for Children and Youth with Handicaps, September 1988, p. 3.

Rimm, Sylvia B. *How to Parent So Children Will Learn.* Watertown, Wisconsin: Apple, 1990.

Ripley, Suzanne. *A Parent's Guide: Doctors, Disabilities, and the Family.* Washington, D.C.: National Information Center for Children and Youth with Handicaps, 1 May 1990, p. 3.

Rogers, Fred and Barry Head. *Mister Rogers Talks with Parents.* New York: Berkley Books, 1983.

Ross, Bette M. *Our Special Child: A Guide to Successful Parenting of Handicapped Children.* New York: Walker, 1981.

Safeguard Those Valuable Papers. Novato, California: Academic Therapy, n.d.

Sarason, Seymour B. and John Doris. *Educational Handicap, Public Policy, and Social History: A Broadened Perspective on Mental Retardation.* New York: Free Press, 1979.

Schaffner, C. Beth and Barbara E. Buswell. *Opening Doors: Strategies for Including All Students in Regular Education.* Colorado Springs, Colorado: PEAK Parent Center, 1991.

Scheiber, Barbara, ed. "For Your 'Rights' Notebook. . ." *Report from Closer Look* (Winter 1975): 5.

Scheiber, Barbara, ed. "Ten Steps to Take . . . When You are in Conflict with Your School System." *Common Sense from Closer Look* (December 1978): 9–12.

Schilling, Robert F. "Helping Families with Disabled Members." In *Chronic Illness and Disability.* Catherine S. Chilman, Elam W. Nunnally, and Fred M. Cox, eds. Newbury Park, California: Sage, 1988, p. 176.

Segal, Julius and Herbert Yahroes. *A Child's Journey.* New York: McGraw-Hill, 1978.

Seligman, Milton and Rosalyn Benjamin Darling. *Ordinary Families, Special Children: A Systems Approach to Childhood Disability.* New York: Guilford, 1989.

Shanker, Albert. "Public Law 94-142: Prospects and Problems." *Exceptional Parent* 10, 4 (August 1980): 51.

Silver, Larry B. *Attention Deficit Disorders, Booklet for Parents,* n.d.

Silver, Larry B. *The Misunderstood Child: A Guide for Parents of Learning Disabled Children.* New York: McGraw-Hill, 1984.

Simon, Rosalyn. "Minority Issues in Special Education: A Portrait of the Future." *News Digest* 9 (1987): 4.

Skaalen, Jon, ed. "Parents May Seek Change in Child's Placement at Any Time, OSEP Says." *The Pacer Advocate* 9, 3 (30 April 1990): 4.

Smith, Gregory White and Steven Naifeh. *What Every Client Needs to Know About Using a Lawyer.* New York: Putnam, 1982.

Smith, Sally L. *No Easy Answers: The Learning Disabled Child.* Cambridge: Winthrop/ Bantam, 1980.

Spiller, Arlene and Bebe Antell, eds. "Believe in Your Rights Before You Begin." *Perceptions* 4, 1 (May 1981): 4.

Timmerman, William. *Preparing Your Child for Work.* Toledo, Ohio: Toledo Society for the Handicapped, 4 April 1987.

To Assure the Free Appropriate Public Education of All Handicapped Children. Washington, D.C.: Office of Special Education Programs, U.S. Office of Special Education and Rehabilitative Services, 1990.

Toombs, Marianne. "Monitoring: The Advocate's View." *LDA Newsbriefs* (January 1990): 8.

Trott, David L. "What Can You Do If . . . The School System Says: 'We Don't Have the Money'?" *Report from Closer Look* (Spring 1980): 1, 5.

Turnbull, Ann P. and H. Rutherford Turnbull. *Families, Professionals, and Exceptionality: A Special Partnership.* Columbus, Ohio: Merrill, 1986.

Turnbull, H. Rutherford III. *Free Appropriate Public Education: The Law and the Education of Children with Disabilities.* Denver: Love, 1990.

U.S. Children and Their Families: Current Conditions and Recent Trends, 1989. Washington, D.C.: Select Committee on Children, Youth, and Families, 1989.

Vitello, Stanley J. and Ronald M. Soskin. *Mental Retardation: Its Social and Legal Context.* Englewood Cliffs, New Jersey: Prentice-Hall, 1985.

Vogel, Susan A. and Joan L. Sattler. *The College Student with a Learning Disability.* Palatine: Illinois Council for Learning Disabilities, 1981.

Walter, Sue. "Public Awareness for Early Intervention Should Be a Family Affair." *Early Intervention* 5, 2 (March 1991): 6.

Warren, Frank and Sandra Hopfengardner Warren. "The Role of Parents in Creating and Maintaining Quality Family Support Services." In *Support for Caregiv-*

ing Families: Enabling Positive Adaptation to Disability. George H. S. Singer and Larry K. Irvin, eds. Baltimore: Paul H. Brookes, 1989.

Webster, Elizabeth J. *Counseling with Parents of Handicapped Children: Guidelines for Improving Communication*. Orlando, Florida: The Psychological Corporation, 1977.

Weisfeld, Victoria D., ed. "Federal Law Guaranteeing Handicapped Children a Free and Appropriate Public Education Successful in Transforming Local School Programs." *Serving Handicapped Children: A Special Report*. Princeton, New Jersey: The Robert Wood Johnson Foundation, 1988.

Wender, Paul H. *The Hyperactive Child, Adolescent, and Adult: Attention Deficit Disorder Through the Lifespan*. New York: Oxford University Press, 1987.

Wetherby, Catherine. *A Parents' Guide to Accessing Programs for Infants, Toddlers, and Preschoolers with Handicaps*. Washington, D.C.: National Information Center for Children and Youth with Handicaps, n.d.

When You Disagree. Columbia, Maryland: National Committee for Citizens in Education, n.d.

Williams, Jane Case. "Special Education and Related Services to Minority Populations with Disabilities." *OSERS News in Print* 3 (Spring 1991): 20.

Wilson, Nancy O. *Parents' Guide to Teacherese: A Glossary of Special Education Terms*. Seattle: Special Child Publications, 1981.

Wing, Lorna. *Children Apart: Autistic Children and Their Families*. Washington, D.C.: National Society for Children and Adults with Autism, 1974.

Wiswall, Joan. "Why Must They Fail?" *LDA Newsbriefs* 24, 5 (September 1989): 3.

Yura, Michael T. and Lawrence Zuckerman. *Raising the Exceptional Child*. New York: Hawthorn Books, 1979.

Ziegler, Martha. "A Parent's Perspective: Implementing PL 99-457." In *Policy Implementation & PL 99-457: Planning for Young Children with Special Needs*. James J. Gallagher, Pascal L. Trohanis, and Richard M. Clifford, eds. Baltimore: Paul H. Brookes, 1989, pp. 87–88.

GLOSSARY

The following terms are selected to help parents and guardians understand the *Education for All Handicapped Children Act* and to serve as an aid to parent–school communication.

- **Accessibility.** A quality or condition wherein people with disabilities have access to ordinary activities of daily life, including employment, transportation, recreation, and education, without being limited by architectural or attitudinal barriers.
- **Access to records.** Public Law (PL) 94-142 states that all agencies that provide services to disabled children must allow parents complete access to their child's educational records, including those used for evaluation and class placement.
- **Accommodation.** A change in teaching methods to meet the educational needs of a child with special needs.
- **Accountable.** A term in law meaning agencies, including schools, report on special education spending.
- **ADA.** PL 101-336, Americans with Disabilities Act of 1990.
- **ADD or attention deficit disorder.** Children with ADD display inappropriate inattention, impulsiveness, and sometimes hyperactivity for their mental and chronological age. Children with ADD often become frustrated. Before they are diagnosed and given the right help, they may experience failure and feelings of inadequacy. Some externalize these feelings with aggression, fighting, or acting out. Others may internalize their feelings, becoming depressed, or develop headaches

or stomachaches. ADD can result in school and learning-related problems.

- **AFDC or ADC.** Aid to Families with Dependent Children.
- **Agency.** A school district, state, or federal department responsible for administering or implementing special education.
- **Amendment.** A change, revision, or addition made to a law.
- **Annual goal.** An IEP contains annual goals that the child should attain in a year and short-term objectives or goals.
- **APE.** Adaptive physical education: physical education modified for a child with disabilities.
- **Aphasia.** Severe difficulty in using language, spoken or written.
- **Appeal.** A written request for a change in a legal decision.
- **Aptitude tests.** These tests provide information about a child's ability to learn in school. They measure understanding, use of language, and other skills.
- **ARC.** Association for Retarded Citizens.
- **Assessment.** A collection of information about a child's learning needs; includes social, psychological, and educational evaluations.
- **Assistive technology.** A device or technology used in education or training to help a person with disabilities gain independence.
- **At risk.** At-risk children and youth have developmental problems that can affect learning. Without special interventions, they are unlikely to complete elementary and secondary school or acquire skills for higher education or employment. Contributing factors may or may not include alcohol/drug abuse, familial poverty, delinquency/truancy, family abuse or neglect, family structure, handicapping or health conditions, inadequate readiness skills, developmental delay, inappropriate school curriculum, inappropriate school placement, limited English, low self-esteem, and pregnancy.
- **Attention span.** The length of time a child can pay attention to the task at hand; affects learning situations.
- **Autism.** A severe disturbance beginning in early childhood characterized by an inability to form meaningful relationships. The child seems insensitive to others, has difficult behavior, is often hard to manage. Some autistic children possess little or no language ability but may show advanced abilities in areas not related to language, such as music or math. Other symptoms include disturbances of physical and social skills and abnormal responses to sensations. The severe form of this syndrome may include extreme forms of self-injurious,

unusual, and aggressive behavior. Autistic children benefit from special education using behavior management techniques designed for specific individuals.

- **Battery of tests.** A group of standardized tests on the same sample of population; the goal is to compare results of tests.
- **BD.** Behavior disorders.
- **Behavior modification.** A step-by-step therapy in which behavior is changed by using a system of rewards and punishments. This approach is applied to teaching and social situations.
- **CA.** Chronological age.
- **Case manager.** The coordinator of services, a case manager works with the family in implementing an IFSP or other intervention plan.
- **CEC.** Council for Exceptional Children.
- **Cerebral dysfunction.** Many terms are used to describe children with learning disorders. In addition to cerebral dysfunction, other terms are minimal brain dysfunction (MBD), minimal brain injury, hyperkinetic impulse disorder, dyslexia, specific dyslexia or specific learning disability, neurologically handicapped (NH), hyperkinetic syndrome, maturational lag, educational handicap, performance disability, problem learner, psychoneurological learning disorder, underachiever, central nervous system disorder, word blindness, congenital alexia, agraphia, dysgraphia, acalculia, dyscalculia, agnosia, aphasia, language disability, ADD or attention deficit disorder, and SDD or specific developmental disorder.
- **Cerebral palsy.** A neurological-muscular disability resulting from damage to the central nervous system, usually before birth, at birth, or early infancy.
- **CF.** Cystic fibrosis.
- **CFR.** Code of Federal Regulations.
- **Child find.** School districts are to locate and identify all children, newborn to age twenty-one, in the district who have disabilities or are at risk for needing special education.
- **Classification.** A child is given a term that describes his or her special education needs. Sometimes called labeling.
- **CNS.** Central nervous system.
- **College Board testing for learning disabled students.** LD students can take college admission tests under special conditions, such as extended test times, readers, and separate testing rooms.
- **Consent.** Parents must give written consent before their child is

evaluated for special education or before he or she receives special education services.

- **CP.** Cerebral palsy.
- **Criterion-referenced tests (CRT).** Tests that measure what a person has learned or can accomplish.
- **Day treatment program.** A daytime program that conducts a clinical assessment of a person's disability and develops an individual treatment plan. Treatment can include physical therapy, occupational and speech therapy, nursing care, vision or hearing services, and/or behavior modification.
- **Decoding.** Reading and listening skills.
- **Deinstitutionalization.** Process of removing disabled people from institutions to integrate them in normal community settings.
- **Developmental disability.** A term applied to children who exhibit problems in development before age 18. Children in our society are expected to perform, within limits, at a set rate. Those who cannot perform physically and/or mentally within these limits are said to have developmental disabilities. Their disabilities include mental retardation, cerebral palsy, neurologically based conditions, autism, and developmental imbalance.
- **Diagnosis.** The science of identifying diseases, defects, conditions, and disorders in order to treat them.
- **Directionality.** Ability to tell right from left, up from down, forward from backward.
- **Discretionary.** Refers to optional or elective programs or parts of a law. Discretionary programs are services *other* than federal grants to states for special education. Discretionary programs include transition, personnel training, and research.
- **Distractible.** Children with learning disorders find concentration difficult because they are attracted to stimuli (noise, activity, movement) around them. As a result, they may be unable to begin or complete learning tasks.
- **Down's syndrome (or Down syndrome).** A genetic condition due to chromosome error that causes moderate to severe mental retardation. Down syndrome children have 47 rather than 46 chromosomes. Originally called mongolism, children born with this condition are characterized by a broad facial structure and a slanted appearance to the eyes. After Langdon Down, a mid-nineteenth century physician.
- **Drug therapy.** Drugs are sometimes used in the treatment of hyper-

activity and learning disorders. The medication a physician prescribes depends on the cause and type of each child's problems. Drugs generally fall into four categories: sedatives, stimulants, tranquilizers, and anticonvulsants. Phenobarbital is a sedative. Stimulants used are the amphetamines, such as Dexedrine®. Ritalin® (methylphenidate) is a mild antidepressant and the most commonly used drug for hyperactivity. Tranquilizers, also called psychotropic agents, are sometimes prescribed for hyperactive children. Two are Thorazine® and Mellaril®. Anticonvulsants such as Dilantin® are used in the treatment of seizures. A recent addition to the drug therapy group is Cylert® (pemoline), a central nervous system stimulant.

- **Due process.** PL 94-142 says parents must be included in a child's IEP or Individualized Education Program. The law says they have a right to participate in decisions affecting his or her placement and education. When school and parents cannot agree on appropriate placement, either has the right to request an impartial hearing. Parents have rights within the hearing process, including an outline of procedures, a right to legal counsel, a right to include results obtained from independent testing, and a right to keep their child in his or her present class setting until the hearing is complete.
- **Dyscalculia.** A learning disorder affecting the ability to do arithmetic.
- **Dysgraphia.** A learning disorder affecting the ability to write.
- **Dyslexia.** The medical/educational term for specific language disability affecting reading. Sometimes referred to as "word blindness," dyslexia means a person cannot read with ability or comprehension because he sees printed words upside down, reversed, blurred, or backward. A person with dyslexic tendencies may confuse meanings of words and phrases. Dyslexia is a condition not related to general intelligence but often occurs with other symptoms of learning disorders, such as hyperactivity and poor attention span. It can be caused by neurological, emotional, constitutional (physical), genetic, or developmental factors or a combination of these.
- **Dysphasia.** Partial ability to use spoken and/or written language.
- **Echolalia.** A parroting of words spoken by others without understanding their meanings.
- **ED.** Department of Education (federal).
- **Educational handicap (EH).** If a child fails to learn within the school environment for any reason—medical, social, neurological, or emotional—he or she is said to be educationally handicapped.

- **EEG (electroencephalogram).** A neurological test made by painlessly placing electrodes on the scalp with a special glue to measure electrical activity within the brain. Often called a "brain wave test," it is used as part of tests and evaluations for children suspected of having epilepsy or brain injury.
- **EHA.** Education for All Handicapped Children Act or PL 94-142. Renamed IDEA in 1990.
- **EKG (electrocardiogram).** A record of heart action taken from a graph recording electrical currents in the heart.
- **EMR.** Educable mentally retarded.
- **Encoding.** Expressing ideas with symbols; expressing oneself through verbal or written language and body expression.
- **Epilepsy.** A neurological condition also called a seizure disorder. Common types are petit mal, grand mal, and psychomotor or temporal lobe seizures.
- **Etiology.** The origin or cause of a disease or condition.
- **FAPE.** Free, appropriate public education.
- **Fluency encoding.** Talking.
- **Formal diagnosis.** After a child is tested by professionals from the fields of psychology, medicine, and education, their assessment of his or her strengths and weaknesses is called a formal diagnosis. Not to be confused with screening.
- **Functional skills.** Personal living skills that enable persons with disabilities to become a "functioning" part of the community. Functional skills depend on the individual, but for a younger child, they usually include dressing, bathing, and finding one's way independently. Adult functional skills may include reading public signs, finding public rest rooms, eating out, or counting change. Functional skills become more complex as people mature.
- **FY.** Fiscal Year. The United States government fiscal year ends June 30 and begins July 1.
- **GED.** General Educational Development. A high school equivalency diploma.
- **Hard signs.** A term used in neurological testing to mean a child performs in very different ways from the average child in central nervous system functions.
- **HCPA.** Handicapped Children's Protection Act of 1986. See Chapter 5.

- **Head Start.** A federal project that provides extensive development programs for income eligible preschool children between ages three and five and their families.
- **Hearing.** Parents are given the right to participate in educational decision making. If school and parents cannot agree on a child's program, either may request a hearing.
- **Hyperactivity.** Overactivity with no apparent need or goal. A hyperactive child is restless and constantly on the move. He or she may exhibit symptoms of learning disabilities, attention deficit disorder (ADD), distractibility, impulsiveness, and excitability. He or she may react to a situation by becoming happier, angrier, and more fearful than the average child. He or she has a harder time settling down in active classroom and home situations. A hyperactive child is not necessarily learning disabled. Other physical, emotional, and environmental factors can contribute to hyperactivity.
- **Hyperkinetic.** Synonym for hyperactive or overactive.
- **Hypoactive.** Some children with learning and/or school problems are consistently underactive, listless, or sluggish, although other physical, emotional, and environmental factors can contribute to this condition.
- **IDEA.** Individuals with Disabilities Education Act. In September 1990, the reauthorization of the Education for the Handicapped Act changed the name from EHA to IDEA. The term "handicapped" in the law was replaced with "children with disabilities."
- **Identification.** Process of locating and identifying children who need special services.
- **IEP and IFSP.** Individualized Education Program and Individualized Family Service Plan. See Chapter 2.
- **IHO.** Impartial hearing officer. See Chapter 5.
- **Implement.** To carry out procedures, as in implementing special education services.
- **Impulsivity or Impulsiveness.** Responding to a situation or stimulus while lacking verbal and/or physical controls. A child may respond impulsively in social situations when he or she grabs or handles objects or asks inappropriate questions.
- **Independent evaluation.** Tests and evaluations obtained outside the school. See Chapter 2.
- **Informal diagnosis.** A teacher works with a child on a daily basis. He

or she formulates an informal diagnosis while evaluating the child's needs and learning patterns. A child does not receive special services, however, without a formal diagnosis arrived at through appropriate evaluations.

- **Instrument.** Evaluation methods and tests are often referred to as instruments.
- **Interdisciplinary.** Refers to resources and information combining several fields of study, including medicine, psychology, and education.
- **Intervention.** A modification, teaching technique, or special material used to help a child learn. Educationally, the term means children with disabilities are identified at an early age and strategies initiated to help them.
- **ITP.** Individual Transition Plan. (Also Individualized Transition Plan.) A written plan that outlines resources and supports the transition of a disabled student into vocational training and employment.
- **LA.** Language age.
- **Labeling.** In our society, children who exhibit or are born with unusual characteristics are evaluated to discover how they differ from other children. If their problems in learning and understanding are severe or if they exhibit hearing or sight impairments or orthopedic disabilities, they are assigned a course of special education. The child attends a special class or receives other interventions and related services directed to his or her needs or condition: hearing impairment, learning disability, etc. The use of these terms as a result of testing, diagnoses, an IEP, and class placement is called "labeling." Now that more than 10 percent of public schoolchildren receive special services, labeling is not as prevalent. Also called classification.
- **Lability.** From the word "labile," meaning emotional instability.
- **Laterality.** A tendency to use hand, foot, and eye on the same side of the body.
- **LEA.** The local school or local education agency.
- **Learning disability (LD).** A disorder in one or more of the basic psychological processes involved in understanding or using spoken or written language or doing math calculations.
- **Learning style.** Each child learns differently depending on his or her behavior, background, and abilities.
- **Least restrictive environment (LRE).** PL 94-142 says a disabled child must be educated with nondisabled children unless it has been demonstrated that he/she would benefit more from a separate placement.

- **LRA.** Least restrictive alternative; same as least restrictive environment.
- **MA.** Mental age.
- **Maturation lag.** A child is behind his or her peers in development.
- **MD.** Muscular dystrophy.
- **Mean.** In testing terms, the average or middle; the average obtained by dividing the sum of scores by their number.
- **Median.** In testing, the middle score in a set of ranked scores.
- **Mediation.** Mediation is a method of resolving differences and settling disputes by using intermediaries between parties.
- **Medicaid.** A government and state program that provides physical and related health care to people with low incomes. Persons with disabilities may qualify for Medicaid on the basis of their income.
- **Medicare.** A government health insurance program designed for everyone over sixty-five years of age and persons with disabilities under sixty-five who have been entitled to Social Security disability benefits.
- **Modality.** The sensory path or mode through which a person receives information; visual modality and auditory modality.
- **MR.** Mental retardation.
- **Multidisciplinary evaluation.** PL 94-142 requires that each disabled child receive an evaluation gathered from a variety of disciplines, i.e., professional fields.
- **Multifactored.** An evaluation covering all aspects of a child's development: health, psychological, and educational.
- **Native language.** Parents have the right to establish the native language of their child. See Chapter 2.
- **NICU.** Neonatal intensive care unit.
- **NIH.** The National Institutes of Health coordinate and support biomedical research into cause, prevention, and cure of disease. A division of Health and Human Services.
- **Norm.** A testing term indicating the typical or normal pattern set for a group or type.
- **Norm-referenced tests.** Tests in which a student's learning and/or accomplishments are compared to those of other students of similar characteristics.
- **Occupational therapy.** Treatment provided by an occupational therapist to help a child with daily living skills. OT includes improving or restoring functions impaired or lost through illness, injury, or depriva-

tion, improving ability to perform functions leading to independence, or preventing further loss of function.

- **OHI.** Other health impaired.
- **Ophthalmologist.** Physician who diagnoses and treats eye conditions.
- **Optician.** A maker and fitter of eyeglass lenses and eyeglasses.
- **Optometrist.** A specialist who examines the eyes and prescribes lenses but not drugs or surgery.
- **Orthopedic.** Refers to treatment of the body's skeletal system.
- **OSEP.** Office of Special Education Programs, U.S. Department of Education.
- **OSERS.** Office of Special Education and Rehabilitative Services.
- **OT-PT.** Occupational therapy and physical therapy.
- **Overloading.** An inability to cope/adapt to busy or stimulating experiences. A child with learning problems may suffer frequent "overloading" in the classroom.
- **P&A.** Protection and advocacy. State agencies that assist parents and caregivers. See Resources, page 253.
- **Part H.** PL 99-457, infants and toddlers program. See Chapter 1.
- **Pediatric neurologist.** A physician who specializes in diseases of children's nervous systems.
- **Percentile rank.** A number that indicates how the child compares with other children who took the test at the same time.
- **Perception.** Understanding. A perceptual disorder is a deficiency in understanding one's environment.
- **Perseveration.** A child who perseverates has difficulty changing to new activities and may continue with old ones long after peers have discontinued. The child repeats words, phrases, and motions after they are appropriate.
- **Phoneme.** Any one of a set of small sounds that represent a language. Sets of phonemes are different for each language.
- **Physical therapy.** Treatment of physical disabilities to help an individual improve the use of bones, muscles, joints, and nerves. Techniques used by physical therapists include the use of heat, cold, water, massage, and exercise.
- **PKU.** Phenylketonuria. A congenital condition of newborns when they are unable to digest the substance phenylalanine, which accumulates in the blood, causing retardation. Treated by special diet if detected early.

- **PL 91-230.** The Education of the Handicapped Act of 1970. This program, known as Part B, authorized education for children with disabilities.
- **PL 93-112.** The Rehabilitation Act of 1973; includes Section 501 Employment of Handicapped Individuals, Section 502 Architectural and Transportation Board Compliance, Section 503 Employment under Federal Contracts, and Section 504 Nondiscrimination under Federal Grants.
- **PL 93-380.** The Education Amendments of 1974. Also the Family Education Rights and Privacy Act (FERPA) or Buckley amendment of 1974. See Chapter 6.
- **PL 94-142.** The Education for All Handicapped Children Act of 1975. Renamed IDEA in 1990.
- **PL 98-524.** The Carl D. Perkins Vocational Education Act of 1984. See Chapter 7.
- **PL 99-372.** The Handicapped Children's Protection Act of 1986.
- **PL 99-457.** The Education of the Handicapped Act Amendments of 1986—infants and toddlers.
- **PL 101-336.** The Americans with Disabilities Act of 1990.
- **PL 101-476.** The Education of the Handicapped Act Amendments of 1990 (IDEA).
- **Placement.** A class, program, and/or related services for a child with disabilities.
- **Placement meeting.** A child's class or placement is determined at a meeting attended by teachers, counselors, parents, and others responsible for his or her tests and evaluations.
- **Policy.** Same as rules and regulations used by states or local school districts to provide special education.
- **Private therapist.** A professional or therapist not connected with a school or agency.
- **Prognosis.** Projected outcome of disease or condition.
- **Program.** Name for a service, special class, and/or therapy used in special education.
- **Prosthesis.** An artificial body part to aid function.
- **Raw score.** In testing, the number of right answers on a test.
- **Readiness.** A child's growth and experiences enable him or her to undertake new learning experiences. As in "reading readiness."
- **Recognition.** To know again. Cognition is to know or comprehend.
- **Referral.** A process of directing a person to an agency for services.

- **Rehabilitation.** Planned program to help a disabled person develop his or her abilities to the fullest.
- **Related services.** Supports to help a child benefit from special education. See Chapter 3.
- **Remediation.** From "remedy," meaning a treatment or correction of a problem.
- **Respite.** Substitute care in order to provide relief and rest for a parent, guardian, or caregiver.
- **Reversals.** Reading and writing errors associated with dyslexia; an individual perceives p for q, b for d, saw for was.
- **Screening.** A group examination given in order to identify those children in need of diagnostic evaluations.
- **SDD.** Specific developmental disorder. A new term for learning disability. Specific developmental disorders include developmental reading disorder and developmental arithmetic disorder.
- **SEA.** The state education agency.
- **Secondary reading disability.** Reading failure aside from neurological reasons due to lack of education, poor motivation, uncorrected sight problem, or health problem.
- **SED.** Seriously emotionally disturbed. Also known as "serious emotional disorder" and/or "severely emotionally disturbed." In PL 94-142, the term does not include children who are socially maladjusted unless it is determined that they are seriously emotionally disturbed.
- **Self-contained class.** A classroom for children who cannot function comfortably in normal settings.
- **Sequencing.** Ability to relate objects, sounds, letters, and/or events in their proper order.
- **Sheltered workshop.** A facility that offers programs of vocational rehabilitation and employment, either paid or unpaid, to disabled workers.
- **Short-term objectives or goals.** The shorter goals used in teaching to help a child accomplish the annual goals.
- **SLD.** Specific learning disability.
- **Soft signs.** Term used in neurological testing to indicate a child performs in slightly different ways than an average child in central nervous system functions.
- **Spatial orientation (also spatial relations).** Ability to understand the relationship between objects and oneself, such as large and small or upside down and sideways.

- **Special Education Regional Resource Center (SERRC).** A federally funded agency that offers teaching aids and materials to teachers, information and counseling to parents, plus evaluation and diagnostic facilities.
- **Special Olympics.** A sports program for disabled people. Special Olympics games include competitions in track and field, swimming, gymnastics, basketball, volleyball, floor hockey, bowling, ice-skating, soccer, winter activities, wheelchair events, and other sports. Special Olympics offers sports clinics in a variety of activities managed by professional and amateur athletes. Local, area, and state games are scheduled through the year. Volunteers who run the games come from schools, colleges, service clubs, parents' groups, youth agencies, sports officials, coaches' organizations, and professional groups in education, special education, and physical education.
- **Spina bifida.** A cleft spine or incomplete closure in the spinal column of newborns that results in disability.
- **SSA.** Social Security Administration.
- **SSI or Supplemental Security Income.** Financial help on a federal and state level for people who are permanently disabled, blind, and aged. Eligibility is determined by financial need for children under eighteen.
- **Standard deviation.** A statistical term, used in special education, it indicates how much a child deviates from the normal score of a group. A child is identified as having learning disabilities if tests reveal there is a severe discrepancy between his or her performance and age-ability levels in speaking, listening, writing, reading, and math. In school districts a learning disabled child may fall two or three standard deviations below the norm or test two or three academic years below grade level to qualify for special education services.
- **Standardized test.** A test developed from testing many students in order to determine uniform scoring procedures.
- **Standard score.** In testing, a term referring to transformed raw scores for purposes of interpretation and comparison.
- **Supported employment.** Paid work in community settings with long-term agency support for individuals with severe disabilities, such as mental retardation, autism, cerebral palsy, mental illness, or brain injury. Supported employment takes place in environments where nondisabled persons also work. Support services include vocational

evaluations, training, vocational rehabilitation counseling, and job coach assistance.

- **Syndrome.** A group of symptoms or signs that, appearing together, indicate a condition, disease, disorder, or disability.
- **TDD.** Telecommunication device for the deaf.
- **Temporal relationships.** Concept of time, such as before and after, yesterday and tomorrow, during and awhile.
- **TMR.** Trainable mental retardation. See Chapter 1.
- **Transition.** One meaning is the passage of child and family from one type of services to another, such as transition from preschool services to school services. Another meaning for transition is the passage from school to independence and/or work. The education amendments (PL 101-476, October 30, 1990) define transition services as a coordinated set of activities for a student that promotes movement from school to postschool activities, including postsecondary education, vocational training, integrated employment (including supported employment), continuing and adult education, adult services, independent living, or community participation. The activities, based on student's needs and interests, include instruction, community experiences, employment opportunities, and, when appropriate, acquisition of daily living skills and vocational education.
- **UCP.** United Cerebral Palsy.

RESOURCES

The following books, periodicals, and a video address family issues and the education of children with special needs:

BOOKS AND VIDEO

As I Am: Portraits of Persons with a Developmental Handicap. $165.00 per VHS. This twenty-minute video, produced by the Metropolitan Toronto Association for Community Living, profiles three young people with mental retardation. They talk about hopes and dreams, their lives, and problems they face. The video, designed for discussion in the field of developmental disabilities, offers basic information on developmental handicaps and presents guidelines for relating to people with developmental disabilities. Substantial savings are offered parent groups or agencies purchasing more than one tape at a time. (Not a rental.) Distributed in the United States by James Brodie Productions, Inc., 366 Adelaide Street West, Suite 706, Toronto, Ontario, Canada M5V 1R9.

Breaking Ground: Ten Families Building Opportunities Through Integration by C. Beth Schaffner and Barbara E. Buswell. Colorado Springs, CO: PEAK Parent Center, Inc. (1989). Personal stories of parents' efforts and success in integrating their handicapped children into regular environments. $10.00 (includes postage and handling [p+h]) from PEAK, 6055 Lehmann Drive, Suite 101, Colorado Springs, CO 80918.

Building Integration with the IEP (booklet) by Barbara E. Buswell and Judy Veneris. PEAK Parent Center, Inc. (1989). How to more fully integrate your child using the IEP. $3.00 from PEAK (includes p+h).

A Difference in the Family by Helen Featherstone. New York: Penguin Books and Basic Books (1980). A reassuring account about family assimilation of a handicapped child. Found in libraries.

Disability and the Family: A Guide to Decisions for Adulthood by H. R. Turnbull, Ann P. Turnbull, G. Bronicki, J. A. Summers, and C. Roeder-Gordon. Baltimore: Paul H. Brookes Publishing Co. (1989). Helps families and children with disabilities make future choices. Discusses family life, leisure, employment, and future living needs. Paul H. Brookes, P.O. Box 10624, Baltimore, MD 21285-0624. (800) 638-3775.

Families of Handicapped Children by Marion Duckworth, David C. Cook Publishing Co. (1988), is an inspirational book that answers practical questions, such as, "My husband says our daughter needs discipline. How do you discipline a handicapped child?" Found in religious bookstores and church libraries.

Free Appropriate Public Education: The Law and the Education of Children with Disabilities by H. Rutherford Turnbull III (1990). $39.95 + $2.00 p+h from Love Publishing Co., 1977 South Bellaire St., Denver, CO 80222. The book provides a legislative analysis (with case histories) of the major principles of PL 94-142.

The Lives of Mentally Retarded People by Daryl Paul Evans (1983, Westview Press, Inc., 5500 Central Avenue, Boulder, CO 80301).

Dr. Evans, a sociologist, addresses education, sexuality, and law, as well as social attitudes toward people with retardation. Found in public and university libraries.

Making the Words Stand Still by Donald E. Lyman. Boston: Houghton Mifflin (1986). A readable explanation of learning disabilities, dyslexia, and "Old-Fashioned Word Blindness" from a teacher who experienced school problems in his youth. Found in libraries.

Meeting the Challenge of Disability or Chronic Illness—A Family Guide by Lori A. Goldfarb, Mary Jane Brotherson, Jean Ann Summers, and Ann P. Turnbull. Baltimore: Paul H. Brookes (1986). A self-help guide for families to identify their needs and strengths. Includes work sheets.

No One to Play With by Betty B. Osman. New York: Random House (1982). A specialist in the field of learning disabilities writes about the social problems of LD children; includes strategies for raising a child's "social quotient." An understanding book about LD children, siblings, and parents. Found in libraries, or $10.00 + $2.50 p+h from Academic Therapy Publications, 20 Commercial Boulevard, Novato, CA 94949.

One Miracle at a Time: How to Get Help for Your Disabled Child— From the Experience of Other Parents by Irving R. Dickman and Sol Gordon, Ph.D. New York: Simon and Schuster (1985). Parents talk about medicine, therapy, and education involving their handicapped children. In libraries.

Opening Doors: Strategies for Including All Students in Regular Education by C. Beth Schaffner and Barbara E. Buswell. Colorado Springs, CO: PEAK Parent Center, Inc. (1991). This how-to book addresses the question "How can we successfully integrate and educate all students in regular classes?" Book is not all-inclusive but assists education team members in increasing quality opportunities for students. $10.00 (includes p+h) from PEAK, 6055 Lehmann Drive, Suite 101, Colorado Springs, CO 80918.

Parents CAN Understand Testing by Henry S. Dyer (1980) explains how and why children are tested, testing procedures, and various terms used in evaluation. The National Committee for Citizens in Education. Send $3.50 + $1.00 p+h to NCCE, 900 2nd Street NE, Suite 8, Washington, D.C. 20002.

Parents Speak Out: Then and Now by H. R. Turnbull III and A. P. Turnbull (1985). Parent-professionals discuss their personal experiences finding help for their children. An update from the 1978 book. $16.95 from Charles E. Merrill Publishing, P.O. Box 508, Columbus, OH 43216-0508.

Profiles of the Other Child: A Sibling Guide for Parents by Frances Dwyer McCaffrey and Thomas Fish. What do siblings of children with disabilities need to know about their brother or sister? Often parents ask what they can do to make sure their other child or children won't get "shortchanged" when one of the family members has a disability. The authors discuss information, equal treatment, permission to be sad, and other topics in this informative booklet from the Nisonger Center at Ohio State University. For a copy, send $2.00 + 1.00 p+h to the OSU/Nisonger Center, Publications Department, 1581 Dodd Drive, Columbus, OH 43210-1296.

Recreation Experiences for the Severely Impaired or Non-Ambulatory Child by Susan P. Levine, Nancy Sharow, Cheryl Gaudette, and Sondra Spector. Springfield, IL: Charles C. Thomas (1983). $14.50 paper. Ideas for parents and guardians.

Respite Care: A Guide for Parents and *Respite Care Is for Families: A Guide for Program Development* are $4.00 each from CSR, Inc., Respite, Suite 600, 1400 Eye St. NW, Washington, D.C. 20005. The booklets answer questions about respite and help families establish their own respite care programs.

SSI—New Opportunities for Children with Disabilities is a 1991 booklet explaining the recent Supreme Court Zebley decision. Written by Joseph Manes and edited by Lee Carty. To order the booklet, write the Mental Health Law Project, 1101 Fifteenth Street NW, Suite 1212, Washington, D.C. 20005. Prepaid orders, including postage: 1–4 copies, $3.00 each; 5–24 copies, $2.50 each; 25–49 copies, $2.00 each.

We Have Been There: A Guidebook for Families of People with Mental Retardation by Terrell Dougan, Lyn Isbell, and Patricia Vyas. Nashville: Abingdon Press (1983). Parents talk about the joys and struggles of living with mental retardation—with practical advice.

When Bad Things Happen to Good People by Rabbi Harold S. Kushner is a sensitive work about coming to terms with personal suffering. The book has been highly recommended by theologians, psychiatrists, and counselors. A thoughtful approach to questions asked by parents of children with disabilities. New York: Schocken Books (1981). In libraries.

Your School: How Well Is It Working? A Citizens Guide to School Evaluation by M. Donald Thomas. NCCE (1982). A handbook to help parents measure the effectiveness of their school by systematically collecting information, analyzing facts, and drawing conclusions. $3.50 + $1.00 p+h from NCCE. Also from NCCE— *Finding Out How People Feel about Local Schools* (1984). Handbook tells how to carry out objective surveys about school district effectiveness. $3.50 + $1.00.

PERIODICALS

Families and Disability Newsletter, H. R. Turnbull, editor. A support and information newsletter published three times a year by the Beach Center on Families and Disability at the University of Kansas. For a free subscription, write the University of Kansas, Beach Center on Families and Disability, 3111 Haworth Hall, Lawrence, KS 66045.

The Exceptional Parent is a magazine of support and information for parents of children with disabilities. Published eight times a year. Found in some libraries. $18.00 a year. Write Psy-Ed Corporation, P.O. Box 3000, Department EP, Denville, NJ 07834.

Sibling Information Network Newsletter, a quarterly, publishes information for and about siblings of persons with disabilities, as well as other issues related to families. Contains networking news and a Pen Pals page for younger readers. $7.00 for subscriptions. Contact Lisa Pappanikou, coordinator, Sibling Information Network, CUAP (Connecticut University Affiliated Program), 991 Main Street, East Hartford, CT 06108.

Chadder is the publication of a support group for parents of children with ADD. The quarterly explores topics such as "Living in the Fast Lane: Parenting Your ADHD Adolescent," by Dr. Arthur L. Robin, Chief of Psychology, Children's Hospital of Michigan. To join the national group and receive the publication, send $25.00 for regular members or $50 for a professional membership to CH.A.D.D., 1859 North Pine Island Road, Suite 185, Plantation, FL 33322.

A DEPENDABLE DOZEN SUPPORT GROUPS

Association for Retarded Citizens of the U.S. (The ARC)
500 East Border St., Suite 300

Arlington, TX 76010; (800) 433-5255
(Refers callers to chapters throughout USA.)

Autism Society of America
8601 Georgia Ave., Suite 503
Silver Spring, MD 20910; (301) 565-0433
(Refers callers to 200 local chapters and state societies across the nation.)

Clearinghouse on Disability Information
Office of Special Education and Rehabilitative Services,
U.S. Department of Education
Room 3132 Switzer Building, 330 C Street SW
Washington, D.C. 20202-2524; (202) 732-1245
(Free information about government help for the handicapped.)

HEATH Resource Center (Higher Education and Adult Training for People with Handicaps)
One Dupont Circle NW, Suite 800
Washington, D.C. 20036-1193; (202) 939-9320
(800) 54-HEATH or (202) 939-9320 V/TDD
(Provides information about college and postsecondary education.)

Learning Disabilities Association
4156 Library Road
Pittsburgh, PA 15234; (412) 341-1515

National Committee for Citizens in Education (NCCE)
900 2nd Street NE, Suite 8
Washington, D.C. 20002; (202) 408-0447
(800) NETWORK (helpline M–F 10–4; Spanish M–F 1–5 for questions about education. *Network* published six times a year.)

National Down Syndrome Society
666 Broadway, Suite 810
New York, NY 10012; (800) 221-4602 or (212) 460-9330

(Sends print information and refers callers to local support groups.)

National Information Center for Children and Youth with Disabilities
P.O. Box 1492 Washington, DC 20013
(NICHCY provides free information to parents, educators, caregivers, and advocates in helping children and youth become participating members of the community. The clearinghouse answers specific questions, refers to other sources of help, sends information packets, and provides technical information to parents and professional groups. Many publications are in Spanish and alternate forms; cassette or braille.)
(800) 999-5599 to order *News Digest* and other materials. Ask for a "Parent Pack" about groups in your area.

PACER (Parent Advocacy Coalition for Educational Rights)
4826 Chicago Avenue South
Minneapolis, MN 55417-1055; (612) 827-2966 (V/TDD)
(800)-53PACER for Minnesota long distance
(Information and advocacy about handicapped children and education. PACER Center offers many nominally priced and free publications and other materials for parents and advocates. Write for publications list.)

Spina Bifida Association of America
1700 Rockville Pike, Suite 540
Rockville, MD 20852; (800) 621-3141 or (301) 770-7222

Tripod Grapevine (support for the hearing-impaired)
2901 North Keystone Street,
Burbank, CA 91504; (800) 352-8888 (V/TDD)
(800) 346-8888 in California (V/TDD)

United Cerebral Palsy Associations, Inc.
7 Penn Plaza, Suite 804

New York, NY 10001; (800) USA-1UCP or (212) 268-6655
(Free quarterly publications, information package, and referrals to
local affiliates nationwide.)

P&A—PROGRAMS FOR PROTECTION AND ADVOCACY

These state agencies can help you with legal matters, administrative issues, and/or find remedies to protect the rights of your
child with disabilities. For information about P&A, or to find an
agency near you, contact:

National Association of Protection and Advocacy Systems
(NAPAS), 900 Second Street NE, Suite 211, Washington, DC 20002.
Call (202) 408-9514 or (202) 408-9521 (TDD).

SAMPLE INDIVIDUALIZED EDUCATION PLAN

School district/County Hillside School year 89/90 Date 5/22/90

Student name Thomas Boyer Date of Birth 4/29/77 Age 12 Grade 5

Parent/Guardian Mr. & Mrs. John Boyer

Address 1515 N. Poplar

Placement L.D. Resource Room Placement date 10/1/85

Last multifactored eval. 5/18/88 Review date 6/6/90

Percent of time in regular program 30% art, music & physical ed; mainstreamed art, music, & gym at 5th grade level.

Supplemental/Related services Speech therapy 9/10/90 to 6/6/91 one time weekly, 30-minute sessions. Therapist Susanna Shears

Tests used Woodcock, W.R.A.T., Key Math, P.P.V.T.-R, TOLD-I: Tests

administered by Dr. Lois Oliver, psychologist

CURRENT LEVEL OF FUNCTIONING

Language arts Reading word recognition 4.0, word attack 3.4, comprehension 5.5, spelling 3.0, written language 2.8 (Tom is working in a 4th grade book with relatively good success.)

Communication status P. P. V. T. -R: SS77, TOLD-I: Listening quotient 82 Spoken language quotient 75. Tom displays communication skills within his low average range of ability.

Mathematics Key Math: computation 4.5, W.R.A.T.: reasoning 2.8.

Social studies Tom participates in current events discussions, grasps abstract ideas.

Vocational Tom worked Tues. & Thurs. noons in the cafeteria with good success.

Social/Emotional Tom is easily frustrated in peer relationships but is socially maturing.

Participation in competency testing program: full __ partial x not __ Tom will take competency & group tests in the Resource Room. Tom will participate in the SLD program in his home school district and will receive related services (speech therapy).

ANNUAL GOALS, INSTRUCTIONAL OBJECTIVES:

A. Tom will improve reading comprehension at the 80% accuracy level. 1. Recite & interpret basal vocabulary. Pronounce words with single/double vowel combinations. 2. Pronounce words with initial final blends & with diphthongs. 3. Find meaning in text reading.
    DATES/SERVICES/EVALUATIONS: 9/10/90 to 6/6/91: Classroom instruction, teacher tests, information evaluation, Woodcock, W.R.A.T.
    Individual(s) responsible: Harold Benson, teacher

B. Tom will spell words at the 5.0 level. 1. Spell words in isolation & in sentences. 2. Write sentences using spelling words. 3. Spell words from lists with same spelling patterns.
    DATES/SERVICES/EVALUATIONS: 9/10/90 to 6/6/91: Classroom instruction, teacher tests, informal evaluation, Woodcock, W.R.A.T.
    Individual(s) responsible: Harold Benson, teacher

C. Tom will score 5.5 on the Key Math test. 1. Regroup when adding column of 4–5 numbers. 2. Increase multiplication & division facts. 3. Add & subtract like fractions. 4. Solve word problems.

DATES/SERVICES/EVALUATIONS: 9/10/90 to 6/6/91: Classroom instruction, teacher tests, informal evaluation, Woodcock, W.R.A.T.

Individual(s) responsible: Harold Benson, teacher

D. Tom will improve study habits. He will complete his assignments in class to 80% accuracy level. 1. Begin assignments sooner. 2. Ignore distractions. 3. Ask for teacher help only after seeing if he can answer questions himself.

DATES/SERVICES/EVALUATIONS: 9/10/90 to 6/6/91: Informal evaluations, 9-week grades.

Individual(s) responsible: Harold Benson, teacher

Parent comments: Parents wish for Tom to continue cafeteria work 9/90 to 6/91

Waiver to be notified by certified mail:

_____ yes _____ no x

signed

Date: 5/22/90

Participants:

Parent Mr. John Boyer, Mrs. Sarah Boyer

Teacher Harold Benson

Representative (& title) Dr. Lois Oliver, Psychologist

Other (& title) Marilyn Paterson, Principal, Hillside Middle School

Chairperson Margaret Johnson, Supervisor Special Education, Hillside.

INDEX

267